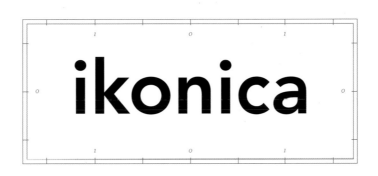

ikonica

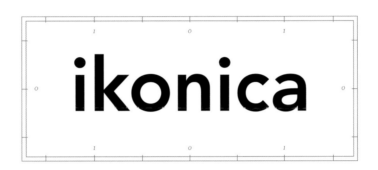

ikonica

A Field Guide to Canada's Brandscape

Jeannette Hanna // Alan Middleton

Douglas & McIntyre
VANCOUVER/TORONTO/BERKELEY

08 09 10 11 12   5 4 3 2 1

Douglas & McIntyre Ltd.
2323 Quebec Street, Suite 201
Vancouver, British Columbia V5T 4S7
www.douglas-mcintyre.com

Design: Cundari SFP
175 Bloor Street East
Suite 900—South Tower
Toronto, Ontario M4W 3R8

Design Production: BF Design

Library and Archives Canada Cataloguing in Publication

Hanna, Jeannette
Ikonica: a field guide to Canada's brandscape / Jeannette Hanna; Alan Middleton.

Includes index.
ISBN 978-1-55365-275-5

1. Branding (Marketing)—Canada—Case studies. 2. Brand name products—Canada. _I.
Middleton, Alan C. II. Title.
HD69.B7H35   2008 685.8'270971   C2007-906384-5

Editing by Scott Steedman
Copy editing by Derek Fairbridge
Cover and text design by Paul Hodgson
Printed and bound in China by C&C Offset Printing Co., Ltd.
Printed on acid-free paper
Distributed in the U.S. by Publishers Group West

Douglas & McIntyre gratefully acknowledges the financial support of the Canada Council
for the Arts, the British Columbia Arts Council, the Province of British Columbia through
the Book Publishing Tax Credit, and the Government of Canada through the Book Publishing
Industry Development Program (BPIDP) for our publishing activities.

Dedicated to Peter, Blair, Russell and Liam who kept the home fires burning...
and to my mother who taught me to always take the scenic route.

A →B

ACKNOWLEDGEMENTS

*It takes quite a community to chronicle a brandscape as diverse and vast as
ours. This project would not have been possible without the insight, support
and roll-up-the-sleeves collaboration of many people. Aldo Cundari provided
the invaluable gift of time. Great navigators helped us refine and finesse the
ideas: Peter Francey, Jeanne Macfarlane, John Hanna, Mary Jane Braide,
Paul Hodgson, Alison Moss, Michael Altman, Jonathan Knowles, Scott Lerman,
Mark Kasoff, Lynne Fletcher, Eli Singer, Joe Pine, Jim Gilmor, Douglas Holt,
Alex Lowy, Malcolm Allan, Ania Szado, Amy Langstaff, Jim Torrance, colleagues
at the CMA Brand Council and all the staff at Cundari SFP. Paul Hodgson,
Clark Spencer, Mike Hosier, Debbie Tsujimoto and Blair Francey designed it
to be smarter and more handsome than we could have hoped. Jeff Jackson and
Shelagh Armstrong contributed wonderful drawings. For their editorial help,
many thanks to: Mandy Harris, Rachel Stuckey, Michael Saouli, Karen Hoffman,
John Kantor, Joanne Mitchell, Alexandra Rybak, Chloe Gravelle and Phillip
Dodd. The exceptional team at Douglas & McIntyre provided astute guidance
throughout the journey. We are especially indebted to Scott McIntyre who saw
great possibilities in the germ of an idea and has been such a stalwart champion
of a brand called Canada.*

CONTENTS

IT'S HIGH SUMMER, 1964. As my father navigates the New York State Thruway bearing northwest, I press my face against the rear window and watch the upstate panorama unfold. Radio host Paul Harvey's distinctive Midwestern cadence fills the car. The rhythm of the road, the thrum of the engine, the syncopation of passing cars— all create a narcotic effect. Senses drift, fade to black.

Is it minutes or hours later that I swim back to consciousness? It's hard to tell. The scenery is deceptively similar. But, like Dorothy, I quickly sense something un-Kansas-like at play. What's happened? We are through the looking glass. The cues are subtle. The roadway signage has traded its familiar graphic anarchy for an oddly restrained orderliness. There are symbols of leaves and forest animals. Odd words like "Imperial" and "Queen" flash by. I'm young and geographically challenged, but one thing is clear: this is someplace else.

PREFACE // JEANNETTE HANNA That first bit of culture shock was more than the musings of some visually precocious kid. Every culture creates its unique codes, symbols and patterns. Our brains are hardwired to instantly register even the subtlest cues when something's different. We catalogue experiences in a complex way, juggling two realities—what the body senses and what the mind construes. Philosophers use the word "qualia," from the Latin word *qualis* meaning "what sort" or "what kind," to describe the raw materials of experience—the unfiltered "knowing" of colours, tastes, smells, sounds, touch—our brains are endlessly processing. Our bodies have immensely astute sorting filters. Our eyes can differentiate millions of colours; our taste buds are calibrated to detect endless subtleties in flavour. One whiff and the nose knows—a new car, fresh coffee, a change of seasons is in the air. One touch tells all— real leather or faux, machine tooled or handcrafted. Our senses are highly attuned to discrepancies between the mind's expectations and the evidence at hand. Back in 1964, the graphics, language, colour and style of a few signposts telegraphed a distinct character of place—all in the blink of an eye. My first, quite literal awakening to Canada's differences still sticks with me because it was so visceral. In a very real sense, it is the genesis of this book.

Everything tells a story, even our own backyard. But our backyard is the last place we look for anything of interest or significance. The Victorians had a very different approach. From today's vantage point, it seems as if everyone in the late nineteenth century was an amateur naturalist obsessively bent on sketching, collecting and cataloguing all manner of information on local fauna and flora, with a patience and perseverance we find hard to countenance today. We can't help but wonder why our ancestors spent so much time creating elaborate arrangements of eggshells, butterflies or beetles in shadowboxes or curio-cabinets. Perhaps they understood what we've forgotten—the precious wonder of familiar home turf.

For transplants from another place, however, everything starts out unknown and unfamiliar. So it shouldn't be surprising that a field guide to Canadian brands would be written by two immigrants. When you come from "away," the landscape of your new home demands close attention. If there are no maps at hand, newcomers must navigate by observation, learning to read the forest first, then the trees. Being uprooted at pivotal points in my upbringing has fuelled a lifelong fascination with the invisible lines that separate outsider from insider: cultural imprinting; social patterns and their meaning, the power of local symbols and the stories behind them. It seemed that I had made a wildly obtuse detour from my studies in philosophy and religion to a career in branding, until a wise person quipped that they are all rooted in a common pursuit: understanding systems of belief. That simple remark became the thread that I've followed through a confounding landscape of brand theories over the past two decades.

That first cross-border expedition eventually led us to a small fishing outpost in Quebec where I was initiated into basics of the bush—canoeing 101, fishing etiquette, recognizing loon calls and moose tracks, the logistics of portages, how to build a fire, the joys of peanut butter and bacon sandwiches. Lesson number one in wilderness

The speed of change

Originally legalized in Canada in 1871, the metric system took more than a century to dominate the landscape. In the spirit of reasonable accommodation, Imperial measures still carry weight with many industries and products.

survival: Don't go out in the woods alone! Before embarking on a reconnaissance trip into the surprisingly uncharted territory of Canada's brandscape, it made sense to find some accomplished companions for the trip—seasoned pros with keen wits and sharp eyes who understand orienteering across complex terrain. I couldn't find a more able partner than Alan Middleton, head of Executive Education at York University's Schulich School of Business. It would be hard to recruit a worldlier traveller, since Alan's role takes him to business centres on nearly every continent. One of England's native sons, he is a consummate chronicler of business and marketing lore as well as an avid student of social history. Paul Hodgson, long-time fellow traveller in design-led expeditions, acts as chief cartographer, typographer and visual guide.

A field guide is, by definition, based on personal reportage. We don't presume to have all the answers—just the benefit of years of observation and experience. We've been in a privileged position to observe many businesses at close range over thirty years and across many different sectors. As field scouts, our role is to gather intelligence, explore promising pathways, identify landmarks and perhaps leave a few inukshuk of our own for fellow travellers.

No trekking through the outback would be complete without some memorable campfire stories. That's why we invited a number of business mavens to share some of their explorations with us, the trials as well as the triumphs. Their personal tales lend rich detail and dimension to our map-making. We're grateful for the time and insights they've offered. Collectively, their stories create a fascinating portrait of the unique dynamics of Canada's cultural and business landscape.

Our hunch is that there are some immensely valuable competitive resources embedded in Canadian culture that our businesses have yet to mine. We just need to know where to dig for them. Sketch pads and notebooks in hand, we sally forth to see what we can discover.

Don't go out in the woods alone!

PREFACE // ALAN MIDDLETON I've been obsessed with this business of brands since my earliest working days, when I decided to apply my training in sociology in the J. Walter Thompson (JWT) advertising agency in London. It was the late 1960s. I was lucky enough to not only work for Jeremy Bullmore and Stephen King, two of the smartest, nicest marketing executives I have ever known, but also to do so at a time that they had become enthusiastic about the work of one of the true greats of marketing academe, Sidney J. Levy.

In his years teaching at the business school at Northwestern University in Chicago, which eventually became the Kellogg School of Business, Levy was a pioneer in applying lessons learned from psychology and cultural anthropology to marketing, particularly the study of brands. Bullmore, the head of the creative department, and King, who had founded account planning at JWT London in 1967, took Levy's thinking even further, into the brand disciplines that still lie behind good brand-meaning management today.

Considering the huge changes in the global marketplace and consumer attitudes to brands in the intervening decades, it is amazing how relevant the thinking of Levy, Bellmore and King are to this day. They have had many followers, but none who have looked at the Canadian brandscape. Enter Jeannette Hanna.

I was on the board of the Royal Ontario Museum (ROM) when, under the leadership of Lindsay Sharp and then William Thorsell, it embarked on a renaissance program that included a full review of its organization's brand. Thorsell and the ROM team appointed communications agency Cundari SFP to manage the brand transition, and with them came their chief strategist and planner, Jeannette Hanna. We quickly became friends, then collaborators when Jeannette approached me to work with her on this project.

As we talked, we recognized that we violently agreed about many things to do with brands, especially three essentials. First, that North America was finally catching up with Levy's thinking and the importance of cultural context in building sustainable brands. Second, we also concurred that the accepted wisdom of current brand models haven't kept pace with the sea change occurring in how consumers interact with the world of commerce. While many of the principles of brand building remain valid, the practices need to be recalibrated. No one was addressing this in a Canadian context. Third, we both felt that that Canada's brandscape could teach us a great deal about this evolution.

We hope this guide will stimulate pride for the accomplishments of our most successful Canadian brands, provide practical lessons from the experiences of others and share a little nostalgia for those brands of yesteryear. Most of all, we hope that it is a useful guide for future managers, researchers and observers engaged in the fascinating world of brand management and meaning.

My tribute is of course to Sidney Levy, Jeremy Bullmore and Stephen King, who started me and many others down this path.

ikonica:

- From the Greek word "eikon" referring to a likeness or similarity.
- Root: Ikonic (someone or something widely admired, often a symbol of a movement or field of activity) + "ca" (standardized abbreviation for Canada).
- Referring to brands, artifacts and symbols that contribute to Canadian culture. They represent shared experiences, ideas and values that particularly resonate with Canadians.

guide:

1 Guidebook to a place.
2 Lead someone in the right direction.
3 Advise or counsel someone, influence their behaviour.

ikonica — a field guide

field:

1 Name given to the background surface in design or heraldry.
2 In physics, unseen forces that exert invisible influences that are only apparent through their effects.
3 Area of open ground marked off for a particular sport.
4 An area rich in exploitable natural resources.
5 A subject area specialty.
6 An area where battles are fought.
7 All of the participants in a race or competition.

brandscape:

1 Term attributed to Professor John Sherry to describe the importance that brands occupy in the everyday lives of consumers.

2 Characteristic group of brand related features in a specific region.

to Canada's brandscape

Canada:

- Second-largest country in the world by area.
- Canada's coast, the longest in the world, borders on three oceans.
- Population: **32,976,026**.
  (Statistics Canada, 2007 estimate)

The conversation often goes like this...

"The thing that drives me crazy is just being
a branch plant for big multi-nationals. How
come there aren't any great Canadian brands?"

"But there are."

"Sure, name three." besides **Tim Hortons**

"What about **Four Seasons** ?"

"Okay, but luxury's a really niche market.
We don't have great consumer brands

like the iPod."

"Isn't that your **Blackberry** ?"

"Okay, but they're anomalies. What have

we produced that's really original?"

"How about **Cirque du Soleil**

"Okay, but

INTRODUCTION One of Marshall McLuhan's lesser-known epithets is, "I don't know who invented water, but it wasn't a fish!" It's so easy to overlook the unique properties of our own habitat. When we live and breathe an environment, it's difficult to stand back and describe its special character, that one-of-a-kind colour, taste, contour or chemistry.

In the past decades, the biggest sea change in our understanding of the world came with our realization of the profound interdependencies of natural systems. Climate change brings that message home every day. We are shaped by diverse forces—from geography and weather patterns, to history and social mores. The premise of this book is the observation that business lives in denial of this basic fact. Trying to understand commerce independent of its context of culture and community is akin to farming oblivious of the variables of climate and local ecology. If you don't understand your environment, growing anything is a highly risky process of trial and error.

Branding in Canada is a great case in point. There must have been more books published on brands and branding in the last decade than any other topic in business. The articles number in the thousands. But for something deemed so critical to the success of businesses everywhere, the bibliography on Canadian brands is almost non-existent. Canadians are curiously inclined to overlook, underestimate and undervalue some of our best natural resources. That's a major liability for business in this country.

So is the fact that the majority of our best practices on the subject have been adopted from US-based packaged goods. The myth is that the American genius for marketing and branding eclipses all others. Why emulate anything else? We disagree, and not because the US models are flawed; it's just that not all of the rules apply here in the same way. We know Canada's makeup—economically, socially and culturally—is different. But how does that shape our most successful brands? A lot? A little? Canadian businesses, trying to navigate competitive challenges at home and abroad, need to know.

One of the challenges is that the little attention the topic has been given here has been doggedly didactic or unconstructive. Naomi Klein's popular *No Logo* (2000) is a political manifesto that discounts any of the intrinsic value of brands. Andrea Mandel-Campbell's 2007 bestseller *Why Mexicans Don't Drink Molson* stridently chides Canada's "inherent conservatism" and dismisses some of our most successful international brands as mere aberrations. According to Mandel-Campbell, Canadians are simply not "players" on the international scene, in part because we don't appreciate brands. We agree that brands are essential tools in the business arsenal. But Mandel-Campbell and many others perpetuate the myth that we suffer from a dearth of brand heavyweights. We beg to differ. This country's real handicap is that we don't celebrate or study our greatest successes; instead, we shrug them off as lucky breaks or freaks of nature.

This is not an exercise in nationalism or cultural navel-gazing. The questions are very pragmatic. Canada is a small economy. If we're going to "punch above our weight" in the marketplace of the global village, indigenous brands need to exploit every advantage. But to play to our strengths, we first have to understand them. Being smugly "not American" is a dead end. Being different is only useful if we know why it matters and where it can take us.

B. Joseph Pine and James Gilmore—the business gurus who penned the bestseller *The Experience Economy* (1999)—argue that "authenticity" has emerged as one of the most important competitive advantages for any enterprise. "Businesses today must learn to understand, manage and excel at rendering authenticity... Authenticity, therefore, centres on (a) being true to one's own self, and (b) being what you say you are to others." So, what does being "true" mean for Canadians? How does our unique cultural climate shape the customer/brand relationship? That's the basic path we set out to explore in this book.

In the process, we've found much more. North of the forty-ninth parallel, the branding vistas hold some fascinating surprises. First, Canada has an impressive roster of success stories to learn from, to share and to celebrate. We do ourselves a great disservice by not chronicling and studying the history of our successes and failures. Next, our initial scouting indicates rich strains of natural resources that homegrown branders have yet to fully exploit. Culture is not simply an environmental factor to consider—it's the bedrock of our brandscape, as formidable as the Canadian Shield itself. The interplay of commerce, community and culture—within organizations as well as in the marketplace—is a constant refrain in the first-person stories we've collected. Our most successful businesses, intuitively or deliberately, have gotten the chemistry right. Even in the by-the-numbers world of high finance, David Goodman, CEO of DundeeWealth, cautions that every organization must protect its sense of purpose and values: "You've got to fight for culture!" he states emphatically.

The most intriguing signs we've found are evolutionary. The contours of the country are changing dramatically on many fronts. Based on the emerging patterns, we have a hunch that Canada could become an exceptional breeding ground for some of the great global brands of the future. Our adaptive abilities, our communitarian instincts and our international outlook are all examples of traits that could give Canadian businesses a huge sustainable advantage in the long run.

Author and journalist Peter C. Newman once wrote, "Being Canadian is an act of faith, something very different, because it is full of potentials that are as yet unrealized." The potential of our unique brandscape is immense. It's about time we charted our own backcountry. Hence, this field guide.

You won't find any "Immutable Laws of Branding" here, because there are none. Instead, we'll provide meaningful context, navigation tips, maps and—most importantly —first-person perspectives from some of Canada's most experienced trailblazers. Anthropologists attest that the best cultural carriers are stories. That's why we've featured personal narratives from a wide cast of prominent brand stewards. Their commentaries have much to tell us about what it takes to succeed in Canada's nexus of commerce, culture and community. The fact that so many of their stories are being told for the first time is a lesson in and of itself.

A GUIDE TO THE GUIDE

Anthropologists study icons (or "ikons," the spelling we prefer) because they reveal so much about a specific culture. Going back to the seventh century, ikons referred to images—typically religious—that carried great mystical or spiritual significance. Today, we apply the word to any kind of important and enduring symbol. Ikons serve important roles as "society's fundamental compass points—anchors of meaning," writes brand analyst Douglas Holt. True ikonic brands go beyond business benefits to tap—and feed—deep, cultural roots. We intend to explore those Canadian cultural connections in this book.

A field guide is a particularly apt metaphor for Canadians. Vast landscape is an integral part of our national identity. "Wilderness to us is more than just empty space out there," observes James Polk in *Wilderness Writers*; "it is part of every Canadian's idea of himself and his country. Even if he has never been out of downtown Montreal or suburban Vancouver, in his imagination he belongs to a place of thundering rivers, untrodden forests, spacious plains, sublime icefloes, and untamed animals."

This field guide aims to orient fellow travellers towards unique properties that shape the business of brands in this country. It is a practical primer on how to decipher and take best advantage of some of our defining features.

The guide format includes:

Origin of the Species: Historical context highlighting Canada's prime movers and native species as well as the inevitable road kill;

Habitat 101: Research-based analysis of the ecosystem and its inhabitants;

Genius Loci: A primer on our natural resources;

Brand Experience Atlas: Executive insights on navigating Canada's brand terrain, and

Climate Change: an Ikonica brand management primer for adapting to the evolving business climate.

The field guide metaphor is more than a clever organizing device. Underlying all our thinking is the conviction that the business of branding also has important lessons to learn from biology, physics and life sciences. "If nature uses certain principles to create her infinite diversity and her well-organized systems," writes Margaret Wheatley in her book *Leadership and the New Science*, "it is highly probable that those principles apply to human life and organizations as well. There's no reason to think we'd be the exception."

Science writer Janine Benyus has spawned a whole new category of innovative collaboration between science and business that she calls "biomimicry." In her book by the same title, she writes, "Organisms have evolved ways to work smarter, not harder." We can follow their lead. The web of relationships embodied in the Internet, for example, is a crude approximation of how most natural systems organize their communications. Looking for the secret to sustainable corporate culture? A type-three ecosystem could be your mentor—old growth forests figured out how to manage identity and change eons ago.

There are important implications for brands originating from Canada and spreading internationally, as well as for transplants operating in Canada. The intense loyalty that Tim Hortons inspires in devotees across Canadian society transcends the savvy of its "Always Fresh" marketing. The secret ingredient in "Tim's" phenomenon becomes apparent when CEO Paul House describes the communitarian spirit that permeates the entire enterprise. While Tim Hortons thrives in the Canadian landscape, its success in the US market is still a wait-and-see proposition. Four Seasons Hotels and Resorts, on the other hand, is an extraordinary global success story that, we will argue, draws deeply on its Canadian values. We'll also explore the challenges that "outsiders" face adapting to this market even when, as in the case of Siemens, they have been in Canada for nearly a century.

The executives interviewed for *Ikonica* demonstrate the power of great storytelling, be it to rally staff around a compelling vision, to communicate relevance and meaning to customers or to capture the zeitgeist of a time and place.

Noted Canadian philosopher Charles Taylor has written that people "make sense of their lives as an unfolding story in a way that gives meaning to their past and direction to their future." From a brand perspective, as social marketer Ric Young says so succinctly, "Best story wins."

Two fifteen rush. Bustling
a lot of movement. Women
visiting mothers daughters,
elderly. Retro pieces.
meeting place. Happy sounds
of people
conversing

FROM A BRAND PERSPECTIVE, AS SOCIAL MARKETER RIC YOUNG SAYS SO SUCCINCTLY, "BEST STORY WINS."

ONE WORD. MANY MEANINGS.

What it is...
A symbol of:
- legal ownership
- identity (personal, tribe, community)
- accountability (e.g. government)
- performance, reliability, risk reduction
  (e.g. standards)
- trust (familiarity)
- character and values (reputation)
- relationship
- perceptions
- quality of experience
- promise of value
- commitment
- a movement or idea set
  OR all of the above

brand

What it's not...
- a logo
- an advertising campaign
- a service or product

"A brand is a person's gut feeling about
a product, service or an organization."
MARTY NEUMEIER, *THE BRAND GAP*

"A brand is both the memory and future of its
products... Products are mute. A brand is what
gives them meaning and purpose."
JEAN-NOEL KAPFERER, *STRATEGIC BRAND MANAGEMENT*

"Brands are units of social consumption...
(They) create packets of meaning—in the form
of stories—which we can apply to our lives."
GERALD ZALTMAN, *HOW CUSTOMERS THINK*

Mark of Authenticity

For millennia, brands have been guarantees of
quality and authenticity. Brand management reaches
all the way back to the first known civilizations in
Sumeria and Egypt, where producers stamped their
marks on bricks. Ancient China, Mesoamerica,
Greece and Rome all had symbols of quality on goods.
The Romans had had enough bad experiences with
the transactions of goods to give us the phrase *caveat
emptor*—"buyer beware"! In Medieval Europe, guild
marks took on the mantle of quality control. By the
fourteenth century, legislation enabled the precursors
of patent attorneys to ply their trade protecting those
marks. Fast forward to the sixteenth century, when
the term "brand" came on the scene. The old
German word "*brandaz*"—which means, "burning
wood"—was given to the authenticity marks whisky
distillers burned onto their wooden barrels with
hot irons to distinguish their product from cheap
substitutions sold by unscrupulous tavern owners.
In North America, Proctor and Gamble and
other companies began promoting their products
to the public in earnest in the mid-to-late 1800s.
Proctor and Gamble is credited with developing
the modern concept of brand management in the
1950s. The success of their roster of "fast moving
consumer goods" launched the late-twentieth
century obsession with brand-centric marketing.

Medieval guild mark

I

ORIGIN OF THE SPECIES

"Discover from whence you come and whither you go."

WHAT'S BRED IN THE BONE Creation myths are stories that help us understand the present by connecting us to our roots, the conditions that forged us and shaped the world we know. Like all living things, brands evolve with each new generation. From tiny, inauspicious beginnings, some thrive and grow far beyond their home turfs while natural selection leaves others to be devoured by stronger competitors. Some simply can't adapt fast enough to changes in the climate and gradually become extinct. Mutations and crossbreeding periodically create whole new life forms. For any brandspotter, it's important to understand "what's bred in the bone"—how our historical climate has shaped our brandscape and the diverse life forms that have taken root here.

COUREURS DE BRAND For anyone searching for the origins of North America's love affair with brands, it is not hard to make the patrimony case for the Hudson's Bay Company. Every Canadian school kid knows that the story dates back to 1670, when "The Governor and Company of Adventurers of England trading into Hudson's Bay" was formed by Royal Charter (with a little help from King Charles II's cousin, Prince Rupert). The Company of Adventurers was made "Lords and Proprietors" of forty percent of modern Canada. That makes "Hbc" the oldest commercial corporation in North America, and one of the oldest companies in the world. Our progenitor brand masterfully weaved together the threads of commerce, culture and community in a way that has had profound implications for Canada.

Fashion was at the heart of the venture right from the beginning. Europe had developed an insatiable demand for dashing beaver hats (ostrich trim optional) in the eighteenth and early nineteenth centuries. The Hudson's Bay Company's raison d'être was to secure a steady supply of this most precious of pelts. By 1748, beaver pelts had become the recognized "Standard of Trade"—our first official currency (one beaver pelt got you a pound of black lead or two pounds of sugar).

It's easy to understand why these *chapeaux* were all the rage. Beaver hats were water-repellent, making wide-brim styles highly functional in the pre-umbrella era. Beaver had unique cachet as well. In some circles it was purported that wearing a beaver hat made you smarter. Rubbing the oil in your hair was said to boost your memory, and it was also rumoured that wearing a beaver hat could restore a deaf man's hearing. Hbc-ers understood the value of good PR from the start. The company promoted itself by presenting complimentary beaver hats (total cost £34) to important men in London to encourage investment in the enterprise.

In 1780, "The Company" launched another fashion ikon, one that survives to this day: the point blanket. The "point" system had been invented by French weavers in the mid-eighteenth century as a means of indicating the finished overall size of a blanket. The distinctive white blankets with coloured stripes were very popular with First Nations because they provided great camouflage in winter. While the green, red, yellow and indigo of the familiar stripes (sometimes referred to as "chief's blankets") were simply colours that were easily produced using dyes at the time, they also had symbolic significance for Hbc's Aboriginal customers. Green means "new life";

*Modifications
of the beaver hat.*

red often connotes the battle or hunt; yellow relates to the harvest and to sunshine, and blue represents water. The Plains people often wore point blankets instead of buffalo robes and used them to make coats. The Metis adapted the blanket into the *capote*, a wrap coat with a hood and fringing.

As the fur trade declined and new immigrants came in search of land and gold, The Company transformed its trading posts into shops stocked with a wider variety of goods than the locals had ever known before. A new type of client emerged: customers who paid with cash, not skins. Canada's retail life had begun.

By the 1800s, Hbc's influence had swept across the commercial landscape like prairie wildfire. In the 50 years from 1821 to 1870, The Company controlled the entire western half of Canada as its sole domain. From the necessities of life—such as liquor, canned salmon, coffee, tea and tobacco—Hbc built a thriving wholesale business.

Its large land holdings took Hbc into real estate. This began with homesteads for newly arrived settlers, then evolved into commercial property holdings and development as well as shipping and natural resources, especially oil and gas. That diversification, in some form, lasted until the economic downturn of the 1980s, when Hbc was forced to rethink its priorities and non-retail businesses were sold off. Today, the Hbc family encompasses a roster of retail monikers that include The Bay, Zellers, Home Outfitters and more. In 2006, South Carolina billionaire Jerry Zucker bought controlling interest in the business and stepped in as Governor and CEO.

Canadian brand history has some key themes and one of them is the large footprint the original players left, not just on the burgeoning economy but on our national character as well. In a speech to the Empire Club, journalist Peter C. Newman gave an example of how much our history has shaped our values: "The reason we are so deferential goes right back to the frontier because the deference came from those Hudson Bay posts and later the CPR [Canadian Pacific Railroad]. Most of the people on our frontier lived in company towns and when you live in a company town you defer to the authority of the company. It made us very different from the Americans because the American frontier had no corporate infrastructure. There it was every man and woman for themselves. There was no Hudson Bay Company, no CPR; it was really a wild west with 69 Indian wars. We didn't have any [wars] and the Hudson Bay Company even had a motto: Never shoot your customers."

ALL IN THE FAMILY A small roster of family dynasties has left a profound imprint on the nation, and John Molson is a prime example. The beer that still bears his name was the first product of Canada's second oldest company and North America's oldest brewery. Molson founded the company on the banks of the St. Lawrence River in Montreal in 1786. Like Hbc, the company's commercial success led to rapid diversification—into lumberyards, steamships and more. The Molson Bank received its charter in 1855; it merged with the Bank of Montreal in 1925. Molson was an astute businessman with a strong sense of community commitment. He was the driving force among citizens who founded Montreal's first public hospital, a major shareholder in the private company that built Montreal's first permanent theatre and a major investor in Canada's first railroad.

HUDSON'S BAY COMPANY STAFF CODE OF CONDUCT 1878

Godliness, cleanliness and punctuality are the necessities of a good business.

The firm has reduced the hours of work, and the clerical staff will now only have to be present between the hours of 7:00 a.m. and 6:00 p.m. on weekdays.

Daily prayers will be held each morning in the main office.
The clerical staff will be present.

Clothing must be of a sober nature. The clerical staff will not disport themselves in raiment of bright colours, nor will they wear hose, unless in good repair. Overshoes and topcoats may not be worn in the office, but neck scarves and headwear may be worn in inclement weather.

A stove is provided for the benefit of the clerical staff. Coal and wood must be kept in the locker. It is recommended that each member of the clerical staff bring four pounds of coal each day during the cold weather.

No member of the clerical staff may leave the room without permission. The calls of nature are permitted and clerical staff may use the garden below the second gate. This area must be kept in good order.

No talking is allowed during business hours.

The craving of tobacco, wines or spirits is a human weakness, and as such, is forbidden to all members of the clerical staff.

The owners recognize the new Labour Laws, but will expect a great rise in output of work to compensate for these near Utopian conditions!

(Source: Hbc.com)

*Five pound bank note
from the Scotiabank
Group Archives,
Numismatic Collection
Dated: 1837*

MONEY MATTERS The Canadian government's protectionist policies have favoured a few big institutions. The history of the Bank of Montreal—founded in 1817 as the country's first financial institution—is in many ways the history of early Canada. Until the Bank of Canada was formed in 1935, it acted as Canada's central bank, providing primary funding for nation-building initiatives such as the first transcontinental railway. All the "Big Five" banks and many of our insurance businesses emerged in the 1800s to underwrite Canada's burgeoning trade: Halifax merchants united to create the Bank of Nova Scotia in 1832; in 1864, a group of local competitors launched the Merchants Bank, later renamed the Royal Bank of Canada; the Bank of Toronto— today's TD Canada Trust organization—appeared in 1856, the Canadian Bank of Commerce (CIBC) launched a decade later in 1867.

TOASTMASTERS Canada's socially tolerant values have been a boon to Canadian business for many years. The Temperance movement of the late 1870s maintained popular support until after World War I, when most provinces repealed Prohibition laws. Canada's tolerance of the "demon drink" during the 1920s, while Prohibition was still in full swing in the US, created boom times for our brewmasters. A popular song of the day rhymed:

> *Four and twenty Yankees, feeling very dry*
> *Sailed across to Canada to get a case of rye*
> *When the case was opened, they all began to sing*
> *To hell with the President and God save the King!*

You didn't need a distillery to benefit from the "dry" years in the US. Pharmacist John J. McLaughlin found his own formula for success with a recipe for Canada Dry Pale Ginger Ale. McLaughlin's bubbly concoction became the mixer of choice in the Prohibition years because the soda masked the taste of home-brewed hooch. New York was his first US distribution beachhead in 1919. Today, although the brand part of the Cadbury-Schweppes roster, many bottles and cans still feature a map of Canada.

Canada's success in building valuable beverage brands is tempered by the fact that so many have been acquired by foreign interests. Molson Breweries has gone through various owners and is now part of Molson Coors, based in Denver, Colorado. Labatt Brewing, established in London, Ontario in 1847, is now owned by InBev, a Belgian company that can trace its own roots back to 1366. Sleemans Breweries' ancestry dates to 1834, although the current company was only started in 1988; it is now owned by Sapporo of Japan. Seagrams was founded in Waterloo, Ontario in 1857 by the Bronfman clan and, while the brand name continues in the entertainment industry, its alcoholic beverage brands are now owned by Pernod Ricard of France. The Hiram Walker distilling company was founded in 1858 and began producing Canadian Club whisky from its plant in Walkerville, Ontario in 1890; it too is now owned by Pernod Ricard.

WHEELERS AND DEALERS Prime Minister William Lyon Mackenzie King once complained that, "If some countries have too much history, Canada has too much geography." The sheer scale of the country has always meant that transportation, natural resources and communication would be major industries. The McLaughlins are another example of a large family that has dominated Canada's brandscape. John J. McLaughlin's brother Robert Samuel "Colonel Sam" McLaughlin took control of the family's carriage and sleigh factory—the largest in the British Empire of the day—and steered it into the automobile business. In 1908, he arranged with William Durant, the founder of General Motors, to use Buick engines. The McLaughlin-Buick brand became world-renowned. When Durant offered McLaughlin the rights to Louis Chevrolet's new vehicle, General Motors Canada was established in 1916.

Cars had been rolling off assembly lines in Windsor since 1904, when the Ford Motor Company of Canada was established, just one year after Henry Ford had launched his enterprise in Detroit. Parts were shipped across the river by the wagonload. Headquartered in Toronto, ZENN Motor Company may be Canada's ride to a new era of transportation innovation. Its ZENN (zero emission, no noise) car is a fully electric low speed vehicle (LSV) that's gaining momentum internationally as a stylish, earth-friendly gad-about auto.

Historically, Canada's seminal transportation corporate brand is Canadian Pacific (CP). Formed in 1881 as the Canadian Pacific Railway Company, it was the first rail service to cross the country and its trunk lines soon became the lifeblood of Canada's expansion. To attract the settlers whose travel and freight would keep the railroad sustainable, CP officials began major marketing campaigns extolling the opportunities of the West. Later diversification brought hotels, airlines and more under the CP brand, but today CP is once again a railway company moving both freight and passengers across North America. The other major railway, Canadian National (CN), was founded by the federal government in 1919.

Air travel came into its own after World War I. By the end of that conflict, it is estimated that twelve thousand pilots returned home, many of them unemployed. This was the beginning of the bush pilot's golden age. In 1937, CN opened a new subsidiary, Trans-Canada Airlines, the precursor of Air Canada. The first transcontinental flight that year took seventeen hours and thirty-four minutes. Six decades later, deregulation opened the skies to a new breed of low-cost carriers including the highly successful WestJet. The vast Canadian landscape inspired other transportation innovations. Joseph-Armand Bombardier started as an inventor and manufacturer of the snowmobile in 1937. While the Bombardier Recreational Products Company still exists, it has been spun off from the main Bombardier Inc. organization, a global player in both the ground and aerospace transportation industries.

POWER BUILDERS Canadians have never been shy about taking on the world. Most Canadians are unaware that the global powerhouse that was Brascan—the asset management company Brookfield—began in 1899 when William Mackenzie and others took over an old mule-drawn tramway in São Paulo, Brazil and transformed it into Brazilian Traction, Light and Power Company, known to Brazilians as "The Light." Today the Brookfield empire encompasses international investments in power, property, infrastructure, resources and financial services in the US, Canada, the UK and Brazil.

From trains to planes

Canada took flight, commercially, in 1920. As a subsidiary of CN Railways, Trans-Canada Airlines (our first carrier) reached altitude in 1937.

origin of the species

The phoenix-like fable of the Reichmann family has been grist for many bestseller exposés. The three brothers, Albert, Paul and Ralph, arrived in Canada from Europe in 1956, and had soon parlayed their modest Olympia and York tile company into one of the largest private real estate companies in the world. The breathtaking moxie of their vision to revitalize a little-known stretch of the Thames riverfront in London turned Canary Wharf into one of the most renowned urban development projects of the late twentieth century. Although its ultimate success vindicated the Reichmanns' vision, financing the project became their Waterloo; Olympia and York collapsed under the weight of its debt and the brothers largely lost control of the company that they had created.

First air express delivery, Leaside. Deliveries are to T. Eaton Co. in Toronto.

KEY CONNECTORS Canada Post is the prime mover of our communications industry. The British Government ran mail service in Canada from 1775 until 1868. Canada's first adhesive stamp, the "Three-penny Beaver,"—designed by Renaissance man Sandford Fleming, the father of standard time—was introduced in 1851. It was the first promotion of the beaver as a national ikon. The Post Office Department of the Government of Canada was created in 1868, just one year after Confederation. The Post was quick to exploit the advantages of air transport; the first airmail delivery flew letters from Toronto to Montreal in 1918. In 1981, the Crown corporation we now know as Canada Post was formed. Its identity, designed by Paul Arthur, incorporated the bilingual moniker "Mail/Poste." Years later the corporation's "shareholder" (Parliament) added the word "Canada" to help publicize its national service role. Today's postal service not only encompasses the largest retail network in the country and a controlling interest in Purolator but a sophisticated suite of logistics and technology businesses as well.

Canada's telecommunications history is dominated by the legendary name Bell. Three countries claim Alexander Graham Bell as their own—Scotland, Canada and the US—and there is much disagreement as to who invented what, when. The US Congress passed a resolution recognizing the Italian Antonio Meucci as the inventor of the telephone, while Canada's House of Commons gives credit to Bell, who is said to have made the first call in Brantford, Ontario, on July 26, 1874. The first long distance call was to nearby Paris, Ontario, in 1876, and the famous two-way conversation with his assistant Thomas Watson took place later that year in the US. From its beginnings in 1880, the Bell Telephone Company of Canada has evolved to become the BCE/Bell organization. In 1895, their telecom equipment business was spun off as the Northern Electric Manufacturing Company, now global giant Nortel.

Telus can trace its roots back to the Alberta Government Telephones organization set up in 1907. It has gone through several acquisitions and mergers, with BC Tel, Quebec Tel and Clearnet, to reach its current position as one of the country's largest telecommunications carriers. The newest star in the communications arena is Research in Motion (RIM), founded in Waterloo, Ontario, in 1984. In 1999, its wireless, phone/email device Blackberry took the world by storm as the status lifeline of the über-connected.

MEDIACASTERS In the early twentieth century, state-of-the-art "wireless" connection meant radio. In the 1920s, the medium was still a novelty and listeners could only dial into US stations. To encourage homegrown programming, the government founded the Canadian Radio Broadcasting Corporation in 1932. Four years later it was re-dubbed the Canadian Broadcasting Corporation. About 100,000 Canadians had TV sets by the time the CBC ventured into television in 1952. Colour hit the airwaves in 1966, the same year instant replays came to Hockey Night in Canada. CTV joined the ranks of broadcasters in 1961, and the 1970s and '80s brought broadcast innovators such as Citytv and MuchMusic onto the scene.

Rogers Communications' corporate DNA is likewise based in radio, as the Rogers Vacuum Tube Company, founded in 1925. The communications company Maclean-Hunter, acquired by Rogers in the 1990s, began in 1887 as a publisher of trade and consumer magazines. The Thomson organization, started in the 1950s in Timmins, Ontario, built a global newspaper empire and then transitioned into the highly successful professional information company it is today. Quebecor Inc. was established in the 1950s by Pierre Péladeau and is now a major media company and one of the world's largest commercial printers. Winnipeg-based CanWest Global has built a huge media empire from its acquisition of Southam Newspapers (founded in 1904) and Alliance Atlantis in 2007. The latter owns numerous TV brands and is a producer and distributor of TV and movie programming; it was created in 1998 when two organizations that had been gradually developing since the 1970s merged. Anyone under the delusion that the history of Canadian business is boring can now enjoy the rise and fall of Conrad Black's Hollinger International media empire in the form of tell-all, made-for-TV movies.

RESOURCEFUL ROOTS Resource industries have always had deep roots in the national brandscape. Imperial Oil was established in 1880 when sixteen refiners joined forces in London, Ontario. In 1900—at a time when there were fewer than 200 cars in the country—Imperial was delivering "automobile gas" by horse-drawn wagon. It opened the country's first gas station in 1947, and its lone oil rig in Leduc, Alberta, launched Canada as an oil powerhouse. Imperial is now majority owned by ExxonMobil, although thirty percent of its stock is still traded in Canada. Irving Oil, founded in 1924, remains a strong energy brand in Eastern Canada. Suncor Energy, now with huge Alberta tar sands operations, was founded in 1917 in Montreal and is now headquartered in Alberta. Husky Energy, now largely a natural gas supplier, was founded as Husky Refining in Calgary in 1938 and is now owned by Li Ka-shing's Hutchison Whampoa Company.

Petro-Canada was founded as a Crown corporation in 1975, in response to the oil shock of 1973, when prices quadrupled but little benefit was going to Canadians. The company soon became one of the largest players in the sector, and a popular symbol of Canadian nationalism, an image it reinforced through its prominent sponsorship of the 1988 Winter Olympics in Calgary. EnCana debuted in 2002 after the merger of PanCanadian Energy and Alberta Energy. Alcan, a major player in the global aluminium industry, was founded in Montreal in 1902. It was acquired by Rio Tinto in 2007.

Mail to go

Blackberry's early interface transformed the face of mobile communications.

Forestry is another resource that made giants of businesses such as MacMillan Bloedel, now owned by US monster Weyerhaeuser. Joseph Kruger established Kruger as a fine paper business in Montreal in 1904; today his grandson Joseph Kruger II heads operations that include forest and wood products, specialty publication papers, Scott Paper consumer brands, recycling and energy.

HOMEGROWN SERVICE Since it was founded in 1922 in Toronto, Canadian Tire has withstood competition and major changes in the marketplace to remain a vital Canadian brand ikon. Brothers John W. and Alfred J. Billes used their combined savings of $1,800 to buy Hamilton Tire and Garage Ltd. in Toronto's east end. The brothers stocked a small range of repair parts, tires and batteries, plus a homemade brand of antifreeze. A big part of their early earnings came from leasing parking spaces in their heated garage. People began to write to the store in search of hard-to-find auto parts, so the brothers produced their first catalogue in 1928. Canadian Tire Money, featuring the colourful Sandy McTire character, was first introduced in 1958; A.J.'s wife, Muriel, suggested the scheme as a response to the promotional giveaways many gas companies were offering at the time. Today, domestic loyalty to Canadian Tire is such that nine out of ten adult Canadians shop there at least twice a year and two out of five do so every week.

The RONA organization has grown to be a smart contender in the hardware category as well. To get around a monopoly that was threatening their supply access, a number of hardware store operators joined forces in 1939 to create Les Marchands en Quincaillerie Ltée. Several years later, Rolland Dansereau and Napoléon Piotte took charge of the business, which became Le Groupe RONA Inc. In 1962, member-merchants acquired all shares in the company and adopted the current cooperative system. There are now more than 620 stores and more than 25,000 employees in the RONA network.

The ever-remarkable Tim Hortons has been a major success in both Canada and the US since it opened its first store in 1964. Few could have imagined that a 1,500-square-foot coffee and donut outlet in Hamilton, Ontario, would be the launching pad for a giant North American operation. The partnership of Ron Joyce—the franchisee of store No.1—and National Hockey League legend Tim Horton is well known. A large part of "Tim's" success is the way the brand has been deeply embedded in local communities. Tim Horton Children's Foundation sends thousands of children, whose families couldn't otherwise afford it, to its camps each year, and the Timbit Minor Sports Program supports a variety of local youth activity programs. After a decade as part of Wendy's, Tim Hortons completed an initial public offering in 2006. There are now 2,640 Tim Hortons restaurants in Canada and more than 305 in the US.

SUPER SHOPKEEPERS Our shopkeepers have succeeded with substance and style. The holdings of the Weston Group, founded by George Weston in 1882, now include a dairy, bakery and retailing; in the UK it owns the prestigious department store chain Selfridges. Loblaws became part of the family in 1947, and in 1986 the stylish Holt Renfrew brand

Making your dollar go further…

Canadian Tire money remains one of Canada's most popular loyalty schemes.

was added. The scale of Bata's global footprint as a retailer and manufacturer of shoes is also extraordinary. The business was originally founded in 1894 in what is now the Czech Republic. Thomas Bata Jr. fled the Nazi regime in 1939 and moved the head office to Canada. Bata now has retail presence in more than fifty countries, production facilities in twenty-six, and has sold 14 billion pairs of shoes in its first century!

Begun in 1973 as a tiny store in Toronto selling its Negative Heel Shoe, Roots now plies its popular fashions through more than 125 stores in Canada and the US and twenty locations in Asia. As outfitters to Canada's 2004 Olympians, it added panache to the country's competitive muscle. Like the Bata family that preceded him, immigrant Frenchman Aldo Bensdoun is building a global shoe empire from his adopted home, Montreal. Since opening his first store in 1978, the Aldo Group's brand footprint extends to nearly forty countries. Club Monaco fashion brand was launched in Toronto in 1985 and acquired by Polo Ralph Lauren in 1999. Umbra's casual, contemporary home accessories are turning heads—and sales—at more than 25,000 retailers in seventy-five countries.

Quebec is home to three of the most successful food and drug store organizations in Canada. In 1947, a buying group of small retailers was established that would eventually grow into Metro Inc. In 2005, they purchased the Canadian business of A&P, making them one of the largest grocery retailers in Canada. Jean Coutu established his pharmacy in Montreal in 1969 that, by growth and acquisition, has become one of the largest drug store chains in North America. In 1980, Couche-Tarde established a convenience store business in Montreal. Since then, by acquisition of chains such as Becker's and Mac's in Canada and others in the US, they have grown to become one of North America's largest convenience store chains.

Shoppers Drug Mart was established by Murray Koffler in 1960. While its ownership went offshore for a while, in 2000 it returned partially to Canadian hands through investments in some of the large pension funds.

Florenceville, New Brunswick, is home to McCain, the world's largest producer of french fries and other "oven-ready" foods. Brothers Harrison and Wallace McCain launched their empire in 1957. When Wallace was ousted as co-CEO in 1994, he headed to Toronto to take over Maple Leaf Foods, another international food powerhouse with several flagship consumer brands, including Maple Leaf, Schneiders and Dempster's.

Boston Pizza's genesis was a long way from the Charles River or the Boston Common. The mass-appeal restaurant chain's actual roots reach back to Edmonton, 1964, when Greek immigrant Gus Agioritis opened his Boston Pizza and Spaghetti House. By 2005, the growing franchise had surpassed $500 million in annual sales.

VOYAGEURS IN STYLE Canadians are great travellers and so are their brands. In the world of luxury hotels, two of the world's major players have strong Canadian roots despite widespread international ownership. Fairmont Hotels and Resorts was actually established in 1907 in San Francisco. In 1999, Canadian Pacific (CP) Hotels acquired the chain and adopted Fairmont's name for its own ikonic hotel properties, including Victoria's Empress, Chateau Lake Louise, Banff Springs, Quebec City's Chateau

From its Florenceville, New Brunswick roots, McCain Food has taken on the world of convenience foods.

A 3.94

B 4.74

V 2.95

U 2.95

X 1.19

T 1.29

B 9.95

C 12.95

E 16.95

F 3.95

1.19

H 5.89

J 3.89

K 7.89

L 4.98

EATON'S MAIN STORE
AND
EATON'S ANNEX, MAIL
ORDER AND FACTORY
BUILDINGS, TORONTO.

ALAS POOR EATON'S, WE KNEW THEM WELL.

The passing of the Eaton's department store chain is an example of how, unless a brand understands the real meaning that it offers customers, it will die, regardless of any emotional attachment its customers may feel towards it.

Back in 1869, Timothy Eaton had the good idea to open a store that sold a cornucopia of items. He'd noted the earlier successes of Bon Marché in Paris and Jenners in Edinburgh, both launched around 1838. By 1849, Harrods was flourishing in London and within a few years Marshall Fields and Macy had taken root in the US. Why not try Canada? Eaton established his Toronto store in 1869, with fixed prices rather than haggling, and aggressive advertising trumpeting "sound goods, good style and good value." The rest is familiar history: the "Goods satisfactory or money refunded" promise; a store chain that moved from general merchandise to almost everything you could imagine.

The famous catalogue, launched in 1884, became an essential ikon on the Canadian brandscape. At the time, the CP railway was opening up the West and the country was still predominantly rural. Eaton recognized that outside the major centres lay vast untapped markets hungry for fashionable, factory-made clothes and new gadgets for the home. The railway allowed for reasonably speedy distribution of purchases. For rural customers, the catalogue helped dissipate some of the sense of isolation. Generations of immigrants depended on the publication as their English language primer. It was the perfect textbook, providing a huge, illustrated assortment of everyday items; knowing "Eaton's English" put you well on the path to functional literacy. For more than a hundred years, the arrival of the new season's catalogue was a major national event. Rivals came and went, but none embedded themselves so deeply in the Canadian psyche.

The T. Eaton store thrived as Canada grew. Smart old Timothy kept innovating to maintain quality and to keep his brand fresh in the area of product selection. He kept up his advertising and direct mail activity to keep customers informed and loyal to Eaton's. He built stores in formats and locations that reflected the trends in population movement.

Unfortunately for Eaton's, the shopping world changed seismically in the 1960s and '70s. New consumer aspirations and, most importantly, new retail formats emerged. Eaton's owners and management made a series of fatal mistakes by trying to sustain a traditional department store business model at a time when there was no longer a differentiated benefit in doing so.

Eaton's is a sad but important lesson in branding. A brand is a promise of benefits that must evolve over time. Eaton's owners fell in love with the idea of a department store as their brand, when they should have fallen in love with Timothy's original concept of providing goods and services conveniently to people in a way that offered "sound goods, good style and good value."

FOUR SEASONS
Hotels and Resorts

Frontenac and Toronto's Royal York. The name change reflected the new international focus of the company and gave recognition to its international properties. Through its Middle Eastern investors, it also owns the Delta Hotels chain.

Four Seasons Hotels and Resorts remains the top luxury hotel chain in the world. Established in 1960 in Toronto by Isadore "Izzy" Sharp, the business has grown from a single modest motor lodge in Toronto to more than seventy of the world's most luxurious properties in more than thirty countries. The exclusive brand now also graces a number of lifestyle offers, from vacation ownership properties and private residences to cruises and one-of-a-kind leisure escapes. Despite its new US and Middle Eastern owners, the company's home office remains strongly grounded in Canada.

Mountain Equipment Co-op (MEC), Butterfield and Robinson, and Tilley Endurables have all created their own highly regarded brands in the outdoor/adventure/travel sphere. MEC was conceived in 1971, within the cozy confines of a storm-battered tent, when a small group of students agreed they needed a place to buy gear not carried by conventional retailers.

BIG VISION CULTURATI Canadians also have a penchant for innovative spectacle. The larger-than-life IMAX experience grew out of technology developed for Expo 67 in Montreal. As of 2006, there were 280 IMAX theatres in forty countries. Cirque du Soleil was the brainchild of two former street performers, Guy Laliberté and Daniel Gauthier. The concept circus was piloted in Quebec in 1984 as part of the 450th anniversary celebrations of the arrival of explorer Jacques Cartier on Canada's shores. Cirque du Soleil has since grown to be a worldwide operation of live performances, TV shows, DVDs and CDs.

Canada's other cultural "name brands" are too numerous to mention given the international success of various arts and pop culture ambassadors that run the gamut from Avril Lavigne to David Cronenberg. If Canadian literature were a brand it would be one of our most successful exports with names such as Atwood and Munro celebrated around the globe. But beyond the covers of high-culture literature, a grippingly steamy page-turner is always in demand, and Harlequin Enterprises is there to fan the flames. The giant of romance fiction publishes in twenty-four languages in more than a hundred countries around the world. Founded in Winnipeg by lawyer, fur trader and printer Richard Bonnycastle in 1949, Harlequin started sourcing romance fiction from Mills and Boon in the UK. Potboiler romance turned out to be so lucrative that Harlequin bought the business in 1971. Now owned by Torstar of Toronto, the Harlequin brand also markets through various other imprints including Luna, Mira, Red Dress, Silhouette and Spice.

SPORTING LIFE Two of Canada's most sacred ikons come from the sports arena. The Montreal Canadiens hockey franchise actually predates the establishment of the National Hockey League (NHL). The original team, Club Athlétique Canadien, was formed in 1910 and adopted its now unmistakeable bleu, blanc et rouge jerseys by 1914. The team was one of the "Original Six" franchises that formed the NHL in 1917. One of the others was the Toronto team. Founded the same year as the NHL, it adopted the name Toronto Maple Leafs in 1927.

Canada's two major hockey equipment suppliers have now been sold to foreign investors. CCM (Canada Cycle and Motor Company) was formed in 1899 when four bicycle companies merged; in 1905 it moved into the manufacture of equipment for hockey and other sports. Reebok purchased the company in 2004. Bauer, established in Kitchener, Ontario, in 1927, was the first company to sell ice skates attached to boots. It became synonymous with hockey and several other sports. In 1995, Nike purchased Bauer.

SOCIAL MOVEMENTS Social marketing and sport have an impressive track record in Canada. Fitness has been a major national preoccupation for many decades. ParticipACTION, a non-profit private company launched in 1971, was well known for its innovative social marketing during the 1970s through '90s. A 1973 TV commercial comparing the health of a 30-year-old Canadian to a 60-year-old Swede started a national discussion on the state of physical education here. ParticipACTION established a health promotion model that's been adapted around the world.

Right To Play is an athlete-driven international humanitarian organization that uses sport and play as a tool for the development of children and youth in the most disadvantaged areas of the world. Originally known as Olympic Aid, it was founded by four-time Olympic gold medalist Johann Koss in 1993. Its signature Red Ball, wrapped with the message "Look after yourself, look after one another," was the brainchild of Toronto-based social marketer Ric Young. The organization now has programs in more than twenty countries and is supported by elite athletes from all over the world.

One of the most venerable environmental activist brands was born in 1971 when a handful of brave souls, calling themselves Greenpeace, set sail from Vancouver in a hired fishing boat to protest nuclear weapons tests by gate-crashing a US atomic test in Alaska. Thirty-five years later, Greenpeace is a global environmental organization operating in more than forty countries with more than 2.8 million members around the world.

RED AND WHITE SALUTE The historical personification of Canada has long been the Mountie. The predecessor of the Royal Canadian Mounted Police (RCMP), the North West Mounted Police (NWMP) was created in 1873 by Prime Minister Sir John A. Macdonald to bring law and order to (and assert Canadian sovereignty over) the western and northern regions of the fledgling country, especially in trouble spots such as Fort Whoop-Up where American whisky traders were causing trouble. Immortalized in popular culture—from Sergeant Preston to the cartoon character Dudley Do-Right and the *Due South* TV series—the RCMP's red serge tunics and Stetson hat are almost as ikonic to Canada as the maple leaf.

Right To Play's ikonic red ball carries a powerful message of empowerment to youth in refugee camps and war-torn communities around the world.

PRIME MOVERS

Recognize that name? Their names are emblazoned everywhere. But we seldom stop to wonder about those early pioneers who carved their monikers on the brandscape. Author Pierre Berton argued that Canada is simply, "not a country of hero-worshippers. It's common dogma, in fact, that we've neglected many of the great figures of the past." In their 2002 book, *I Know That Name!*, authors Mark Kearney and Randy Ray profile quite a pantheon of great Canadian brand builders. Our roster of progenitors is substantial and surprising— it's a colourful field of brash upstarts, eccentrics, maverick inventors, savvy entrepreneurs, great humanitarians and shady scoundrels:

Elizabeth Arden
1939

Alexander Graham Bell
circa 1914–1919

Elizabeth Arden
Born Florence Nightingale Graham, Arden was raised on a tenant farm near Woodbridge, Ontario. She moved to New York in 1908 and developed a line of skin creams, tonics and oils that led to the international cosmetics empire. Arden became one of America's wealthiest women. Signature ikon: the Red Door.

Thomas Bata
Started in 1894, in what is now the Czech Republic, the Bata Shoe Company was so successful that it had soon expanded into the rest of Europe, the UK and the US. In 1939, when he was in his mid-twenties, Thomas Bata Jr. moved the business to Canada to escape the Nazis. He and his wife Sonia built the business rapidly. In 2002, the company had forty-eight manufacturing operations and employed 50,000 people across the globe.

Alexander Graham Bell
This story has a familiar ring. The son of Scottish immigrants, Bell landed on Canada's shores in 1870. He later moved from Brantford, Ontario, to Boston. In 1880, Bell Telephone of Canada was incorporated. Bell himself said, "Of this you may be sure, the telephone was invented in Canada. It was made in the US."

Henry Birks
The Birks had been making cutlery for the British upper classes since the sixteenth century. Jewellers by trade, Henry's parents immigrated in 1832 to Montreal, where son Henry was born in 1840. He opened his own jewellery shop in 1879, soon followed by his own manufacturing plant. Offspring William, John Henry and Gerald added the "and sons" to the company name in the 1890s. Signature ikon: the Blue Box.

Eddie Black
Black's wasn't always synonymous with photography. In 1930, Eddie sold radios and appliances in his first store in Toronto. The family's first camera store didn't materialize until 1948. When Eddie's sons retired from the business in 1988, there were more than two hundred Black's stores across Canada. Fuji Photo Film Canada Inc. bought the business in 1993. Signature tagline: Black's is Photography.

Joseph-Armand Bombardier
Mechanics were always a passion of Bombardier's. In 1922, at age fifteen, he created his first working snowmobile prototype. Four years later he started Garage Bombardier where he continued to invent variations on the vehicle that eventually become the hugely popular Ski-Doo. Bombardier's firm has grown to become one of the world's most important transportation conglomerates.

William Buckley
During the 1918 flu epidemic, pharmacist "Doc" Buckley whipped up a concoction of ammonium carbonate, menthol and oil of pine, with a pinch of Irish moss extract, to sooth his customers' coughs. The elixir, now

known as Buckley's Mixture, has been a mainstay of medicine cabinets across the country since the 1930s. Many generations of kids were also spoon-fed his more palatable Jack & Jill cough syrup.

Jack and Carl Cole
The Colofsky brothers moved to Toronto from Detroit as young boys. Adventurous retailers, they ran bookstores that also sold an eclectic mix of goods, including hula hoops. But it was the introduction of "Coles Notes," in 1948, that endeared them to students in seventy countries. They sold the rights in the US to a firm that renamed them "Cliffs Notes." In 1995, Coles and Smithbooks merged to become Chapters, now Chapters Indigo.

Samuel Cunard
Born in Halifax, Cunard was a business prodigy. At seventeen, he was managing his own general store then gradually expanded the family's interests into coal, iron, whaling and shipping, ferrying mail between ports along the eastern Atlantic. Cunard introduced many innovations that shaped the future of commercial ship transport and luxury cruising. The Cunard Group became a public company in 1878 and the business continues to set the bar for luxury cruise ships to this day.

Charles E. Frosst
Mr. Frosst's inventiveness has meant fewer headaches for Canadians since the beginning of World War I. That was the time the pharmacist created Frosst 222 painkillers, the first of many medicinal innovations. In the mid-1960s, the business was acquired and became Merck Frosst Canada.

Alfred C. Fuller
The man who would build an empire on brushes hailed from Nova Scotia and was barely literate. The company began with door-to-door sales, backed by the company's famous lifetime guarantee. Early on, Fuller moved the business to the US. Since 1973, Fuller Brushes and more than two thousand other products have been manufactured near Great Bend, Kansas.

James Grand and Samuel Toy
Grand started his office supplies business in Toronto in 1882, delivering his goods door-to-door by wagon. With business booming, he brought his brother-in-law, Samuel Toy, on board. The business stayed in the Grand family for several generations, becoming one of North America's largest office products retailers. In 1996, it was purchased by the US firm Boise Cascade.

James Holt and G.R. Renfrew
These two entrepreneurs bought controlling interest in a fur shop started by William Henderson. In the 1880s, the company was appointed Furrier-in-Ordinary to Queen Victoria. It was the start of a long association with British royalty, which soon extended to fashion royalty. Now part of the Galen Weston empire, Holt Renfrew still represents the haute couture of Canadian fashion retailers.

John Inglis
Inglis immigrated to Canada from the UK in 1850. With two partners, he founded a company that built machinery for flourmills. Son William took over the growing manufacturing work in the late 1890s, and by 1938 the business had shifted to firearms. It wasn't until after World War II that the name Inglis became associated with home appliances. In 2001, Inglis became Whirlpool Canada.

Kenneth Colin Irving
Born in 1899 in New Brunswick, Irving was always an entrepreneur. He started his own oil company in 1924 and within a decade was "Mr. Transportation" in the province. He sold cars, fuel, did repairs and ran the major trucking and bussing firms. But Irving was just ramping up. By the 1980s, the Irving family controlled three hundred companies in the Eastern United States.

James Kraft
One of eleven children, Kraft hailed from a dairy farm in the Niagara region. Investing in a cheese business made good sense in his youth. He moved to Chicago and patented a way to create processed cheese in 1916.

A famous Cunard ship
RMS Queen Mary
Long Beach, 2007

From 1918 to the mid-1940s, per capita cheese consumption jumped fifty percent in the US. Kraft Dinner debuted in the famous Kraft Kitchens in 1937. Kraft was an early advertising innovator, embracing outdoor advertising, radio and TV as each innovation appeared.

John Kinder Labatt
In 1847, John Labatt turned his energies from farming to brewing by investing two thousand dollars in a small brewery on the Thames River near London, Ontario. Annual production was only a few thousand bottles. Today, the company produces more than 817 million bottles a year, including the ikonic beer labels Labatt Blue and Labatt 50. According to company history, John Labatt is also responsible for our annual celebration of the Queen's birthday. However, there is no mention of Labatts being involved in the unofficial re-branding of Victoria Day as "the May 2-4 weekend."

Albert Edward LePage
A.E. LePage began selling real estate in Toronto in 1913 and quickly raised the professional bar for all agents. He marketed himself as a bungalow specialist, introduced placement of descriptive ads in consumer publications and was the first agent to accompany clients on their tours of homes. When he sold A. E. LePage Ltd. in 1953, it was one of the most successful real estate agencies in the Toronto area. The 1984 merger of LePage's with Royal Trust created the largest real estate firm in Canada.

William Nelson Le Page
The son of a Prince Edward Island farmer, Le Page was working with Russia Cement in Massachusetts when he discovered how to transform unwanted fish skins into an adhesive that was soft, pourable and easy to produce. Between 1880 and 1887 fifty million bottles of Le Page's glue were sold worldwide. In 1890, Le Page sold his share of the company and, somewhere along the line, the name was reduced to one word. Now owned by one of the largest chemical companies in Europe,

Colonel J.B. McLean and Horace Hunter with a copy of The Financial Post *1947*

LePage continues to make glue and other adhesives in Brampton, Ontario.

Theodore Pringle Loblaw
This three-dollars-a-week grocery store clerk traded in his early dreams of driving trains, to revolutionize the way we shop for food. In 1920, he and like-minded partner Milton Cork opened their first two stores in downtown Toronto and began introducing innovations such as self-service shopping, product tracking, direct buying and house brands. By 1930, the Loblaws chain included 95 outlets in Ontario and reported annual sales of $18.4 million. Now part of the George Weston empire, the company's President's Choice products give the term "pc" a whole new meaning.

William C. Macdonald
Born on Prince Edward Island in 1831, William Macdonald founded the Macdonald Tobacco Company that would eventually become one of the giants of the industry. It started in 1858 when William and his brother Augustine began importing tobacco and manufacturing tobacco plugs in Montreal. By 1866, William was sole proprietor and the business was flourishing. In 1917, his heirs, the Stewart brothers, added roll-your-own cigarettes to the product line and, in 1928, introduced Export "A" cigarettes to Canada. The company is now owned by Japan Tobacco Inc. and, with its head office in Toronto, continues to sell Export "A."

John Bayne Maclean
His English marks were too low for a career in education, so Maclean turned to journalism instead. In 1887, after a few years reporting for *Toronto World* and the *Toronto Daily Mail*, he decided to establish his own publishing company. His first trade magazine, *Canadian Grocer*, was a success and new titles such as The *Dry Goods Review* and *Druggist's Weekly* continued to bring in profits. Maclean hired Horace Talmadge Hunter in 1903 and eventually made him a full partner. Maclean-Hunter is still publishing *Canadian Grocer* and *Maclean's* magazine continues to serve as Canada's newsweekly of record.

Harvey Reginald MacMillan

Born in 1885 in a Quaker community near Newmarket, Ontario, MacMillan spent the first twenty years of his working life in government in a variety of forestry-related positions. In 1919, he established the H.R. MacMillan Export Company and, by the mid-1930s, held a near monopoly on forest production in British Columbia. When his company merged with Bloedel, Stewart and Welch, MacMillan Bloedel became one of the largest forestry firms in the world. MacMillan remained chairman until the age of seventy-one and did not retire from active participation in the business until he hit eighty-four, the same year he was made a Companion of the Order of Canada.

Daniel Massey

Daniel Massey imported the first mechanical threshing machine into Upper Canada in 1840 and his barn soon became a farm implement workshop. He and his partner moved these activities into a foundry and the Massey Manufacturing Company prospered. With his son Hart Massey at the helm, the company had a reputation for innovation and quality work. Massey Manufacturing merged with competitor A. Harris, Son and Company in 1891 and, with four of Hart's sons still involved in the business, merged again with the Ferguson Company in 1953. The name Massey Ferguson was adopted in 1958 and is still emblazoned on farmers' ball caps across Canada.

John McIntosh

None of us would ever have taken a bite of his apple if John McIntosh hadn't rescued a seedling he found while clearing bush on his farm near Prescott, Ontario, in the spring of 1811. Growing an apple empire is a slow business and it took John, his son Allan and grandson Harvey until 1835 to produce apples on a major scale. It wasn't until 1870, twenty-five years after John's death, that the apple was officially introduced and named. Today McIntosh apples account for more than half of the seventeen million bushels of apples produced in Canada each year.

John Molson

John Molson was an ambitious young man who immigrated to Canada in 1782 and found his first entrepreneurial home in a brewery on the St. Lawrence River. He produced his first four thousand imperial gallons of beer in 1786 and the thirsty colony of Montreal guzzled them gladly. Molson went on to diversify into lumber, railways, steamboats, hotels and banking.

Samuel Moore

There's genius in knowing a good idea when you see it, and when John Carter showed Samuel Moore the benefits of inserting a simple piece of carbon paper between two pages of a sales book in 1882, Moore recognized its potential. Over the next forty years the Moore Group introduced the one-time carbon, continuous folded forms, web-fed lithography and carbonless paper. Thirty-one years after his death in 1948, Moore was inducted into the Canadian Business Hall of Fame. Today Moore's international network sells its products in fifty countries.

William Neilson

William Neilson went from bankruptcy in 1891 to establishing a dairy dynasty when he and his wife began delivering homemade ice cream door to door in Toronto during the summer of 1893. Their product line grew to include those ikonic treats Eskimo Pie and the chocolate bars Crispy Crunch and Jersey Milk. William Neilson Ltd. grew to become the largest producer of ice cream in the Commonwealth and the largest manufacturer of chocolate in Canada. The company was sold to George Weston in 1947. Today, the business is back to its roots as one of the country's biggest dairies.

John Redpath

Redpath arrived in Canada in 1816 as a skilled stonemason and made his first fortune as a building contractor in Montreal. In 1854, at age 57, Redpath decided to invest his profits in his family's future and chose sugar as a growing field with no competition. In

McIntosh apples

A Massey Ferguson MF 135 Tractor

1859, John Redpath and Son Canada reported a profit of $90,000. The company stayed in Redpath family hands until Tate and Lyle Sugars Group of England purchased it in 1959.

P. L. Robertson
In 1908, Peter Robertson began to manufacture a square recess in the head of a screw that revolutionized the fastener industry. The first patent was issued in 1909 and expired fifty-five years later, in 1965. The screws and screwdrivers he invented still carry his name. Today, Robertson Inc. is a global supplier of standard and specialty fasteners based in Milton, Ontario.

Edward S. "Ted" Rogers, Sr.
In 1925, Ted Rogers Sr. introduced his batteryless radio, the world's first alternating current (AC) radio tube, powered by ordinary household current. This breakthrough became a key factor in popularizing radios. In 1927, he founded CFRB (Canada's First Rogers Batteryless) radio station.

Joseph Emm Seagram
Born in 1841 in Upper Canada, Seagram got his first taste of distilling when he went into business with Wilhelm Hespeler. By 1880, Seagram had bought out all his partners and began to produce best-selling brands such as Seagrams 83, Old Rye and White Feather. Joseph E. Seagrams and Sons Ltd. was a family run business from 1911 until 1928, when the Bronfman family added it to their growing empire. The company took full marketing advantage of the 1939 royal visit to launch its premium brand, Crown Royal.

John H. Sleeman
John H. Sleeman was an experienced and ambitious brewer when he immigrated to Canada from England and set up his first brewery in St. Catharines, Ontario, in 1836. Within 15 years, he had moved to Guelph to start the successful Silver Creek Brewery. It continued to thrive under son George. But when grandson Henry was caught smuggling during Prohibition, the brewery was forced to shut its doors. The family recipes lived on,

however. In 1985, great-great-grandson John W. Sleeman reincorporated the Sleeman Brewing and Malting Company and Sleeman's Cream Ale, Original Dark and Honey Brown Lager began to flow once again.

Ernest D'Israeli Smith
E.D. Smith took his first step to becoming jam-maker to Canada in 1877, when he took over the family farm in Niagara from his ailing father. He saw huge opportunities in the rapid population growth around Toronto to expand his land holdings and diversify his operations. The E.D. Smith and Sons factory opened in 1905, producing the first pure fruit jam in Canada. Smith's work ethic, vision and reputation for honourable dealings eventually led him all the way to a seat in Canada's Senate.

John William Sobey
J.W. Sobey learned how to build things on the family farm in Pictou Country, Nova Scotia. He moved his family to Stellarton in 1905 and worked for two years on the construction of the Stellarton mine. Then he bought a meat business, sold his product door to door and opened his first shop in 1912. In 1924, with son Frank at his side, Sobey began offering a wider range of grocery items in a growing chain of stores. Father and son nursed their business through the Depression and in 1947 opened their first supermarket in New Glasgow, Nova Scotia. Since a $1.5 billion takeover of the Oshawa Group in 1998, Sobeys is now the second-largest food distributor in Canada.

Rose-Anna Giroux and Arcade Vachon
In 1923, this couple left their village of Saint-Patrice de Beaurivage, Quebec, to buy a bakery in Sainte-Marie-de-Beauce. Since then, kids across North America have indulged in the confectionery magic of Jos. Louis, May West and 1/2 Moon/Lune branded treats. Today, Vachon is part of the Saputo family of products, though its plant still remains in Ste-Marie-de-Beauce.

Hiram Walker
Driven by Prohibition and lured by cheaper production costs, Hiram Walker abandoned

Robertson screw

Zellers
Ottawa, Ontario

Detroit in 1858 and bought land near Windsor, Ontario, where he set up a milling and distilling business. The whisky he produced was so enjoyed by gentlemen members of clubs that he labeled it "Club" to distinguish it from the rest. By the 1880s "Club" was so popular in Canada he decided to expand into the American market. Lobbying by his American competitors forced him to identify his whiskey's country of origin and in 1890 "Canadian Club" was born. Today it is sold in more than 150 countries and is one of the best-known liquor brands in the world.

George Weston

George Weston began his working life at age twelve, hauling 120-pound sacks of flour, stoking the wood-fired oven and tending the kneading machine of a small bakeshop on the fringes of Toronto. He then apprenticed with baker and confectioner G.H. Bowen and by age seventeen, owned two of Bowen's bread routes. In 1897, he opened the "Model Bakery" and was soon selling his bread in five hundred stores. In 1911, he merged all his interests into the Canada Bread Company. Son Garfield expanded it into a thriving international business and today, headed by grandson Galen, it oversees more than seventy-five companies with sales of more than $20 billion.

Walter Zeller

Walter Zeller did his groundwork thoroughly, beginning as a stock boy in several chain stores and climbing up the ladder in a variety of jobs in both Canada and the US. Zellers Ltd. was incorporated in 1931, and by the end of its first year in operation its twelve stores had reached $2 million in sales. The slogan was "Retailers to Thrifty Canadians." With that in mind, Zeller weathered the Depression well. In 1952, he began to affiliate with other chain stores, including Federal Stores and W. T. Grant Company. By 1981, the company was owned completely by the Hudson Bay Company. Today there are 350 Zellers stores across Canada.

ROADKILL

Famous Canadian brands that have become extinct

Aikenheads

Avro Arrow

Canadian Airlines

Dickie Dee Ice Cream

Eaton's

Gooderham and Worts

Heintzman Pianos

Massey Ferguson

McLaughlin Motors

Simpson's

Wardair

Woodward's

LAND OF INVENTION

In his book **Ideas in Exile**, *J.J. Brown writes, "The story of the disasters and triumphs of Canadian invention is for the most part the story of the struggles of individuals to achieve recognition from an indifferent society." Nevertheless, the world is a better place because of some great Canuck ingenuity.*

Alkaline long-lasting battery

Ardox spiral nail

Basketball

Birchbark canoe

Blackberry

Bloody Caesar

Canadarm

Electric oven

Electric wheelchair

Electronic music synthesizer

Five-pin bowling

Green plastic garbage bag

Hockey goalie mask

JAVA programming language

Lacrosse

Light bulb

Pablum

Paint roller

Poutine

Radio voice transmission

Robertson screwdriver

Ski-Doo

Snow blower

Standard time

Telephone

Wonderbra

Zipper

Paul Bunyan: The origins of the tall-tale, gargantuan logger are cloudy but many attribute them to French-Canadian loggers who called him Paul Bonjean.

Bonhomme: Quebec Winter Carnival's snowman mascot.

Windigo: Evil figure of Algonquian legend.

Sasquatch: Canada's best-known monster; a mythical, hairy creature that stands three metres tall.

Ogopogo: The fabled aquatic monster of British Columbia's Okanagan Lake.

Winnie the Pooh: The Canadian bear cub christened "Winnipeg" that inspired British author A. A. Milne to write his famous children's stories.

Superman: Canadian cartoonist Joe Shuster drew the original man of steel.

Johnny Canuck: Comic-book strongman introduced in 1941.

Ookpik: Inuit souvenir owl made of sealskin.

Dudley Do-right: klutzy, square-jawed Mountie cartoon character from the classic *The Rocky and Bullwinkle Show.*

Glooscap: Legendary "transformer" of the Wabanaki First Nation who's credited with creating natural features such as the Annapolis Valley.

2

HABITAT 101

"A land not to be wooed in a day, but in a long courting."

~ THOMAS SAUNDERS, 1949 ~

PAINT BY NUMBERS When *Fire and Ice: The United States, Canada and the Myth of Converging Values* was published in 2003, Michael Adams, President of Environics Research Group, was able to draw on more than thirty years of market research to paint a fascinating portrait of how Canadians and Americans have followed very different evolutionary paths.

Adams asserts that he wrote the book to counter what he felt were erroneous assumptions in the press that American and Canadian cultures were converging and the distinctions of culture were blurring. Despite the appearance of many similarities, for Adams the heart of the matter is how Canada and the US are shaped by a different set of underlying values that spell very different cultural outcomes. He describes values as, "the basic learned motivators of human behaviour. While we come into the world with genetically coded instincts common to all human beings, such as the sex drive, our culture has an overwhelming influence on what we come to value in life." Culture, like gravity, is impossible to see but its force is undeniable and inescapable. To understand our brandscape, we need to understand how culture and values are essential building blocks of our habitat—the equivalent of brand soil, light and climate.

The challenge Adams puts forward is to look beyond the surface idiosyncrasies of culture and analyze the bedrock below: "Most Canadians, like most Americans, can be spotted in their natural habitats driving cars, consuming too much energy and water, spending a little less time with their nuclear families than they would like, working a little more than is healthy, watching television, and buying some things they could probably survive without. But differences—both subtle and marked—do exist, and do endure. Some are external (gun control, bilingualism, health care), but many only exist in the minds of Canadians and Americans—in how they see the world, how they engage with it, and how they hope to shape it."

It's easy to overlook some of the fundamentals. For example, we often forget that Canadians are far more urbanized than Americans. More than one third of all Canadians live in one of three metropolitan areas: Montreal, Toronto and Vancouver. Our urbanism has a distinctively multicultural flavour as well. Canada has the highest per capita immigration rate in the world. But it's highly concentrated in our cities. For example, in Toronto forty-six percent of all residents have mother tongues other than English.

Our historical bias for "peace, order and good government" has given us the security to acknowledge the value of interdependence. To be interdependent means recognizing the essential equality of the "other." One of the consequences of our highly urbanized, hyper-multicultural communities is the reinforcement of that interdependence, breeding a pragmatic, we're-all-in-this-together tolerance for differences. One of the unintended consequences—and benefits—appears to be an ability to welcome change, to embrace diversity, to find common ground with others.

A 2002 Pew Research Centre Poll that studied 38,000 people in forty-four countries quantifies just how different Canada is in this respect: Canada is the only country where a majority (a huge majority of seventy-seven percent!) said that immigrants have a good influence on the country. Where the lion's share of citizens of forty-three other countries sees a threat from "others," we see positive opportunities, by a large margin!

PROFILE CANADA

SCALE: Second-largest country in the world in area (after Russia).

ECONOMY: Gross National Income: eighth largest world economy; converted to purchasing power parity as a measure of value, Canada ranks sixteenth in the world. Primarily industrial and urban. Service industry employs about three-quarters of Canadians. Oil and logging industries are also key. Since 2001, Canada has maintained the best overall economic performance in the G8.

POPULATION: 32,976,026 (Statistics Canada, 2007 estimate).

MEDIAN AGE OF POPULATION: 39.5 years.

DISTRIBUTION: About three-quarters of Canada's population live within 160 kilometres of the US border. Canada has 34 ethnic groups with at least one hundred thousand members each (2001 census). Canada's aboriginal population is growing almost twice as fast as the rest of the Canadian population. Canada has the highest per capita immigration rate in the world.

RANKINGS: *UN Human Development Index:* (weighs a long healthy life, knowledge and a decent standard of living): Canada ranked fifth in the world; US ranked tenth; UK ranked fifteenth. Canada was ranked the number one country 10 times out of 18 between 1980 and 2006. *2006 ranking:* Canada placed sixth behind Norway, Iceland, Australia, Ireland and Sweden but still ahead of the US (eighth), France (sixteenth) and the UK (seventeenth).

BRAND EQUITY: Canada is seen favourably on a wide range of dimensions: *2005 Anholt Nations Brand Index:* Canada ranked sixth after the UK and Switzerland; ahead of Italy, Sweden, Germany, Japan, France, Australia and the US (based on sum of perceptions across six areas of national competence: tourism, exports, governance, investment and immigration, culture and heritage and people/human capital)

BRAND FINANCE VALUATION: Canada had a brand value of $1,106 billion or 111 percent of GDP. Canada scored particularly well in good governance, in respecting its citizens' human rights, and in helping towards international peace and security.

GINI INDEX FOR EQUAL DISTRIBUTION OF INCOME: With an index of 100 being total inequality and 1 being perfect equality we score 31.5 compared to France at 32.7; UK 36.8; US 40.8.

TI 2005 CORRUPTION PRACTICES INDEX: Transparency in business dealings: Canada scores 8.5 on a 10 point scale, ranks fourteenth; UK scores 8.6, ranks eleventh; US scores 7.3 and ranks twentieth. Competitiveness in business: Canada ranks sixteenth.

Like any species, brands are spawned from, and sustained by, their habitat. So we start with a brief snapshot of Canada's unique cultural climate and terrain. While not all the facts are new information, taken together in the context of culture and brand-building, they provide compelling evidence that Canada's brandscape has its own unique contours, especially when juxtaposed with US market profiles, the locus of most of our brand theory.

Our culture of group rights, public institutions and deference to authority has always stood in contrast to America's preoccupation with individualism, private interests and mistrust of authority. However, Canada's social landscape has altered considerably in the past few decades. Today, we're far less deferential to authority and far more open to change than our American counterparts.

Adams echoes a 1999 speech by journalist Peter C. Newman, who was discussing his book *The Canadian Revolution*: "Canadian values have shifted from deference to defiance, from deference to authority, to defiance of authority… This is the good news because when you become self-reliant, when you depend on yourself, instead of having faith in all this other stuff, you become first of all much more interesting; you become a person who is much more adventurous, willing to take risks. It is very un-Canadian but it's true and it's happening."

Both Adams and Newman argue that it's our lack of attachment to history and our diffused sense of identity that make us very adaptable. In his earlier book on Canadian social values, *Sex in the Snow*, Adams wrote: "Canadians have a sort of flexible 'geophilosphy,' more pragmatic and less rooted in history and more in the multicultural, multimedia reality of their everyday existence." That seems born out in more recent Environics studies in which Canadians scored high on attributes like "Adaptability to Complexity," which is defined as: "Tendency to adapt easily to the uncertainties of modern life, and not feel threatened by the changes and complexities of society today. A desire to explore this complexity as a learning experience and a source of opportunity."

Much of Adams's commentary on these differences seems counter-intuitive at first. But he describes how, "people who have a greater sense of personal security (financial, emotional, familial)… feel their personal and professional decisions matter, and they're confident that they're able to navigate the world in all its complexity. This sense of control and comfort with complexity leads people to a greater sense of engagement with their communities and the world around them." Ron Inglehart's World Values survey supports the premise that typically, as a society's affluence increases, its social values become "postmodern," meaning there's greater acceptance of change and diversity, as well as greater individual autonomy.

What's intriguing is the fact that our traditional conservatism has actually morphed into its polar opposite. Adams notes the irony of our evolution vis à vis developments in the US and ponders why an initially conservative society like Canada has ended up producing, "an autonomous, inner-directed, flexible, tolerant, socially liberal, and spiritually eclectic people while an initially 'liberal' society such as the United States has ended up producing a people who are, relatively speaking, materialistic, outer-directed, intolerant, socially conservative, and deferential to traditional institutional authority. Why do these two societies seem to prove the law of unintended consequences?"

Similar themes are evident in other research addressing Canadian attitudes relating to gender, youth and immigrants. For example, a famous study by Geert and Gert Jan Hofstede tracks attitudes and behaviours in more than seventy countries. One of the measures the study tracks is a masculine/feminine index. "Masculine" is ascribed

NORTHERN LATITUDES

A sampling of research contrasting Canadian and US attitudes from surveys conducted between 2000 and 2004.

Source: Environics, *Fire and Ice* by Michael Adams

Canadians 18%	Americans 49%	Agree a father of a family must be master in his own house
Canadians 12%	Americans 24%	Feel violence is all around them
Canadians 67%	Americans 52%	Relate to non-conformists
Canadians 29%	Americans 36%	Feel it's important that people admire the things they own
Canadians 34%	Americans 54%	Feel a car says a lot about a person—it should reflect personal style and image
Canadians 62%	Americans 40%	Feel a car is just an appliance—something to get from point A to B
Canadians 29%	Americans 41%	Derive great pleasure from looking at ads
Canadians 17%	Americans 44%	Believe a widely advertised product is probably a good product

to cultures where emotional gender roles are clearly distinct: men are supposed to be assertive, tough and focused on material success; women are supposed to be more modest, tender and concerned with the quality of life. A society is called "feminine" when emotional gender roles overlap; men and women are supposed to be equally modest, tender and concerned with the quality of life. In the Hofstede rankings, where number one equals the most "masculine" culture (the honour goes to Slovakia) and number seventy-four is the most "feminine" culture (Sweden), the US lands the nineteenth spot; Canada weighs in with a ranking of thirty-three, representing significantly more equity in its social gender roles.

Environics research on youth compares two very distinct youth cohorts or "tribes" in each country with the evocative descriptors "Aimless Dependents" (apathetic, tendency to nihilism) and "New Aquarians" (energetic and idealistic). The social values trend lines are startling:

Proportion of 15-18 year-old population described as Aimless Dependents:
1992: Canada: 27%, US: 34%
2004: Canada: 18% US: 47%

Proportion of 15-18 year-old population described as New Aquarians:
1992: Canada: 7%, US: 12%
2004: Canada: 14% US: 5%

Source: "The Kids of Free Trade," *Marketing Magazine*, May 16, 2005

Michael Adams's commentary on the findings, published in *Marketing Magazine*, notes, "Young people in Canada today are, in their values, more distinct from their American age peers than are their parents or grandparents. And the differences are growing."

The immigrant perspective may not be as dramatic but it provides some interesting cues as to how our openness to change and diversity is nurtured through the attitudes of the eighteen percent of the country that is foreign-born. In an article in *The Globe and Mail* from March 2005, Adams points out that immigrants are typically—and understandably—less attached to nationalism and regionalism. Because their identities are mixed, they tend to view themselves as citizens of the world. But they are, according to Adams, "vastly more interested in cultural pluralism… new Canadians are enthusiastic about interacting with diverse others, agreeing with statements like, 'I learn a lot from meeting people who are different from me.' and, 'Other cultures have a lot to teach us; contact with them is enriching.' " For new Canadians under thirty, the importance of minority cultures is assumed. Adams quips, "Their motto could be 'the other 'R' Us.' "

Adams sees deep implications in these cultural sample cores: "In many ways, it is Canadians who have become the true revolutionaries, at least when it comes to social life… Canadians are at the forefront of a fascinating and important social experiment: we are coming to define a new sociological 'post-modernity' characterized by multiple, flexible roles and identities while Americans, weaned for generations on ideals of freedom and independence, have in general not found adequate security and stability in their social environment to allow them to assert the personal autonomy needed to enact the kind of individual explorations—spiritual, familial, sexual—that are taking place north of the border."

HABITAT FIELD NOTES The portrait Adams paints of contemporary Canadian values is well supported by other research at home and abroad. While the insights into specific audience segments will not be new to many marketers, the larger questions of our evolving brandscape—the trends and implications—hasn't garnered much discussion in the business press. For brand-watchers and business leaders the first lesson is the most obvious. As Michael Adams summarizes, "You cannot speak to Canadians as if they were Americans, not just because it is politically incorrect but because they have different values and priorities and live in a very different context."

The question is, "Do brands grow differently with this kind of northern exposure?" One could use this kind of data to counter the "branch plant" mentality that American businesses often have towards Canadian operations. But as Adams points out in our interview, we are a small market. It doesn't make economic sense to localize every form of communication. For some products and categories, Canadian cultural filters will be less relevant than other determinants of relevance—whether it's first-time parents looking for a brand they can trust or pop culture aficionados looking for a badge of status.

In our next chapter, we'll explore how and where these cultural markers are most relevant to brand development—for customers, employees, partners, communities and other stakeholders—at home and abroad.

First Person Singular

Michael Adams

Habitat: President, Environics Research Group

Field Notes: We asked Adams to elaborate on what factors have contributed to the evolution of Canadian culture and how they are relevant for branding and marketing.

Bloodlines: Michael Adams is the co-founder and president of Environics—a group of research and communications consulting companies with offices in Canada and the US. Since 1970, Adams's work at Environics has focused on monitoring and interpreting the impact of social trends on public policy and corporate strategy. His best-known books include *Sex in the Snow*; *Fire and Ice: The United States, Canada and the Myth of Converging Values*; *American Backlash: The Untold Story of Social Change in the United States* and *Unlikely Utopia: The Surprising Triumph of Canadian Pluralism*.

On autonomy and values...

It is ironic that Canadians, this peace-oriented, pro-government, shy, deferential people have over time become more autonomous than Americans. For Canadians, autonomy extends to all spheres of life: you decide for yourself, I decide for myself. At work, it's about having some control over your projects—being able to exercise initiative and creativity—not having someone looking over your shoulder because they're higher in the office pecking order. At home, it's about flexible leadership. It used to be that everything revolved around Dad, the breadwinner. Today, maybe Dad takes transit to work because Mom needs the car to get to meetings. Everyone's interests and activities matter; it's a matter of compromising, doing what makes sense for everyone. Autonomy extends to identity too: gender identity, ethno-cultural identity, religious identity, even age identity. Canadians want to live lives they define for themselves—the lives that make them happiest. It's not about fulfilling a social role defined by someone else, or climbing up a status hierarchy and getting a Rolex once you arrive. It's about experiences, relationships, and personal freedom.

On autonomy and inter-dependence...

You can only be truly autonomous with interdependence. The myth of American individualism is that autonomy is possible only with independence. Get away from the bad guys; put Grace Kelly into the carriage; ride off to the ranch; stand guard. This vision of the individual is a dream of being master of your domain. When you're master of your domain that means you're removed from the rest of society and if anyone comes on your land they probably mean you harm. Safety in this kind of model is not neighbourhood watch; it's Dad keeping a gun in the nightstand. Dad has to be tough and strong in order to protect his family from outside encroachment. In Canada, there is less deference to patriarchy because Dad is just a guy you live with and maybe love; he's not the police chief and the fire chief and the four-star general.

The two countries' different ideas about freedom really come out when you hear guns discussed. When there is a shooting in Canada, people tend to call for tougher gun laws; Canadians' automatic reaction tends to be collective: that we should be creating a *culture* of safety and non-violence. When there is a shooting in the United States, people tend to argue that the victims (or other "good guys") should have been carrying guns. It's not about a culture of safety, it's about empowering *individuals* to fight back.

Even though Canada is a very big place, we live close together: huddled in cities and along the US border. Our five big cities represent almost half the population. Being urban means living close to a lot of people, which means trusting people: trusting them not to attack you in the street, trusting them to make reasonable amounts of noise, trusting them to respect your privacy. The public domain is underpinned by this generalized trust and the sense that we are interdependent and do better when we share than when we retreat and guard our little plot. In Canada the public domain is very robust: parks, libraries, public education, public healthcare—the things we all use and trust each other to use responsibly.

On the idea of a "Canadian Dream"…
The Canadian dream is at once simple and ambitious: it's the dream of getting people from all over the world together in one place without killing each other. The Canadian dream is compassionate meritocracy: you make your own way, but you don't leave others in the dust. America is a more rugged, one might even say Darwin-istic, meritocracy: you make your own way and the other guy's problem is not something you worry about. Of course the American system is tremendously motivating for people. That narrative of someone going from the log cabin to the White House, from rags to riches, the self-made man who doesn't owe anything to anyone is very compelling. But there's research to show that there may actually be more social mobility in Canada and Europe than in America these days; the trip from the

log cabin to the White House is perhaps not as smooth as it once was.

On culture, values and the workplace…
I think HR [human resources] in Canada is quite different from the United States. Lots of companies try to transplant their HR model from one country to the other and find that it just doesn't work. I think a lot of the trends in Canada are driven by our commitment to gender equality. Forward-thinking Canadian companies are looking quite hard at how to accommodate women, including mothers. In America, childcare, like a lot of things, is seen as more of a private issue: you had the kids, so you figure it out yourself.

And it's not just women who are treated differently in the two countries. In Canada, many young men in traditionally high-pressure, high-personal-cost careers are saying, "I want to be around for my kids. Sure, I'll work on the weekend, but not the whole weekend—and I'll do it from home. I don't need to be a tough guy bragging about my 100-hour weeks. I'd rather read my kids a story at night than win that contest."

Part of what makes this possible in Canada is our greater entitlements and securities. If you push back at work and say you're not taking on that extra project, your family's health care isn't on the line. In America, if you lose your job it is more catastrophic. I think in Canada people are more likely to expect that their employer will adapt to *their* needs, not the other way around.

Americans and Canadians both say, "My family comes first." That's common to the two cultures. But the Canadian at the meeting is going to tell everybody, "This meeting is scheduled from 5:00-6:00 p.m. I have got to pick up my kid from daycare; go visit my mom in the nursing home; get dinner ready for my family; so I've got to get out of here on time." The American at 6:00 looks at her watch and says to herself, "My family comes first, so I can't leave this meeting. Our livelihood and our healthcare is in the balance." So as 6:30 rolls around, the American is still in the meeting for the sake of her family, and the Canadian is gone—for the same reason.

On immigration and multiculturalism...

A lot of our positive attitude to immigration is an accident of history, not so much moral superiority or anything like that. We don't have a border with a Third World country. But America does. It's a bit easier for us. We have a point system so we attract many of the best immigrants in the world. We are still a place where multiculturalism is not a bad word. Here, multiculturalism operates more as a stepping stone to integration than as a way of keeping people separate. Polling shows that Canadians remain amazingly enthusiastic about multiculturalism. We're the most likely of any country to think that immigrants are good for the country, the most likely to think they help the economy grow (as opposed to "taking our jobs"), the least likely to think immigrants commit more crime than "people born here" and on and on. Because we had to do the French-English compromise from the beginning, we've always been compromising. In the '60s there was nationalism, bilingualism, biculturalism. Multiculturalism was the next step in our evolution. And Canadians really want it to work.

On Canadian skepticism...

Here, I think because of skepticism of the Church, skepticism of dads, skepticism of the Americans, we're always questioning. Part of the evolution of Canadians was falling in love with America. We fell deeply in love with America in the '50s and early '60s and American ikons such as Kennedy and Martin Luther King Jr. All that idealism, that forward-looking, ambitious, idealistic time. We were absolutely enchanted by it. Canadians admired American presidents much more than their own prime ministers. Then, with the war in Vietnam and race riots, we thought, "Oh shoot. There's this other side to our cool cousins." So that was part of our evolution, falling out of love with the American Empire, waking up from the American Dream. Previously, we'd fallen out of love with the British Empire and the French Empire, too. So we were sitting here in the 1970s after all these love affairs, looking at each other, and asking what was left. We had to figure out who we were. People got tired of peering over the fence and feeling like life was always happening somewhere else: at Buckingham Palace or in Life magazine or wherever it was. When we first set out, of course, we tended to define ourselves by who we're not and what we're not. But I think slowly, we're evolving into what we are. But it is evolving slowly because we still, most of the time, are saying what we're not. We're questioning every authority: church, dad, advertising, the boss at work, everyone. But we're rebels, not revolutionaries. The difference between a rebel and a revolutionary is that a revolutionary knows how the world should be. A rebel just doesn't want to be told what to do.

On celebrating success...

We think of ourselves as a branch plant, an extension of American capitalism. Once we were hewers of wood and drawers of water and we still rely heavily on natural resources. But I don't think we think of ourselves as a very ingenious people. Take the spectacular success of the Blackberry. It just doesn't fit with the Canadian narrative, so it's not trumpeted in the way some tech success stories are. (Instead we all obsess over Conrad Black.) The fact that there is not a single book on the market about the Blackberry story speaks volumes about the mental posture in this country. If that little gadget were American, or even Swedish or German, you can bet we'd know the story. Just like we know the story of Sergey Brin and Larry Page cooking up the algorithm for Google in their dorm room. There's a mythology about Google because it fits with the American narrative of entrepreneurialism and innovation: the little guy with a great idea. The Blackberry has taken the world by storm but where's the story? Who's going to tell it?

my ikonica

Mostly they would be writers: Margaret MacMillan, Mark Kingwell, Thomas Homer-Dixon, Alice Munro.

GENIUS LOCI: A PRIMER

IN ROMAN MYTHOLOGY, every woman had her *juno* and every man had his *genius*—guardian spirits that bestowed unique gifts of intelligence and prowess. Over time, cities and entire regions claimed their own *genius loci*—spirit of place. It's a highly democratic notion: every community comes equipped with its own super stewards to protect the soul of the locale. Born of unique history, habitat and culture, they act as mentors and champions of indigenous abilities. Like any self-respecting spirits, *genius loci* are elusive, invisible forces, making them easy to overlook or dismiss. But we discount them at our peril. They symbolize our most authentic gifts: essential attributes and adaptations that enable us, not only to thrive in our surroundings, but also to make a valuable contribution in some way.

We believe that Canada has its very own *genius loci*. Whether Canadians choose to acknowledge them or not, they affect our businesses and brands because they mirror the elemental forces of climate, geography, history and social values that define our collective DNA. What's bred in the bone isn't the only arbiter of destiny, but it profoundly shapes our orientation in the world. Our *genius loci* are useful points of orientation that have been sadly lacking in most business analyses. Unlike stereotypes, they hold up useful mirrors of our cultural mores. The brand-builder's creed is "keep your promises." There's plenty of evidence to suggest that values—our codes of behaviour—drive long-term brand success. Therefore, understanding how cultural values underpin notions of authenticity within Canada's diverse communities is a huge—and largely untapped—competitive advantage.

In the course of our fieldwork, we've uncovered eleven specific characteristics that—taken as a whole—distinguish our brand environment in significant ways. At first, we suspected that these were conceptual mirages, tricks of perception that wouldn't withstand closer scrutiny. But after months of exploration, we're convinced they aren't flukes. They echo too consistently across a broad spectrum of organizations. Observe closely, and powerful patterns emerge in the way the most successful Canadian brands interact with their environment. We'll describe these forms of "genius" and what they can mean in the following chapters. As our case studies attest, our *genius loci* aren't parochial. Many of Canada's most successful brands exploit these traits on the world stage with great ingenuity.

But first, however, let's recalibrate our understanding of the role of brands in the interplay of commerce, culture and community.

AUTHENTIC GENIUS Successful organizations have their own forms of genius: great quality, impeccable service, design prowess or a host of other factors that not only make their offerings desirable but distinguish them from their rivals. Consider any competitive brands: Four Seasons versus Ritz Carlton or Telus squaring off against Bell, for example. On the surface they seem to be parity offerings competing for similar customers in the same market. Some analysts would account for their distinct character in terms of business strategies. Others would refer to the relative merits of their marketing prowess. Those are certainly significant factors. But in each case, the contenders also bring very different histories, culture and values to bear in the way

Genius loci: n.
1. The presiding god or guardian spirit of a place.
2. The body of associations connected with or inspirations derived from a place.

"Genius loci."
Canadian Oxford
Dictionary,
Second Edition

genius loci: a primer

they create customer experiences. However brilliant, business and marketing strategies simply can't succeed if they go against the grain of authentic organizational culture. One of the essential questions we set out to explore is, how does our national culture shape perceptions of authenticity for brands?

As Shakespeare reminds us in *Hamlet*, authenticity has two components. Part A: "To thine own self be true." Part B, so the soliloquy goes, is not being "false to any man." Both are essential elements of a brand—how true a business stays to its own sense of purpose and how it's perceived as authentic by others. Brands don't *create* authenticity—they simple reflect the coherence that organizations bring to what they say and what they do. In more prosaic words, it's how consistently a business actually "walks the talk"—internally with its employees and externally with its partners, customers and the public.

E. Joseph Pine and Jim Gilmore, business gurus of *The Experience Economy* fame, make the case that "rendering authenticity" is one of the most critical factors for success in almost any business today. Their get-real manifesto, *Authenticity: What Consumers Really Want*, lays out a new Maslow-style hierarchy of buyer needs that moves from basic availability to affordable price, product quality and, ultimately, authenticity. "Consumers and business-to-business customers now purchase offerings based on how well those purchases conform to their own self-image… People no longer accept fake offerings from slickly marketed phonies; they want real offerings from genuinely transparent sources."

Focusing on authenticity seems particularly relevant for the Canadian market. Based on Environics research we have clear evidence that Canadians are more skeptical about advertising than our neighbours to the south. One of the most consistent responses we heard in our interviews with business leaders is how finely attuned Canadians are to over-hyped marketing. It brings out our contrarian instincts.

From a corporate culture standpoint, authenticity is a prerequisite for employee engagement. During our interview, Pine noted that most organizations don't realize the value of their culture as a competitive advantage: "Your corporate culture very much defines who you are as a company and what it means to be true to self. The essence of authenticity is respect for your heritage, a sense of purpose and your values. Corporate culture is the sum of your body of values. Not many organizations understand this. They hire consultants and say, 'Help us come up with our values.' You already have values. You need to *discover* what they are. If they need to change, that's long, hard work. But you can only start by acknowledging what they are today. There are limits to what you can do that are defined by your heritage, your origins and your history."

Pine's last point is an important one for Canadian brands. Authenticity also means being clear about what we are *not*. There are limitations inherent in our DNA. With finite resources and global competition, indigenous brands can't afford to be bland. Equally important, the people behind them need to be highly engaged, especially in the service sector that represents such a high proportion of Canada's economy. In fact, understanding and nurturing corporate culture emerges as one of the fundamentals of business success in our field research. It's a constant refrain in all our executive interviews. CEO Clive Beddoe attributes WestJet's commercial success—in an industry littered with financial casualties—to its "extreme culture." In our interview he asserts, "Culture and brand are one and the same. The culture creates the brand… What has amazed me is just how powerful this really is and how few people understand it. Until you live it, breathe it, and are part of it, it's almost impossible to grasp."

Because culture is something that we live and breathe, it's also hard to deconstruct. Each organization operates with its own unique lens of values, traditions, history, aspirations, purpose, competencies and experiences that evolve over time. But corporate culture must also draw from, and be meaningful to, the communities it serves. It may seem self-evident to say that commerce can only exist in an ecosystem of culture and community. But it is shocking to realize how little understanding business leaders have of how all the pieces connect. In Canada and elsewhere, businesses used to operate on a very simplistic view of cause and effect, the if-we-build-it-they-will-come approach. Marketers interceded with another form of hubris—it's all about the sell!

> **"CULTURE AND BRAND ARE ONE AND THE SAME. THE CULTURE CREATES THE BRAND… WHAT HAS AMAZED ME IS JUST HOW POWERFUL THIS REALLY IS AND HOW FEW PEOPLE UNDERSTAND IT."** *Clive Beddoe*

MIND THE GAP In the mid-1950s, marketers began promoting a world view far different from the age of authenticity. The notion of everyday customers morphed into "consumers" and bigger, better consumption became the name of the game. The language of marketing devolved into military-style strategies for mass manipulation. In the early '70s, Al Ries and Jack Trout epitomized the guerilla-warfare attitude in a popular marketing treatise entitled, *Positioning: The Battle for Your Mind.* For Ries and Trout devotees, the book promised strategies on how to ensure your brand message—"wheedles its way into the collective subconscious of your market—and stays there," as one promotional blurb trumpeted. "Wheedling" into the collective consumer subconscious became a high-stakes, zero-sum game of marketing dominance. The presumption then was that sheer advertising muscle would ultimately triumph in the market, and in our minds. We consumers were largely oblivious to the billion-dollar battles being waged by titans of industry to lord over tiny areas of our grey matter. For North American marketers, when the end game was simply staking out "mindshare," who needed to worry about authenticity or culture?

With endless repetition, we will remember the phone number for a pizza delivery service, the latest campaign slogan for a beer label or the catchy jingle for an attraction. But brute force marketing has its limitations. For one thing, it's expensive. Return on investment is devilishly hard to measure, and pumping up awareness doesn't automatically translate into purchases. Eventually, even some of the biggest mindshare proponents became battle weary. Niall Fitzgerald, former chair of Unilever, admitted that marketers can't simply lob, "messages and memorability into the skulls of the audience."

MIND YOUR MEANINGS Marketers have spent decades obsessing over why and how we "consume," forgetting that people are not simply "consumers" focused solely on personal gratification. In his book *Culture and Consumption*, Canadian anthropologist Grant McCracken illustrates how much people use the material world to assert personal and social values: "They are seeking not meaning with a capital 'M,' the existential notion of the term. They are looking for small meanings, concepts of what it is to be a man or a woman, concepts of what it is to be middle aged, concepts of what it is to be a parent, concepts of what a child is and what a child is becoming, concepts of what it is to be a member of a community and a country. These are the projects that preoccupy us on a continual basis."

They preoccupy us because we're hard-wired for *meaning*. Neuroscientist Michael Gazzaniga, in describing how the two sides of our brains cooperate, explains that, "the interpretative mechanism of the left hemisphere is always hard at work *seeking the meaning of events*. It is constantly looking for order and reason, *even when there is none…*" (Emphasis added.) As a species, we're driven to search out patterns and purpose. The left side of our grey matter is preoccupied with satisfying our craving for narrative, stories to make sense of things. Aristotle was right. Nature abhors a vacuum. So do our brains. They act like meaning-seeking missiles that target patterns and symbols as ways to frame our experiences in coherent ways.

In their provocative business guide, *Making Meaning*, authors Steve Diller, Nathan Shedroff and Darrel Rhea make the case that, "… for companies to achieve enduring competitive advantage… they must address their customers' essential human need for meaning… Worldwide, consumers are increasingly seeking products and services that… jive with their sense of how the world is, or should be." In other words, the brands that we value most are ones that feed our hunger for authenticity and belonging. While these are universal themes, how brands interpret them in the Canadian context is critical. What does it mean to jibe with how Canadians view the world?

The real power of ikonic brands is in the way they reinforce shared meaning and identity for entire communities, even generations. Douglas Holt describes their ability to trigger powerful, but unexpressed, "little epiphanies—moments of recognition that put images, sounds, and feelings on barely perceptible desires." Ikonic brands have an uncanny ability to capture the zeitgeist of a time or place. "What gels in the collective imagination of a country," Holt explains, "are the few great performances, those that get the myth just right." That "myth" is the set of stories that cement our collective identity; the *entre nous* experiences that underpin our sense of belonging.

Think how Molson's "I am Canadian" television commercial still reverberates long after Joe, its über-Canuck spokesman, has left the scene. Although he was nothing more than an actor with a clever script, "Joe's Rant" tapped a rich cultural artery. It's success came from the fact that the monologue was served up with "insider" nuance. It was archly Canadian—sly, self-deprecating and politely cutting at the same time. Audiences got the irony. Not only did the TV spot win international awards and become a viral Internet phenomenon, it inspired a frenzy of provincial and international adaptations as well.

JOE'S RANT:

Hey, I'm not a lumberjack, or a fur trader…
I don't live in an igloo or eat blubber, or own
a dogsled… and I don't know Jimmy, Sally
or Suzy from Canada, although I'm certain
they're really, really, nice. I have a prime
minister, not a president. I speak English and
French, not American. And I pronounce it
"about," not "a boot." I can proudly sew my
country's flag on my backpack. I believe in
peacekeeping, not policing; diversity, not
assimilation, and that the beaver is a truly
proud and noble animal. A toque is a hat.
A chesterfield is a couch, and it is pronounced
'zed' not 'zee', 'zed'! Canada is the second
largest land mass! The first nation of hockey!
And the best part of North America!
My name is Joe! And I am **CANADIAN**!

Sixty-second TV spot first aired in 2000
Advertiser: Molson Breweries
Agency: Bensimon Byrne D'Arcy
Creative Director/Writer: Glenn Hunt
Director: Kevin Donovan.
Actor: Jeff Douglas (Douglas moved to Los Angeles
in the wake of the commercial's success.)

The commercial won various advertising industry
awards including a 2001 Bessie.

STUDIES IN CHARACTER Authenticity, the lifeblood of ikonic brands, can't be manufactured. By definition, it's rooted in something genuine and relevant that the organization brings to its markets. Every organization needs to define "What's authentic to us?" A product or service itself may not be original but the character of its brand experience certainly can be. Procter and Gamble's Robert T. Blanchard, in his 1999 *Parting Essay*, argued for the importance of brand character: "People have character… so do brands. A person's character flows from his or her integrity: the ability to deliver under pressure, the willingness to do what is right rather than what is expedient. You judge a person's character by his/her past performance and the way he/she thinks and acts in both good times, and especially bad. The same is true of brands."

Marketers often define brands in terms of customer perceptions. But that's only half the yin-yang equation. Authenticity starts with an organization's vision of its role in the world and the value it creates. No focus group ever imagined a Cirque du Soleil. But audiences embrace its originality with such passion because each performance is such an authentic, high-wire act of creative risk-taking. A sense of creative purpose is what powers its brand.

Social marketer Ric Young is passionate in his interview about how great brands are fuelled by purpose and meaning: "You have self-knowledge and you're not timid about acting from that core. But we run our organizations and our societies as though meaning's not important. We're not vigilant and intentional about it." Running our organizations and our societies as though meaning's not important is an astute assessment of what's missing from most business analyses. Like fresh water and clean air, too often we take these necessities of survival for granted. For ikonic brands, nurturing meaning is job number one. Grant McCracken explains that every manager must become a de facto meaning-manager because, "badly constructed, badly managed meanings confuse the consumer, diminish brands, damage careers, generate losses, and help pull stock prices down." Eaton's is a prime example. The venerable department store simply lost touch with the meaning it had enjoyed in Canadian culture for generations.

THE POWER OF PURPOSE No organization can sustain itself without addressing fundamental questions about purpose ("What do we do?"), character ("How we do it?") and relevance ("Why does it matter?"). Canadian business leaders know from experience the downside of a cynical, man-the-lifeboats culture that resists change. What's been less clear is the upside—especially financial—of investing in corporate culture. But the evidence is emerging, and it's compelling.

In our interview with Chaviva Hošek, President of the Canadian Institute for Advanced Research (CIFAR), she describes new insights into personal, social and organizational health factors that show a tangible connection between work that matters and the bottom line. The way to motivate people, Hošek explains, is to have something together and feeling trust in, and from, management." Where management lives by strong organizational values, authenticity thrives. And it pays huge dividends, as

Hošek illustrates: "If you measure it against pay, through regression analysis you can show that a one point improvement in trust in the workplace is worth more than a thirty-percent increase in salary."

While there may be no line for it on a balance sheet yet, "doing the right thing" has very real market currency as well. Business analysts are taking note of the authenticity dividend that accrues to organizations that do more than give lip service to their social commitments. Market watchers, who are paid to be skeptical, recognize the systems effect on an organization's ability to sustain revenues if, for example, they are plagued with ethical, labour or environmental risks. Numerous investment firms are now indexing stocks of companies with strong social responsibility platforms. In 2007, it was the fastest growing segment of the investment community internationally. In Canada, the category grew more than seven hundred percent in two years, from $65.5 billion to $503 billion.

As we'll see throughout our interviews, the link between a deep sense of purpose, beliefs and market success is very real in practice as well as theory. "Once you look at a brand as a belief system," according to Patrick Hanlon, author of *Primal Branding*, "it automatically gains all the advantages that enterprise strives for: trust, vibrancy, relevance, a sense of values, community, leadership, vision, empathy, commitment, and more… Believing is belonging. When you are able to create brands that people believe in, you create groups of people that feel they belong." The lesson here is important. Like any natural system, brandscapes operate on simple rules. Authenticity breeds belief (culture). Belief breeds belonging (community). Belonging breeds loyalty—the holy grail of commerce.

AS TIME GOES BY… The other simple but inescapable rule is that time waits for no brand. Organizations often underestimate the fact that cultures and communities are constantly morphing. Ikonic brands must develop adaptive strengths and feedback sensors to keep them highly attuned to their turf. But being adaptive is the kind of risky business that many branders avoid. Doug Holt chides marketers who systematically strip their brands of the "messiness of society and history in search of its purified essence." It's exactly that "messiness" of time and place that gives the brand its relevance. The process is tricky because brands have a cultural presence and meaning independent of the organizations that created them. The social life of a brand is impossible to anticipate. Research in Motion, for example, couldn't have foreseen that "Crackberry" would become the colloquial for Blackberry because of its addictive reputation.

For Holt, the great brand builders are those that develop a "cultural activist organization… a company that is organized to understand society and culture, not just consumers." Even the word "consumer" deflects consideration of our social connections. When branders define audiences strictly in terms of their consumption proclivities, it's easy to ignore how culture and community fit into their experience. Holt envisions future brand managers as genealogists who understand their brand as, "a cultural artifact moving through history. They must develop sensitive antennae to pick up tectonic shifts in society… To create new myths, managers must get close to the nation."

Getting close to the nation brings us full circle, re-examining our own history, culture and the unique powers of our *genius loci*.

Canadians have forever been defined by the country's intense climate and geography. Today, the realities of globalization, competition and market fragmentation make our brandscape even more challenging. But, as we shall hear throughout the coming chapters, ikonic Canadian brands thrive because they adapt to difficult conditions with such ingenuity. The riskier the market environment becomes, the more finely honed character and identity need to be. As Grant McCracken advises, "The solution to a diverse market of conflicting expectations cannot be fainthearted risk management. Blandness is no place of safety. Indeed, as markets splinter, it is more dangerous than it has ever been before."

When Michael Adams quips, "I don't think we think of ourselves as a very ingenious people… It just doesn't fit with the Canadian narrative," he touches on one of our collective brand challenges. Like McLuhan's fish, we subvert our strengths and assets simply because they are so elemental for us. (Canadians often respond with Woody Allen-esque bemusement to the fact that there are a number of major US universities with thriving Canadian Studies programs. "Why?" is the typical response.)

GENII-OLOGY Canadians can't claim exclusive rights to any one characteristic in the same way that Canada doesn't own the franchise for dramatic mountains, vast prairies, arctic tundra or windswept shorelines. Nevertheless, the sum total of all that extraordinary geography creates something unique in the world.

The following field report sketches eleven forms of communal genius that we've encountered. Our premise is that these attributes are important orienteering markers for any business navigating our brandscape because they shape our ecosystem of commerce, culture and community in essential ways. We can't claim that this is a definitive compendium. Our analysis is inductive—based on observations of hundreds of indigenous brands and the cross-section of leaders from businesses, organizations and service firms we interviewed. Certainly, no one ikonic brand embodies all of these attributes. Nevertheless, we were surprised at how consistently these themes surfaced, unprompted, in our discussions. Our *genii loci* are powerful spirits of place, as inspiring and elusive as the Northern Lights. As you read the "First Person Singular" viewpoints in the following chapters, their spirits spring to life in colourful and dramatic ways.

LATITUDES OF GENIUS

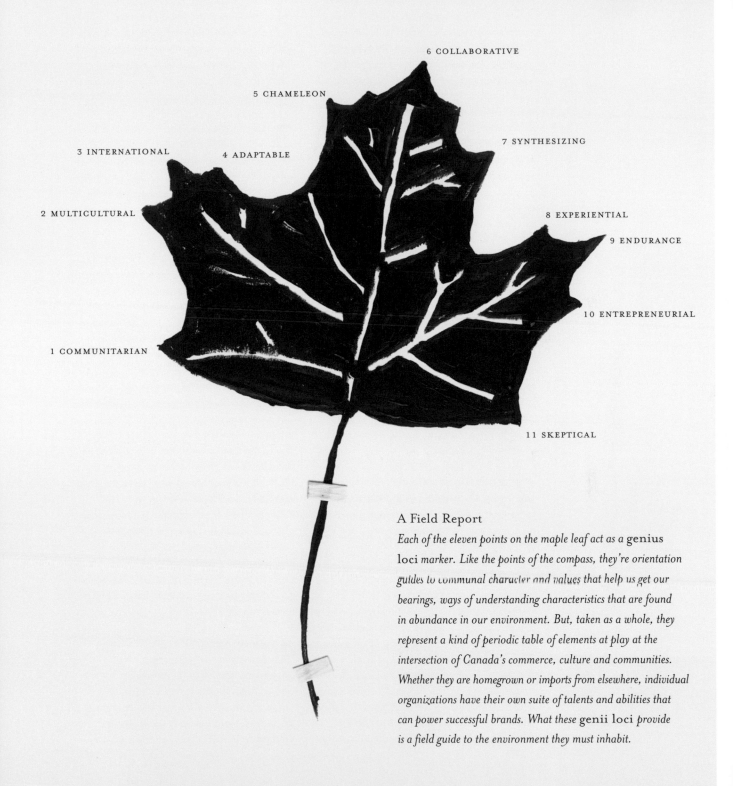

6 COLLABORATIVE

5 CHAMELEON

3 INTERNATIONAL   4 ADAPTABLE

7 SYNTHESIZING

2 MULTICULTURAL

8 EXPERIENTIAL

9 ENDURANCE

10 ENTREPRENEURIAL

1 COMMUNITARIAN

11 SKEPTICAL

A Field Report

Each of the eleven points on the maple leaf act as a genius
loci *marker. Like the points of the compass, they're orientation
guides to communal character and values that help us get our
bearings, ways of understanding characteristics that are found
in abundance in our environment. But, taken as a whole, they
represent a kind of periodic table of elements at play at the
intersection of Canada's commerce, culture and communities.
Whether they are homegrown or imports from elsewhere, individual
organizations have their own suite of talents and abilities that
can power successful brands. What these* genii loci *provide
is a field guide to the environment they must inhabit.*

1 COMMUNITARIAN Our True North is communal. Canada's history, scale and urban character reinforce a collective respect for communities and the public "commons." There is a strong egalitarian streak in many of our most successful brands. Tim Hortons is an example of how an ikonic Canadian brand plays the just-one-of-us community card particularly well. Every order of coffee and donuts comes with a large dollop of "always there" neighbourhood connections. It's the same with Canadian Tire, WestJet and others: everyone's welcome but, please, park your pretensions at the door. Co-operatives are significant, mainstream businesses here—think The Co-operators (insurance); Vancity (bills itself as the fourth largest financial co-op in the world), and Mountain Equipment Co-op (whose membership represents almost one-tenth of the Canadian population). Given our culture of shared responsibility, it's also not surprising that community engagement is highly valued by the public. In international studies, Canadians are in the vanguard of empowered and active consumers demanding that corporations be more socially accountable. We expect our brands to "walk their talk" with conviction. Recent research shows that one quarter of Canadians always or often take corporate social responsibility into account when making everyday purchases and investment decisions.

2 MULTICULTURAL Our bicultural genesis has forced us to learn the value of accommodation. That Canada is a very multicultural society today is merely a statistical fact. What defines us is how avidly we embrace our diversity. We lead the world in viewing multiculturalism as a positive benefit, by a huge margin. The Aga Khan recently located his Global Centre for Pluralism here because of his contention that, "of all the modern industrialized societies, Canada is by far the most effective and by far the most successful in its pluralism, and therefore there was something very serious to learn from Canada." What we see as mere entertainment, others see as intrepid risk-taking. The launch of CBC's *Little Mosque on the Prairie* sitcom garnered international attention

because it was seen as so perilous by outsiders. The *New York Times* called it, "new and perhaps treacherous terrain." Marketers may grumble about having to accommodate diversity in everything from customer service to packaging and technology solutions, but that versatility is a great asset for Canadian firms serving niche segments, cultivating regional markets or challenging multinationals at home and abroad.

3 INTERNATIONAL Canadians are very realistic about our place in the world. We know we're not the centre of the universe. Fred Schaeffer, President and CEO of McCain Foods Canada, believes, "Canadians make some of the best ex-pats because they are more externally focused, more open to ideas outside of their culture." Like all small economies, we've always been forced to look beyond our borders to sustain growth, which makes us adept at building bridges across borders. We have a strong track record abroad as good business partners. In a 2007 study, the University of Toronto's Institute for Competitiveness and Prosperity notes that many Canadian firms are leaders in their fields internationally, albeit in increasingly narrower markets. The study compares the number of Canadian companies that ranked in the top five in the world in their particular sectors during the past decade. In 1985, thirty-three Canadian firms claimed that distinction; by 2007 the number had jumped to seventy-two, with hefty average revenue gains as well. Roger Martin—the institute's head and Dean of U of T's Rotman School of Management—urged corporate Canada to focus on growing internationally competitive companies. "It's the defining thing," Martin quipped. "You either go out and play the game, or have the game brought to you."

4 ADAPTABLE Our cultural adaptability shows up in research on several dimensions: tolerance for ambiguity, comfort with complexity, willingness to experiment. These are also the attributes of a resilient, whatever-it-takes business survival instinct. Entrepreneurs in Canada have to be highly versatile and self-reliant to overcome the challenges of competing in a welterweight economy. Organizations like Mountain Equipment Co-op, Roots and Umbra have been driven to innovate through supply chain management, design, marketing, distribution and community-building as a way of offsetting potential market liabilities. As mass markets become increasingly fragmented, knowing how to play the edges effectively to serve specialized, niche communities is a great asset.

5 CHAMELEON Playing "Spot The Canadian," noting homegrown celebrities who've made it abroad, is a national pastime. We can be smug—and validated—when other cultures embrace Canadian entertainers, broadcasters or artists as one of their own. Unlike their US counterparts, whose value proposition is often overtly "American," many ikonic Canadian brands succeed by camouflaging themselves in the local culture. Boston Pizza and American Apparel are two overt examples of Canadian businesses operating undercover with Yankee monikers. The Brits claim McCain as one of their own— the best chips in the world would have to be from the UK. Research in Motion's Blackberry belongs to wired citizens of the world. The "gold standard" of luxury hoteliers, Four Seasons Hotels, adapts easily to every cultural context. On home turf, contrast the way Second Cup withstood the Starbucks juggernaut. While Starbucks enforces strict guidelines for its retail presence, Second Cup, Canada's largest specialty coffee retailer, allowed shops to burrow into a neighbourhood based on a corporate philosophy where quality, consistency and diversity are entirely compatible. Second Cup exteriors were often highly localized—a café in the heart of a gay community welcomed its local brethren quite differently from a business-centric urban core outlet. Chameleons don't preen like other creatures; their genius is responding quickly to changes in the environment. (Perhaps it should be no surprise that Canadian Tyler Brulé, the international taste maven, dubbed his first highly successful style magazine *Wallpaper*.)

6 COLLABORATIVE Our natural instinct for collaboration shapes our brandscape in several ways. Coming from an unforgiving, unpredictable climate, we know the wisdom of not going it alone. Playing well with others is essential when your survival depends on cooperation. Collaboration can also give organizations "critical mass" when there are big challenges that are too complex to handle solo. Canada has great strength as a convener. Our knack for getting disparate players to the table gives us more clout internationally than our population size and resources would warrant. Fair play matters. In his interview, one very insightful CEO characterizes this difference in the way US and Canadian businesses compete: For Americans, success is "killing the competition"; in Canada, it's "fighting to a draw." Ensuring everyone gets a piece of the action is a very pragmatic survival response. When today's competitor could be tomorrow's collaborator, it makes sense not to pursue a "scorched earth" policy that might limit your options in the future.

7 SYNTHESIZING Ikonic brands know how to connect the dots. Integrating diverse influences into a coherent whole is an important complement to being collaborative. It requires a particular genius to cross-pollinate seemingly disparate elements into successful new hybrids. From food to fashion, Canada's cool factor has been its ability to fuse ideas and trends. Dave Nichol parlayed Loblaw's President's Choice private label into a globetrotting, culinary docent for millions of North Americans. We see potential in the mundane. Umbra created a burgeoning "home fashion" market that rivals Ikea's global reach by marrying signature stylists—Karim Rashid became the first of many—with the most utilitarian of objects, including garbage cans, picture frames and the lowly window shade.

8 EXPERIENTIAL The Canadian leaning towards intrinsic versus extrinsic values translates into a bias for experiences. It's a small but telling point that BMW Canada diverges from its US counterpart on that one key word… from the promise of "The Ultimate Driving

Machine" to "The Ultimate Driving Experience." Michael Adams argues we're becoming a people who see, "vitality—the ability to experience lives of energy and intensity in a more ethical world—as the most desirable end in our society." There's a strong streak of nomad and wanderlust in our psyche. Our youth, weaned on multiculturalism and broadband access to the world, are travelling in overwhelming numbers. Canada has been unusually fertile ground for a number of ikonic travel brands: Four Seasons Hotels and Resorts, Fairmont, Butterfield and Robinson, Mountain Equipment Co-op, even Tilley Endurables. Compare Four Seasons with one of its biggest competitors, Ritz Carlton. While both compete in the über-luxury category, the Ritz experience tends to more traditional trappings of the grand hotel, an extrinsic show of hot-and-cold-running marble and gilt. The genius "luxe" of Four Seasons, as any brand loyalist will tell you, is a service ethos that's steeped in experiences of personal wellbeing, not just *things*.

9 ENDURANCE Our ikonic brands endure through a special alchemy of patience, tolerance and a last-man-standing contrarian streak that's been bred in our bones. Whether it's because of geography, climate, history or immigration, forbearance is one of our strong suits. The unofficial motto of the Canadian Federation of Independent Businesses is, "we don't give up and we won't go away." In Canadian history, the large footprint of family-run empires—Batas, Bronfmans, McCains, Westons and so on—also encourages taking the long view. So does our economic reliance on the worlds of finance and natural resources. In timber and insurance alike, Q1 results are far less critical than ten-to-twenty-year scenarios. You'll hear patience and endurance echoed throughout many of our interviews, from Rogers to Manulife.

10 ENTREPRENEURIAL The myth is that Canadians are allergic to risk. Not true, if stats on entrepreneurism are any measure. Corporate Canada has been largely dominated by upstart entrepreneurs and family dynasties. Research from the Sauder

School of Business indicates that there are one million family-owned firms in Canada. They account for over eighty percent of all businesses, forty-five percent of Canada's GDP, fifty percent of employment and seventy-five of job creation. A nation of immigrants and self-starters, Canadians have always been savvy about playing in the white (not snowbound) spaces between big, established industries. Many an ikonic brand was formed from what authors W. Chan Kim and Renée Mauborgne have dubbed "Blue Ocean Strategy," the art of scouting and capitalizing on previously unmapped opportunities. Canada has a long ikonoclastic tradition of just such "challenger" brands. Who knew one could build an international empire from frozen fries, transform a depleted circus tradition into a vibrant art form, redefine mobile devices or make cable television hip?

11 SKEPTICAL Hubris does not play well north of the forty-ninth parallel. In fact, satire is one of our most successful exports. Celebrity is cool, but only to a point. The maple leaf crowd is more likely to be watching from the back of the pack—interested but not easily won over. As a nation of "doubting Thomas" types, our BS radar is finely tuned. Advertising may be entertaining but the percentage of Canadians who believe a widely advertised product is probably a good one is extremely low relative to our American counterparts. This is the home of *Adbusters*, the magazine dedicated to exposing the hype behind the headlines. Authenticity counts. Ikonic brands not only win over skeptics, they inspire fierce loyalty when they get simple, but telling, details of authenticity right. For example, Mountain Equipment Co-op's rigorous commitment to green business practices inspires great loyalty from its outdoor-loving members. The brand's contribution of more than five thousand new words to the French lexicon for extreme outdoor sport has made it an international hero of francophones internationally and paid huge dividends at home with Quebecers.

Ric Young

Field Notes: Young's passionate critique of brands as belief systems digs deep into the brandscape terrain, separating the "fools gold" from the mother lode of story, meaning and possibility for Canada's future.

Habitat: Principal, E Y E

Bloodlines: Ric Young runs a self-described "social projects studio," founded in 1993, where he develops long-term, often large-scale, social issue projects designed to foster social innovation through public engagement or, as Young puts it, "change the world in some way or another." His clients include corporations such as Shell Canada, Adidas and AstraZeneca as well as numerous not-for-profits. They all come to Young to develop strategies, campaigns and partnerships that produce groundbreaking social initiatives the likes of Frontline Health, Right to Play and True Sport. Young has also been the strategic force behind a number of public dialogue projects: The Society We Want, with Canadian Policy Research Networks; Our Millennium, a nationwide community engagement program with Community Foundations of Canada; Template for Transformative Dialogue, for the Toronto Community Foundation; the Banff Dialogues, a series in which important thinkers from the art, science, business, environment and society communities explore the role of creativity. In addition to stints on the boards of the Canadian Centre for Philanthropy and the Calmeadow Foundation, Young currently serves on the board of EcoTrust Canada, the advisory board of Right To Play and Imagine Canada's corporate citizenship committee.

On brand and meaning…

It's almost impossible to understand brand unless you think of brand as narrative. When a brand is a reductionist exercise, you squeeze all meaning out of it. I think brands are the weirdest things in the entire universe. Everybody talks about branding. But I don't know that anybody has a shared idea about what a brand is. An astonishing amount of money, productive energy, good talent and corporate strategy goes into doing this thing called branding. What people are talking about is actually that alchemy where a thing goes from being inert to having magical properties. There's a magic theatre that happens in the best of brands.

Where do you really make meaning? Inside yourself. And I'm not just saying that as a metaphor. Take the Nike Swoosh. I knew some of the people who were at Nike. They said, "We didn't do research. We sat in a room until we got passionate about something. When we were totally passionate, in love with the thing, we thought we could take it out to the world and we took our chances." I asked the founder of a hugely successful US ad agency, "How do you do it? How did you make an organization that's so consistently creative?" He said two things: Work relentlessly to get the question right, to know what real problem you're solving. Have utter clarity on that. Then, bring your own truth to it. The best story wins. Martin Luther King… Nelson Mandela… were not doing focus groups to speak powerfully to the people that they needed to engage. That power came from something that they did within. The hardest thing is to live close to truthfulness. That's where real power comes from, that's where real strength comes from. Instead the world has a whole industry to do this manufacturing of meaning. Which is, in the long run, exactly the opposite. It's a hemorrhaging of meaning.

You can't speak truthfully, unless you've thought truthfully. Instead what we get are code words that are completely loaded and completely empty. You know… commitment to excellence, customer focus or the value statements of just about any corporation. Two years and five million dollars of consultants and you could do a search and replace on any of them and they would apply to probably 90 percent of corporations. Why go through this whole exercise to get at words that make them sound exactly the same as everybody else? When everybody has to have a card in their wallet to remember what the six key values of the organization are, that tells you that nobody knows… there's no truth being told because it's not connecting at a meaning-making level. They bring in branding experts to figure out, "Okay, now what's the cloak we wear? Now that we've gone through this therapy that's produced not a single insight about ourselves, now we're going to figure out who our couturier should be. So, we put on a cloak that is meant to differentiate ourselves when all we have done is to prove that we can't understand one thing about ourselves that actually makes us different. Look at corporate reports, look at most advertising, listen to most CEO speeches, look at most press releases… Where do you see an expression of character?

Real leaders, without any intellectualizing and philosophizing, actually understand what brand is, in the way that brand is character. Character that is charged with a sense of soul. Clever makeover artists don't come along and breath soul into people or things or organizations. That's acquired through living a life of meaning. That's acquired by not selling your soul at every choice you make. Character is expressed through actions. You have to live in relationship and in response to the world. Great leaders know that. Second tier leaders think that there is a

plan, and an imposition of a plan and that it's all manufactured and controlled. Show me one great business that has evolved over time, especially in changing times, simply according to plan. The actions we take both reveal and shape our character. The stories and narrative that we give to the swirl of events in our lives reveals us.

What does integrity mean? That we're nice guys? Integrity means that you have coherence and consistency and you know who you are. You have self-knowledge and you're not timid about acting from that core. We run our organizations and our societies as though meaning's not important. We're not vigilant and intentional about it. We're not smart about it. And yet, if you talk to real leaders, this stuff matters to them. No one can now think that they win just because they created an extra billion dollars. So what. That's a game that's been played a hundred times. There's no distinction in that. Real leaders want to punch above their weight in the universe. They want to have lasting impact. They want to change things. They are necessarily involved in meaning systems.

On Canada's growth…

I went away when I was twenty years old to live in England. Like Madame Bovary, I always thought life was elsewhere so, I'm a reluctant patriot. But I actually deeply believe that Canada could be what I would call a successful society in the Twenty-first Century. The qualities that exist in Canada, that we are not conscious of, or that we are embarrassed by, are exactly the qualities we need. We should recognize them as competencies and strengths and unique characteristics of this place, which, both by design and by accident, we are fortunate enough to have. To me, they are qualities of civility, and a basic recognition of what I call the "between," that civic space. People laugh at Canadian manners—that respect for the space between people—but there's enough elasticity in Canada that we can accommodate multi-identity systems. Those are qualities that make us incredibly poised to be a leader and an exemplar in the world. It's not just a peace giver and it's not just because this'll be a kinder, gentler place. It's because Twenty-first Century creativity is necessarily collaborative. Nobel Prize winners are now teams, rather than individuals. The Twenty-first Century world is necessarily a multi-identity world. We've figured out how to create respectful and relatively harmonious living systems where people with multiple identities can co-habit.

But this is exactly the kind of stuff that Canada is oblivious too, or embarrassed by. And so part of Canada, like every middle child or aspiring artist, actually wants to imitate other forms of power. Every struggling writer, before he or she discovers their own voice, wants to be a writer that they admire and so they are imitative. The transformation to true artistic strength is a recognition of your own voice, the thing that maybe you are embarrassed by, or horrified by, the thing that is unique. It goes right back to what we were saying about branding and integrity... the coming to terms with that which is you, with authenticity, and recognizing in that how to be strong. That's where Canada fails, and has behaved like a provincial place. But it doesn't have to now because it's just made the remarkable accomplishment of a remarkable society, with incredible strengths. We just don't see the strengths yet. The journey of adulthood is to try to understand who you really are, and to find those things that are inside you that are strong.

Well-being connects to—this is why I think it's so Canadian—what I was talking about the civic space. Well-being itself is so deeply tied to the strength and quality of the connective tissue amongst us. That's not a moral statement—it's practical and empirical and scientific, when you look at population health studies. The pursuit of individual stature and happiness at the expense of the well-being of the social fabric... it's a mug's game because you can't be well within if your not part of a social fabric. We have to understand that cultures express themselves, like character, through the things that they pay attention to and the things that they do. Our health care system may not be sustainable in the way that it is... I don't know. But, why is there such a hue and cry when we want to dismantle it? Because we're not just dismantling the pragmatics of health care, we are dismantling something of our culture, our character, what it means to be Canadian. Places are not just physical. They are relational. And the relationship between place and identity is profoundly important. Meaning making and future making go hand in hand.

"CULTURES EXPRESS THEMSELVES, LIKE CHARACTER, THROUGH THE THINGS THAT THEY PAY ATTENTION TO AND THE THINGS THAT THEY DO." *Ric Young*

4

BRAND EXPERIENCE ATLAS

God is in the reciprocity

LAY OF THE LAND Not only was Samuel de Champlain an intrepid explorer, he was also an experienced map-maker with a fine hand for telling detail. Beyond their practical navigational facts, his finely wrought sketches of New France's earliest outposts also capture expressive attributes of the land and its newly rooted settlements. Our field notes so far include bits of history, habitat and a roster of guardian spirits. Inspired by Champlain's astute eye, the "Experience Atlas" illustrates the lay of the land as we've encountered it. The topographic range is quite broad: We've explored brands of various pedigrees—some newly spawned, others more than a century old—across the spectrum of business, public sector, arts and not-for-profits. Compiling an atlas gives us the opportunity to do several things: chart different brand arenas; identify some of their distinguishing characteristics, and highlight some over-arching patterns.

Brands represent complex systems of relationship, identity and meaning. What's emerged from all our scouting is a simple observation: Ikonic brands thrive because of their ability to connect commerce, culture and community in authentic and meaningful ways. Reciprocity is the key. Employees want to know their work is somehow connected to meaningful goals. Communities want a fair deal economically (e.g. jobs and investment) but not at the expense of their social values as Wal-Mart and Starbucks—organizations that have felt the sting of local push-back—will attest.

Our atlas allows us to compare and contrast how culture and community shape commerce in different scenarios. What's fascinating is to compare how successful brands, even within the same sector, weave these strands together in unique ways that create very different outcomes. Before we unfold our atlas, let's first explore how the territories of commerce, culture and community relate to each other.

COMMERCE Commerce, quite literally, begins with relationship. Combine the Latin prefix *com* (together) with *merx* (merchandise) and you're in business. The whole purpose of any enterprise is, of course, to create value. The important questions are how organizations create value and for whom.

There are shelf-loads of books describing the economic multiplier effect of strong brands—higher margins, more loyalty, greater resilience and so forth. Well-schooled brand managers know the fundamentals of "exceeding expectations" of clearly defined target groups with good value and reliable performance. But ikonic brands up the ante to create worth in ways that parallel Jim Collins' *Good to Great* business bestseller. Collins uses a humble woodland creature to describe the single-mindedness of organizations that make the leap from acceptable to exceptional. Good-to-great organizations are, he writes, "more like hedgehogs—simple, dowdy creatures that know 'one big thing' and stick to it." The hedgehog metaphor becomes the centerpiece of the good-to-great business model. Its three moving parts have all the hallmarks of mythic narrative: a hero's quest to be "best in the world" at something; a specific set of well-oiled tools to get the job done (the "economic engine"), and the chutzpah to succeed, born of deep, authentic passion for the task at hand.

In his own hand...

Champlain's sketches of Quebec, published in 1613.

Ikons of greatness

*Although they share
a similar profile, beavers
and hedgehogs are
biologically quite distinct.
Hedgehogs are shy
insectivores while our
national ikon is a highly
social, industrious creature
renowned for its building
prowess and adaptability,
equally at home on land
and in water.*

While Collins's theme of greatness garnered lots of traction in corporate boardrooms, many organizations treat his analysis as a simplistic recipe for success. The economic tools inevitably absorb the lion's share of attention because they're the most concrete and quantifiable components. The narrative—"we'll be best in the world at (fill in the blank)"—is quickly dispensed with in a mission statement that's enshrined in lofty text. Passion is interpreted as a form of cheerleading with all the campy accoutrements of slogans and mnemonics… ("What's that spell? S-e-r-v-i-c-e!")

Great brands, like truly great organizations, dig deeper. In the past, stellar market leaders just had to excel at being relevant and distinct, best-in-class in some way. But with customers and shareholders demanding corporate accountability and ever-more skepticism in the employee ranks, authenticity has become the great new divide. Internally, superficial cheerleading can't nurture the deep passion that grows from meaning and trust. Externally, corporate values are also affecting market value as more analysts do the math on trading short-term returns for long-term viability. Ikonic brands infuse the best-in-class quest with a powerful sense of purpose that fortifies competitiveness while strong character fuels the economic engines of differentiated products and services. Not trying to be all things to all people enables businesses to focus their resources based on clear priorities.

The interesting trait that many of Canada's ikonic brands share is how broadly they interpret the notion of value. Shareholder return is the priority. But in the big scheme of things—especially in a culture where endurance is a strong suit—building other forms of social and cultural capital serves long-term business imperatives as well. For Canadian business, paying attention to the "com" in commerce isn't just about good-neighbourliness. Our relative economic size and don't-go-it-alone survival instincts make it a prudent strategy for risk-averse organizations.

CULTURE Every organization pays lip service to the sentiment that, "people are our greatest asset." There are often, of course, huge disparities between walk and talk. Our field reports also demonstrate that ikonic brands thrive in fertile corporate cultures; cultures that coalesce around explicit demonstrations of purpose, values and meaning. These are places where identity, codes of behaviour and social rites nurture a sense of belonging and the climate of trust is continually stoked by stories and actions that inform everyday "moments of truth." Peter Robinson, CEO of Mountain Equipment Co-op, states plainly, "the culture you earn is the one you practice every day."

Trust, belief and belonging are magnetic forces that are critical success factors for organizations. Researcher John Helliwell, a Fellow of the Canadian Institute for Advanced Research (CIFAR) and Professor Emeritus of Economics at the University of British Columbia, is spearheading groundbreaking work that's studying well-being in the workplace. It was Helliwell's research that identified how improving trust in management by one point, on a ten-point scale, can be the equivalent of a thirty percent change in income for employees. It turns out that authenticity and trust are not "soft" business values at all. The implication is one that executives (and their corporate boards) should note carefully. Management's credibility as models of corporate values can have a huge economic impact on the organization.

In our interview, Helliwell points out that employee engagement and efficacy are intrinsically tied to trust. Engagement is more that simple consultation. "People at all levels must feel it's their enterprise," he explains. Those who feel a sense of ownership take initiative. Initiative leads to willingness to shoulder responsibility. Responsibility fosters cooperation for collective success. Once the goals and roles are clear in high-trust environments, people know how to get the job done. More importantly, as Helliwell asserts, "People have to be prepared to take risks not for themselves but for others. That takes confidence. It requires you to believe that the other person takes your interests seriously, not because it's going to make them money but because they are your interests. That basic human point is so often forgotten in business."

Aeroplan CEO and President Rupert Duchesne provides a very practical demonstration of that point in his interview: "When you hold people accountable for what they're doing, they realize that they're part of an organization that cares about performance, that cares about its customers. We've seen extraordinary statistics come out of the call centres since we've done that. Productivity five years ago was fifty-three percent. It's now in the low eighties. That's the active work time versus paid time. You don't get that through people being ordered what to do. You get it by persuading them this is a good thing to do."

Culture can't survive on trust alone. It needs to be nurtured or it will wither and atrophy just like any natural system. Jane Jacobs, the noted urbanist, was very succinct on the subject of culture: "Use it or lose it," she intoned in *Dark Age Ahead*. As we will see, ikonic brands play close attention to managing the meaning of their brand. Much like any traditional religion, carriers of meaning take many forms starting with genesis stories right through to creeds, symbols and totems, language and rituals. Each element plays an important role in reinforcing cultural continuity and cohesion.

GENESIS STORIES In the beginning… Whether it all started in a garage (Canadian Tire) or on a mountaintop tent in a blizzard (Mountain Equipment Co-op), a compelling genesis story is a memorable lesson in overcoming great odds to serve a timely need or powerful vision. It can speak to hope, imagination, ingenuity, perseverance or simply guts. That taproot story and entrepreneurial spark become authentic touchstones for all subsequent generations. The strengths that enabled the enterprise to survive adverse conditions from its origins can be reinterpreted over time to suit future challenges as well.

CREEDS The creed is a capsule "gospel according to…"—core principles that fuel brand experiences internally as well as externally. Every organization needs its shorthand for communicating core principles: Here's what we believe; how we make a difference in the world; the challenges we've overcome, and the qualities that make us succeed. Creeds act as the golden rules that underpin doing things "right."

SYMBOLS Symbols are the sensory connectors and expressions of culture. From logos and trademarks to a range of physical and aesthetic touches, these are essential ingredients in the "secret sauce" that distinguishes experiences. The Blackberry—with its minuscule keyboard and interface—launched a whole new category of communication devices. Cirque du Soleil's yellow and blue striped tent is a bold symbol of the wonders within. Even devices as twee as Sandy McTire, the jaunty Scot who graces Canadian Tire money, can add instantly recognizable heritage and warmth to a brand's character.

RITUALS, LANGUAGE Ikonic brands pay close attention to the power of storytelling, language and ritual to nurture culture. There are no employees at WestJet, only WestJetters. WestJetters serve guests, not passengers. The airline's finance and accounting teams resides in a self-described "bean land." Celebrations of great service abound. Aeroplan celebrates its best customer experience stories under the moniker "Aeroplan Moments." It routinely engages staff in rapid-fire brainstorming sessions dubbed "guerrilla workshops" to encourage on-brand innovation. Word-of-mouth is the most potent affirmation of a great brand's culture. The litany of exceptional service stories that are transmitted with all the efficiency of wildfire among Four Seasons loyalists have made their employees, especially the concierge staff, legendary in traveller circles.

Genesis stories, creeds, myths, symbols and rituals are all powerful tools for sustaining corporate culture which is, by definition, organic and messy at times. Internal ballast is all the more important in times an organization is coping with great turbulence. Expressions of belonging help to clarify purpose, renew identity and reinforce core values. Some values may be more aspirational than others but they all have to be clearly rooted in demonstrable "moments of truth" that exemplify the character that the organization is striving to become.

With robust corporate values, organizations can be more flexible because employees know how to improvise appropriately when the inevitable anomaly pops up. The modus operandi becomes less controlling but more coherent. When WestJet's Clive Beddoe describes how staff made good on lost luggage containing a bride-to-be's wedding dress he adds proudly, "They don't have to ask. They just do what they know is right. What makes people feel that this is a great place to work is that they have that licence."

Scott Lerman, founder of Lucid Brands and counsel to many Fortune 100 businesses, underscores the importance of getting the cultural meaning right internally first: "Not every product can be profound. But character can be a defining trait." He recommends that CEOs, "go out and talk to the people who care about the business. After all, don't you want people that are passionate about what makes you great? If we can learn to listen to our own people and to understand what makes them engaged and passionate then maybe we have learned enough to start to do that with strangers."

COMMUNITY   The Japanese don't think of corporations as just impersonal entities whose main function is to provide services and goods; they personify them as places where people work. Advertising is a litmus test not just of product but also relationship—"Do I want to do business with these people?" In deference to those community values, Japan is the only country in the world where Procter and Gamble, one of the most product-centric global organizations in existence, signs off its ads with a corporate—not product—message that reflects its organizational values.

Commerce is ultimately dependent on nurturing strong relationships not just with individual customers but also communities as well. Whether they're defined by geography, special interests or simply shared passions, ikonic brands are diligent in fostering and protecting their community connections, the shared sense of entre nous and belonging. Community-building is far richer territory than the simple buy-ten-get-one-free mechanics of typical loyalty programs. Tim Hortons, Vancity and Cirque du Soleil all use quite different strategies to build community relationships. The important thing is that community is an integral part of their business strategy, not an afterthought. Community connects represent high-trust contracts that warrant great respect. For Cirque du Soleil, the two million fans who've enlisted to be part of its Club Cirque network represent a invaluable resource that must be carefully protected.

One of the defining characteristics of the Canadian marketplace is its size. With only 33 million souls within our borders—less than the population of metropolitan Tokyo—individual organizations can have a huge footprint on the national scene. One in ten Canadians, for example, is a member of Mountain Equipment Co-op. (If Co-op members acted as a block of voters, they would represent the fourth largest polity in the nation.) Nearly one-third of the populace uses Royal Bank of Canada (RBC) for some type of financial service. In terms of brands, we share considerable common ground.

Canadians may be comfortable with fewer institutions of bigger reach but we also hold them to account more than our counterparts in most other countries, according to the research firm Globescan. By international standards, Canadians have higher expectations of brands to "do the right thing." Our consumer empowerment and activism rankings are also strong. In its 2006 annual report, Scotiabank took special note of this trend: "Recent research shows that one-quarter of Canadians always or often take CSR (corporate social responsibility) issues into account when making everyday purchases and investment decisions." A study by Ipsos Reid and Marketing Magazine tracking consumer environmental attitudes found overwhelming public concern that organizations are shirking their green obligations. Seventy-seven percent said that most companies do not pay enough attention to their own environmental responsibilities.

The rising tide of public expectation about the social role of business also mirrors advice from corporate strategy pundits about the value of pursuing enlightened self-interest in social issues. As Douglas Holt argues, ikonic brands are built by engaged organizations that see their brands as actors with valuable roles to play on the cultural stage. Many of the organizations we interviewed are passionate supporters of that position. Mountain Equipment Co-op's "Big Wild" wilderness protection advocacy and McCain's nutrition and wellness stance are just two examples of marrying strategic and social priorities.

In their widely discussed Harvard Business Review article, "Strategy and Society," authors Michael Porter and Mike Kramer make a compelling case for getting involved: "When a well-run business applies its vast resources, expertise and management talents to problems that it understands and in which it has a stake, it can have greater impact on social good than any other institution or philanthropic organization... It is through strategic CSR that the company will make the most significant social impact and reap the greatest business benefits."

Making a real difference for communities also pays extra dividends in bolstering employee engagement and internal culture. Fred Schaeffer of McCain Foods reminds us that, "We should not be ashamed of the fact that businesses make money. What matters is how you want to make money. Having principles and making money are not an oxymoron. If your principles resonate with that majority of the population then they'll have a magnetic pull for people. If you're vanilla, you're not going to have a real strong attraction with anyone."

THE FOURTH DIMENSION As in physics, brands are subject to their own space/time continuum. The evolution of organizations and the threads of social history are the woof and warp of one another. Ikonic brands are in a constant state of evolution. To remain relevant, they must be active partners in an elaborate dance of collective meaning. As Douglas Holt puts it, these are brands that see themselves as players in history who don't manage a stable brand image as much as negotiate an evolving one. Negotiate is an apt verb. It implies astute navigation as well as ongoing dialogue. Hubris kicks in when organizations mistake past success as validation of a commercial monologue, not a communal dialogue. Brands that have powerful meaning to one or more generations—Hbc and Eaton's are two great Canadian examples—have no automatic claim to the loyalty of future generations.

ATLAS OF STORIES A useful atlas is more than just a collection of maps. It offers a variety of perspectives and context to create a multi-faceted primer. Our objective is not to arbitrate which brands deserve ikonic status but to showcase organizations that offer useful learning about Canada's brandscape. The range of brands we've included is deliberately eclectic—small and large, new and old, from a variety of sectors and types of organizations. Like Champlain's sketches, these first person narratives add authenticity and practical insights to our brandscape cartography.

We've grouped our interviews so that we can compare and contrast them based on ten different themes:

VOX POPULI: The role of public services in reflecting Canadian voices and values
GRANT JOHNSON | *Federal Identity Program*
JOHN BOZZO | *CBC*

FAMILY ROOTS: Three different brands shaped by family ties
FRED SCHAEFFER | *McCain Foods*
LINDA HAYNES | *ACE Bakery*
DAVID GOODMAN | *Dynamic Funds*

COMMON GROUND: Uncommon touch for the common good
PAUL HOUSE | *Tim Hortons*
MICHAEL ARNETT | *Canadian Tire*

MOVERS AND SHAPERS: Canuck cool meets mondo flair
ROBERT SARNER | *Roots*
LES MANDELBAUM | *Umbra*

STORYTELLERS: Taking the cultural pulse
WILLIAM BOYLE | *Harbourfront Centre*
PIERS HANDLING | *Toronto International Film Festival Group*

FELLOW TRAVELLERS: Navigating brand building routes
ROBERT MILTON | *Air Canada*
RUPERT DUCHESNE | *Aeroplan*

WEALTH WONKS: Comparing a wealth of alternatives for creating value
SLOAN DINNING | *Vancity*
BARBARA STYMIEST | *RBC*
JOHN DOIG | *Scotiabank*

THE MOBILIZERS: Making community connections that count
RUSS KISBY | *ParticipACTION*
JUDITH JOHN | *Mount Sinai Hospital*

CULTURAL CONNECTORS: Brands as change agents
DIRK MILLER | *Siemens Canada*
STEPHEN GRAHAM | *Rogers*

LEADING ROLES: Lessons in leadership
CHAVIVA HOŠEK | *Canadian Institute for Advanced Research*
WILLIAM THORSELL | *Royal Ontario Museum*
CLIVE BEDDOE | *WestJet*
MARIO D'AMICO | *Cirque du Soleil*

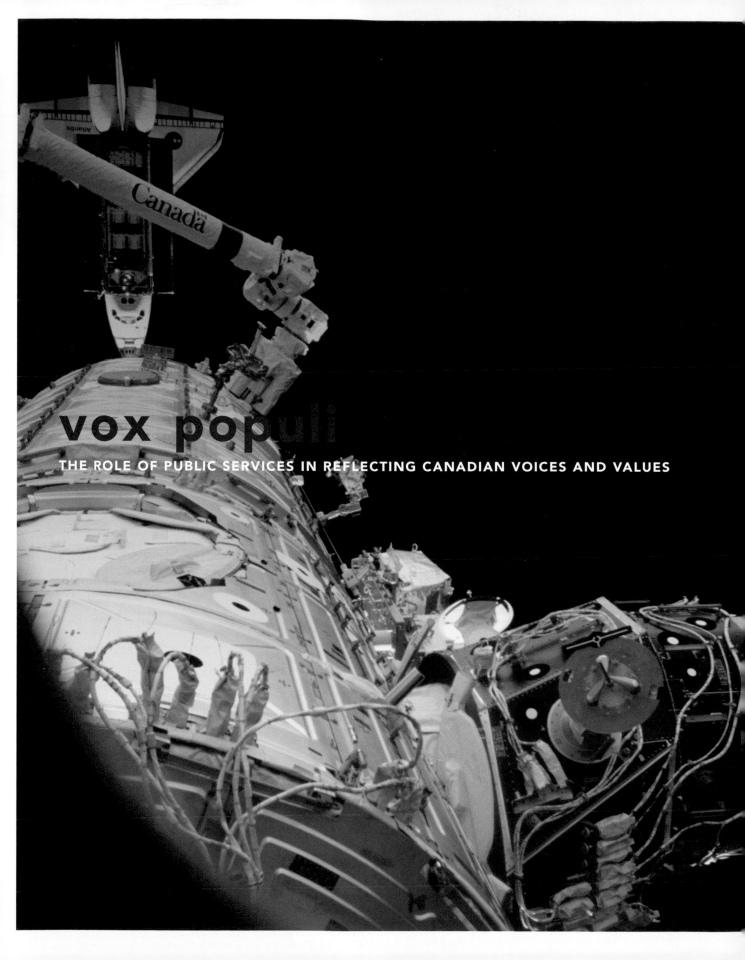

vox populi

THE ROLE OF PUBLIC SERVICES IN REFLECTING CANADIAN VOICES AND VALUES

THE LONG, WHITE REFLECTIVE ARM
reaches out into the void with highly
engineered precision while inhabitants of the
tiny blue planet spinning below watch with
awe. Emblazoned across what looks like a
well-starched sleeve is a single word in black,
graced by a tiny red ensign—Canada. We
may take them for granted but our national
ikons—from tiny maple leaf patches sewn on
backpacks being lugged all over the globe to
the Canadarm at work miles above it—play a
profound role in defining who we are. Our
national symbols are relatively young. It's hard
to remember that the country didn't even
have its own official flag until 1965. The maple
leaf, or l'unifolié (French for "the one-leafed"),
has much deeper roots as an emblem used
by les Canadiens at the beginning of the
eighteenth century. It caught on slowly as a
national symbol. In 1868, the maple leaf was
included in the coat of arms of both Ontario
and Quebec and not added to the Canadian
coat of arms until 1921.

Ikons evoke powerful emotions. After
decades of debate, the furor over choosing
a new flag became so intense that George
Stanley, the man responsible for our national
standard, had to endure death threats from
incensed citizens. (Its proper heraldic
descriptor or blazon is, "Gules on a Canadian
pale argent a maple leaf of the first.") Adopting
a flag, however, was only the first step in a
long process of clarifying and codifying our
ikons of nationhood and government.

Canada's Federal Identity Program (FIP),
is one of the largest corporate identity
initiatives ever undertaken by a national
government. The FIP program is a powerful
testament to order and good government
The rationale for a comprehensive approach
to the identity of federal programs goes right
to the heart of democratic ideals: citizen can't
judge the quality and scope of the services
rendered by their government if they aren't
readily identifiable and accessible. The
objective is to make the work of government
more visible and coherent as well as easier
to navigate. Citizens can't make officials
accountable if it's not clear who does what.
Launched in 1970, FIP now covers some

160 Government of Canada institutions, over
20,000 facilities and innumerable applications
—everything from forms, vehicles and signage
to websites, food aid packaging and passports
—in all regions of Canada and abroad.

Before there was a flag to rally 'round,
Canada had found a voice for the young
nation in the Canadian Broadcasting
Corporation. The Aird Commission of 1929
recommended the creation of a national
broadcasting company, similar to a public
utility, that would be capable of, "fostering
a national spirit and interpreting national
citizenship." The Crown corporation, one
of the country's largest cultural institutions,
didn't make its formal debut until November
1936. Today, what began as radio transmissions
has mushroomed into twenty-eight services
offered on radio, television, the Internet and
satellite radio, as well as through its record
and music distribution, wireless and messaging
services. Radio itself is now served up in
English and French plus eight Aboriginal
languages as well as numerous other
languages for overseas consumption.

Both the FIP and the CBC illustrate the
powerful inter-dependencies of identity,
culture and community. "CBC's job is to hold
up a mirror to this fascinating place," the
corporation's John Bozzo explains, "in a way
that supports the democratic and cultural life
of the country."

The nuances of Canada's Federal Identity
may seem arcane to non-designers but the
program has been lauded internationally for
its breadth, professionalism and resilience. Its
small, unsung team of stewards takes pride in
contributing to a more accessible, accountable
government for all. The CBC stands as a
lightning rod for omni-directional public
opinions on the appropriate role of
communications in feeding culture, community
and commerce. Every hour of every day our
public voice-box channels the ideas and
vicissitudes of the Canadian experience at
home and abroad. It's a tough, but lively
juggling act—one that plays out across our
brandscape every day. Both organizations
exemplify our strong communitarian values.

Grant Johnson

Habitat: Senior Advisor Federal Identity Program, Strategic Communications and Ministerial Affairs, Treasury Board of Canada Secretariat

Field Notes: The Federal Identity Program (FIP) was launched in 1970 in response to a 1969 Task Force report entitled "To Know or Be Known" that criticized the lack of visibility and clarity in the government identity standards (or lack thereof) that was causing public confusion.

Bloodlines: From an early age Johnson was curious about visual systems and symbols. He studied visual communication at Nova Scotia College of Art and Design and did an analysis of the Government of Canada's identity during postgraduate studies in classical rhetorical theory and semiotics.

Canada

On size and scale…
The size and scale of FIP is much larger than it was thirty-five years ago although I think it remains pretty close to the original vision. Today FIP applies to the identification of roughly 20,000 facilities, 40,000 transportation craft, several hundred thousand employees, hundreds of programs and services spread over ten million square miles. It creates a cohesive visual identity for the Government of Canada across the nation and around the world.

On evolution…
The principles and direction of FIP have remained pretty constant since its introduction in 1970. Like any identity it has under undergone modifications. However the biggest shift occurred in mid-1980s when the identifying symbol of federal institutions was changed from the federal emblem (a red bar and maple leaf) to the flag symbol. At that time, government also placed an emphasis on the titles of institutions to ensure they were as brief as possible and descriptive of the institutions function. This was also a period of further clarification on use of the Arms of Canada as an identifying symbol.

On profile…
The introduction of the "Canada" wordmark to the program in 1980 had a big impact on government's overall identity. On the one hand it made it a little more complicated to manage (two symbols for each institution rather than one), but it also provided a mark that was more visually succinct and compact in its design and nimble in its application. The use of the wordmark on the Canadarm is probably the highest profile application. The symbol is also prominently displayed on government rail cars, international food aid, a variety of ships and military craft including the Snowbirds.

National Design Council
1961–1985 R.I.P.

In the 1960s, an influx
of European-trained
graphic designers helped
shape the face
of contemporary
national ikons.

Canadian Centennial
1967

Canadian Metric
Commission
1971

The current Arms of Canada.
Originally created in 1921,
it was updated in 1956
and 1994.

On identity management…

The community of FIP practitioners across government has definitely evolved. Today there are fewer professionals with design backgrounds in the field and there is an accelerated rate of employee movement. So, this means the program requirements need to be conveyed to a more generalist user group who may have less overall experience managing identity issues. With the advent of the web, we know more people have access to FIP information and tools but we actually have less knowledge of who "they" are and what knowledge they posses. Our list of stakeholders has broadened as well, from what would have been a small group of designers, sign makers and publishing units originally, to a diverse list of professionals in each department and across government.

The principles of the program have essentially remained the same since the beginning: to ensure Canadians can recognize their federal government and its activities at a glance by means of clear and consistent identification. FIP shows Canadians their government and their taxes at work. The underlying philosophy is that government must be visible to the public it serves if it is to be accountable, and its programs and services to be accessible. There are two other hugely important principles of FIP: the obligation to project the equality of status of the two official languages, and ensuring overall cost-savings through standardization.

Priorities, circumstances, technology and ways of operating change and each can have an influence on clear identification. For example, the government has become much more involved in partnering and collaborative arrangements with external institutions to better leverage resources of both parties in key program and service areas. This has required a shift to ensure the federal government's role remains clearly visible for Canadians.

The underlying design principle of FIP is to efficiently convey the message without becoming part of the message. Where design standards are mandatory such as signage, clarity and legibility are maximized so the message can be understood by the public at large. For example, the use of text messages, neutral high-contrast colours and simple layout grids help ensure that the information is conveyed directly without encumbrances of style. Non-verbal signage is strictly limited to CSA/ISO symbol sets and Braille is a requirement for points of emergency egress.

A second important principle is the projection of the visual equality of the two official languages. English and French must always be displayed using the same font, weight, colour and size. A side-by-side format is considered more visually equal than an over-and-under format and is mandatory for departmental identification and all forms of signage.

On identity versus marketing…

The "Canada" wordmark had its origins as a "place brand." It was developed by Jim Donahue in 1965 as part of an advertising campaign for the Canadian Government Travel Bureau. The symbol evolved to become an official mark of government in 1980 and today it is the dominant mark of government to signal its presence and identify government programs, services, assets and activities. By its very design, it is possible for one to see the wordmark as a symbol of the country even though it remains strictly an official mark of government. In terms of concrete activities aimed at branding Canada as a destination for travel, investment, etc., that remains the role of federal institutions with that mandate. It is not an aim or function of the government's identity program. Government initiatives intended to brand Canada are not necessarily aimed at Canadians but rather aimed at benefiting Canadians through increased tourism and investment from other countries, etc.

The principles of FIP are rooted in the broader principles of government—providing factual, objective and impartial information. FIP supports the principles of accessibility and accountability by ensuring government is visible. We are careful to protect the integrity of government's official symbols and to avoid blurring the lines between identification and marketing or promotion. The aim is to ensure jurisdiction and authorship are clear without persuasive attributes. And since government's identity is based on the flag, coat of arms and name of the country, we have an obligation to act responsibly.

On measures of success...
Success measures are difficult for a program this size. FIP is implemented and managed day-to-day within dozens of departments, agencies, tribunals and corporations. The policy and standards are managed here at the centre and we maintain working relationships across government. Consultations, both internal and external, are key to keeping tabs on what is working and what needs a little help. Our bottom line is whether the public recognizes their federal government at work for them.

On future challenges...
Our biggest challenge is supporting our changing community of practitioners. The format and language we use to communicate still resides in the print and design world. We have a lot of work to do to simplify our tools and information while still maintaining consistency. We also have a challenge to maintain the core principles and philosophy of the program while continuing to keep abreast of changing priorities, initiatives and technology.

On lessons learned...
The image cast by government's identity and the principles behind it remain as relevant today as in 1970. I often marvel at the amount of thought and research that went into parts of the system. I also continue to be surprised at the level of passion for government's official symbols. One sees a lot of pride for these symbols within the public service and among a lot of Canadians. I've even received requests from Canadians wanting tattoos of the symbols—I had to decline. Pick your models carefully and resist the urge to compete with the world. Public entities, particularly governments, have broad

constituencies. Effective communication requires clear messaging and plain design. Plain design is the visual counterpart of plain, direct language. This means using short, clear names for programs and services; avoidance of jargon and acronyms, and keeping the lid on symbols and logos that pop up in the organization. That is easier said than done. People also love logos, rather, people love to create logos. It is surprising how early in the evolution of a committee, new service, program or a product the issue of "we should have our own logo" gets raised. Motivation is the single biggest antidote—people have to be reminded regularly how the values of the organization and the principles of communication and identity support only one corporate identity for an organization.

On design discovery...
From a very early age I can remember having an interest in visual systems and symbols sets—railway signals, road markings, street and highway signage, safety markings, etc. In retrospect, these were largely symbols in the public interest—marks that informed, directed or prohibited. I was intrigued by the fact that someone got to design them. I eventually studied visual communication at NSCAD in Halifax, a program that emphasized theory and principle of design. It is rather ironic now, but I chose the Government of Canada's identity as a common theme in my postgraduate studies in classical rhetorical theory and semiotics. A few years ago I was cleaning out some boxes I hadn't sorted through since I was twelve or thirteen and was surprised to come across a small white bag with the "Canada" wordmark on it. I had a strong enough attachment to the symbol even then to put the bag away for safekeeping.

my ikonica
In my work I see the Canadian flag all day, every day but I still never tire of the design. It is a great cohesive, modern and distinctive flag recognized around the world. It looks good abstracted or snapping in a cold February wind, or displayed with the flags of other countries. I think Canada is extremely fortunate that the principles of good design won the day in 1965 rather than the forces of compromise.

John Bozzo

Habitat: Executive Director English Communications, Canadian Broadcasting Corporation (CBC)

Bloodlines: Most of John Bozzo's long career has involved working with major public service brands: Bell Canada, Ontario Hydro, Ontario Ministry of Health and Long Term Care and CBC. While they represent different industries, Bozzo notes that each institution represents an important inflection point in the country's history, culture and public values that speaks to Canadian societal values.

Field Notes: CBC's official birth as a Crown corporation came on November 2, 1936 as the evolution of several earlier public radio experiments including a network developed by CN Railways in the 1920s. Today, programming is delivered in both official languages via national radio and television networks, the multilingual overseas shortwave service and a wide spectrum of web-based content on cbc.ca. Since his arrival in 2004, Bozzo has led a major overhaul of CBC's brand strategy designed to keep it personally relevant to diverse, quality-conscious audiences.

On audiences and diversity...

CBC is a brand rich in history but needs to make the full transition to a modern view of itself. There's an incredible wealth of history imbedded in this culture that you want to honour. But what does that mean in today's world? Whether we like it or not, we're competing with the American cultural space. Canadians are saying, "We expect you to be of the same quality as the US. If it is Canadian and of high quality we will come to the CBC." Our mandate set out in the Broadcasting Act definitely articulates a goal to inform and entertain and enlighten Canadians. However, we sometimes fall in the trap of focusing on national duty rather than national pride and adopting an undertone of "We know what's best for the consumer." We're an incredibly diverse country both regionally and ethnically. We need to find those universal themes that reflect what Canada is, which by its very

nature, has to have diversity built-in. But it isn't diversity from the perspective of, "Let's make sure we've got one black, and one Muslim and so on." That's tokenism. We must reflect this diversity for sure but more importantly we have to cover the issues that matter to our diverse community in the way we tell their stories.

Little Mosque on the Prairie is a great example of something that's very respectful of another culture but also breaks down stereotypes. I don't think you could do that in any other country but Canada. A lot of American interest in the show was driven by, "We could never do this in the US. How did these Canadians up North get away with this?" The interesting difference in our cultures is that we are much more accepting. Where brands fall down on this issue is that they fall into the trap of tokenism, not being truly relevant to the diversity of the country.

THE HOUR

Are you having real dialogue? Is your brand truly relevant? Few brands do that very well. I'm not saying that we are there yet, but we're getting better at understanding the importance of Canada's regional, cultural and ethnic diversity and reflecting that in our work.

The response to *Little Mosque* has been tremendous. It has also reinvigorated a part of the CBC brand that we can compete against the big American shows. If we put something on air that is high quality and resonates with Canadians it will draw large audiences. That's where *Little Mosque* has really helped the brand. People are beginning to say that we're relevant to them again. Personal relevance is one of the most important elements of our brand.

On authenticity...

I firmly believe that companies do not own brands. Consumers own them. If you start from that premise, you need to have the strength and wisdom to let your consumers guide where you're going. That's not to say you don't shape things. That's what brand management is all about. For CBC, the real shift in what makes things authentic or not is whether we start from where the audience is and where they want to take us. Then, our job is to make what we do engaging, informative, entertaining and it has to be high quality. There is no doubt that our news coverage is of very high quality, but people believe our coverage is too focused on areas that don't matter in the everyday lives of Canadians— that we can be too earnest and serious. People think, "They're not going to give me "the news I need or want."

To be authentic, we have to get inside and understand what consumers want. Our news renewal project is designed to get at this issue and to offer news how, when and where consumers want it. Unlike other competitors, we have to look at the entire constituency of Canada. They can choose to appeal to the 25-54 year olds only. We can't. We can target shows to demographic groups, but our programming has to be something that is for all Canadians, offering content across all platforms—TV, radio and Internet. But if we

do it right it can be quite a differentiator for us and a more authentic expression of the brand.

My mentor, Norm Simon, taught me that the real trick of branding is not understanding what people need or want today but anticipating what people will want tomorrow. That's a much harder job. If you do that right, you can actually be ahead of the curve. No research would tell you that you need to develop a half-hour Muslim sitcom and it will be a hit. The real insight with *Little Mosque* was to take an intense interest in the Muslim community and bring it to life through comedy and everyday people struggling to be Muslim in Canadian society.

On reflecting the future...

The strength of the internal culture at CBC is a sense of purpose that we are doing something of public value and that it's a privilege to work here. It's almost like a missionary cause. People work here because they believe in what they are doing. It's rooted in this notion that public broadcasting is an important part of the fabric of the country and we are contributing to that. That's the part of the culture that gels and works quite well. The danger is that it can migrate into a we-will-tell-you-what's-good-for-you attitude. What we tried to do in all of the branding work was to build the brand from an aspirational view… in other words where Canadians want the brand to be.

We started from the premise that in the future world two fundamental principles will be at play: One, content is king. Two, consumers will choose what, how and where they consume media from an ever increasing array of choices and from among the best in the world. If we assume that's the world we're going into, CBC must become a content brand, not a series of delivery platforms. We need to move away from being known as a television brand or a radio brand, but to something that brings you great news, information and entertainment content— when, where and how you want it. If we want Canadians to come to us, we have to give them content they want.

my ikonica

Marshall McLuhan and Jean Vanier. For anyone in communications and advertising, McLuhan is the Godfather of our industry. Vanier took a "brand"—the Catholic Church—that was broken and actually turned a part of it into something that was relevant and meaningful to people. He created an entire following and social organization dedicated to helping the disadvantaged that exists to this day and continues to do a lot of the good work he started.

If you reflect Canadians back to themselves, they will come. Canada is a fascinating country. CBC's job is to hold up a mirror to this fascinating place in a way that supports the democratic and cultural life of the country. Therefore, from a branding perspective we only need two brands. That's why we've merged 17 different brands into one CBC content brand and a sub-brand for CBC News. Everything we do has to fit into one of those brands. We're totally agnostic about the delivery medium.

On measuring success...

Financial sustainability and growth are not sustainable in the long-term without creating customer value and an appropriate fit between the company and its customers—in the case of CBC, audiences. Brand planning and management must begin and end with the customer. Dialogue with the customer is critical if we are to meet not only today's demands but to anticipate tomorrow's. So how do you measure success? At two fundamental levels—the first is shareholder or public value and the second is relevance and brand equity. We have to deliver on the business requirements of financial health and the ability to invest in the future. In the case of CBC this means increased audiences that increase our personal relevance in the marketplace and provide the financial room to invest in more Canadian programming. The second is relevance and equity

generated by the brand relationship. The long-term viability of any company rests on the fundamental trust that is created with its customers, stakeholders and shareholders. Measurement systems that can capture this dynamic relationship are available.

These factors, when put together as a holistic approach to planning and measurement, can provide real insights and dynamic, relevant brands.

On advice to business leaders...

Don't underestimate the importance and the power of the diversity here. You have to understand that these are very different markets so your targeting in Canada has to be much more precise. Don't underestimate the pride that exists in the country either. We don't wear it on our sleeves but there is a great loyalty and pride.

As well, look for holistic solutions to brand issues. Trust, relevance, competitiveness and value all need to be looked at as one inter-related and integrated whole. All too often we jump to the easy "creative or short-term solution." Brands are built over time and are multi-dimensional and so should our solutions.

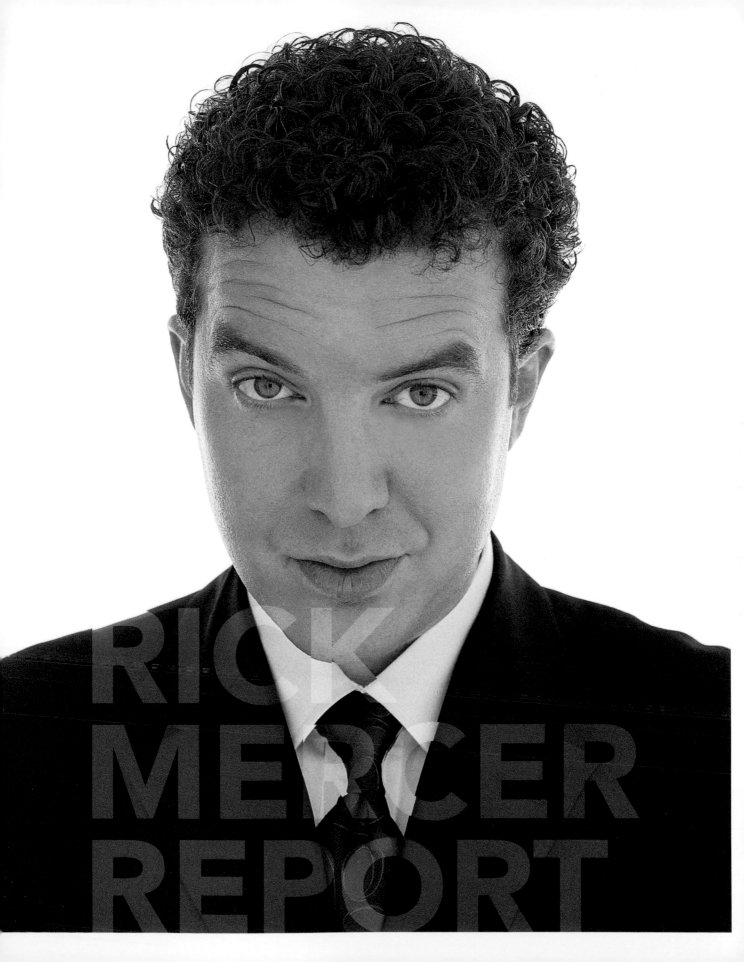

family roots

THREE DIFFERENT BRANDS SHAPED BY FAMILY TIES

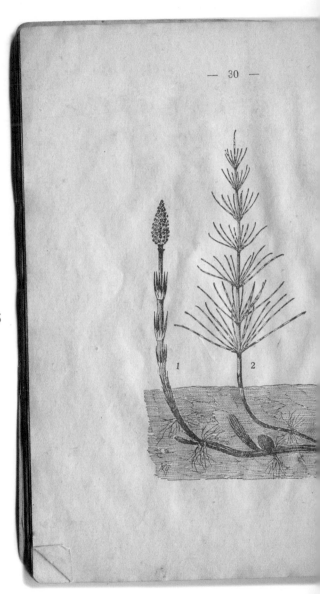

HUDSON'S BAY COMPANY may be our oldest brand but multi-generational clans have powered much of Canada's economy since John Molson first began brewing up business ventures in Montreal several hundred years ago. Entrepreneurism and family ties creates fascinating business dynamics as intergenerational storylines play out, often as headlines in the press. Canada's business history is flush with name brand dynasties peopled with a colourful, larger-than-life cast of visionaries, scoundrels, innovators, opportunists, mavericks and impresarios.

Family-run is no synonym for small enterprise. In 2004, Family Business Magazine published a survey of the 250 largest family operations in the world. The Canadian contingent included familiar names like Magna International, Bombardier, Thomson, Maple Leaf Foods and McCain Foods. Pinning down how much family-owned organizations drive our economy is tricky but the numbers are significant; estimates range as high as sixty-five percent.

Whatever the actual numbers, these organizations represent a significant swath of Canada's most successful entrepreneurs and the brands they create. What's important to understand is how familial histories and personal values shape the relationships of commerce, culture and community. A family-owned enterprise doesn't guarantee a kinder, gentler workplace. On the contrary, great entrepreneurs can be hellishly eccentric, egocentric and unpredictable as bosses. But they often embody many of Canada's ikonic characteristics including the ability to marry their entrepreneurial instincts with endurance and skepticism. Taking the long view—ten-to-twenty year timeframes—instead of being obsessed exclusively with next quarter results is often one of their greatest assets. Being skeptical and entrepreneurial at the same time can give them a contrarian edge competitively. They're prepared to zig while others zag. Being close to the source of the original vision for a business can also reinforce a strong sense of purpose. Community ties are often stronger because of local roots and personal connections.

McCain Foods, Dynamic Funds and ACE Bakery are three highly successful family-run ventures that have built powerful brands in very different ways. McCain represents the great global success story, born of sturdy New Brunswick roots. The family has parlayed simple spuds into an international smorgasbord of food products under the McCain brand. As Fred Schaeffer, President and CEO of Canadian operations, will attest, you-have-my-word accountability is an important trump card in a family-operated business where major deals can be sealed with a handshake.

Dynamic Funds represents only one aspect of the Goodman family's broad canvas of wealth-management services. One of the biggest challenges facing any successful family enterprise is managing the transitions between generations. In taking up the reins of DundeeWealth from his father Ned, David Goodman pays close attention to brand and internal culture, well aware that these are important ballasts for an organization in the midst of change.

ACE Bakery's Linda Haynes tells the story of a simple family passion that rose into a thriving international bakery. For Haynes, fermenting a strong business culture is the same process as leavening quality bread: start with the best ingredients—value, integrity, a sense of community—and bake in the quality every day.

Fred Schaeffer

Habitat: President and CEO of McCain Foods Canada

Bloodlines: A native of the US, Fred Schaeffer joined McCain in 2006 after over two decades at rival Kraft Foods. In 2000, he was promoted to Vice President Marketing and Strategy, Kraft Cheese Division, in the US. He became Senior Vice President of Kraft Foods and President of Kraft Foods Canada in 2002.

Field Notes: From its roots in Florenceville, New Brunswick, McCain Foods has parlayed its spud expertise to become the world's largest producer of frozen french fries and a global leader among food processors. When it celebrated its fiftieth birthday in 2007, the McCain Foods empire had grown to include 20,000 employees and fifty-five production facilities (in twelve countries spanning six continents) that process one million pounds of potato products each hour. The company now sells one-third of the world's frozen french fries products, in over 110 countries. The corporate menu now extends to appetizers, pizzas, vegetables, desserts, entrees, oven meals and other quality frozen foods. The company ascribes its remarkable success to its "cutting-edge agronomy, superior technology and… its unique culture." In 2007, McCain enjoyed the distinction of hitting number twenty-two on the Reputation Institute's annual survey of the world's most respected companies as well as nabbing the number one ranking in Canada. The study surveys consumers in twenty-nine countries. McCain Foods (Canada) employs about 4,000 people in fifteen processing facilities, and enjoys a very large percentage of the total frozen food market share in Canada.

On cultural mores…

Culturally, Kraft and McCain are like apples and pineapples. McCain is very much still a family-run, privately held company. The values associated with that permeate the organization. It comes from a rural New Brunswick community and those agricultural-based values include true respect for others, looking out for each other, a solid work ethic. It's quite refreshing. I'd also say there is a longer-term perspective. In any publicly traded Fortune 500 company the focus is on next quarter. When long range is five to ten years, you worry about very different things. The family worries about ensuring that we have a sustainable business for generations to come versus boosting the stock price for next quarter. It's about making sure that you understand what's going on; that you involve and engage the people around us. Let's do the right thing for the long term. It's a very different mindset.

I link what the family stands for and what the brand stands for. To date, the brand promise has been quality, a brand you can trust—not cheap but a value-oriented brand. It's a Canadian-based brand but internally, people believe in drinking the local wine, embracing whatever culture that you're part of.

Americans tend to be a little bit more internally focused. I have found throughout my business career that Canadians make some of the best ex-pats because they are more externally focused, more open to ideas outside of their culture. For a Canadian brand, that translates to a different, "We would like to be part of your culture and we think we have something to bring," relationship. It's a different approach.

Maritime people are just very down to earth.

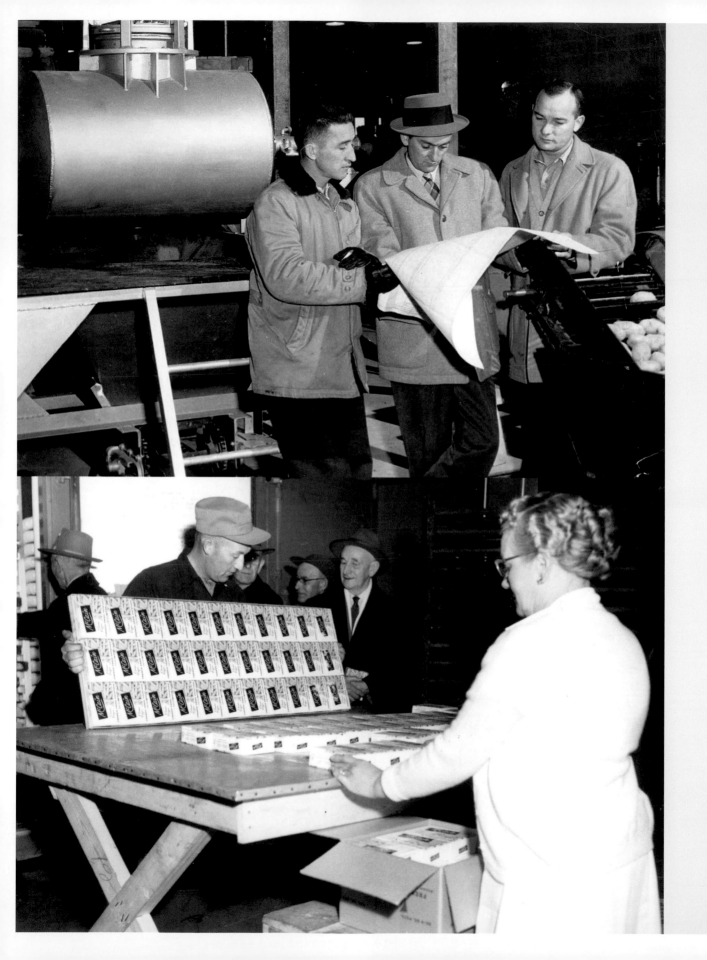

It's say-what's-on-your-mind straightforward. There are no airs about them at all. They're wonderful and inviting. People talk to you in plain English. It's a very straightforward kind of place and that's part of the elegance of the organization.

On brand passion...

Our job is to leverage all our great assets that we have but also think about new attributes. I would like to have more people think of us as innovative. The company has historically been a fast adaptor. I would like to hear more passion about the brand. The analogy that I use is sitting behind a two-way glass and your spouse is on the other side. If you heard them describe you as an old slipper—comfortable, always there when they need you—you would be crushed! We hear things about the brand like: "The brand I grew up with and my mom trusted." We'd rather hear something along the lines of, "It's indispensable to my life!" We want to keep the heritage of quality and value but build on that.

On growth and change...

Harris and Wallace McCain are the two founders of the organization. They were bigger-than-life leaders that drove the business. They carried the strategy in their heads, and then communicated that strategy to the organization. The first transition we're trying to make is from what we characterize as an owner-led business to a more distributed leadership model, one in which everybody is accountable and responsible for driving strategy, growth and innovation.

Leaders that have the greatest impact are those that actually have some tenure, which is rather rare these days among CEOs. It takes time to build a culture. Longevity is a double-edged sword. You have the benefit of people that have a longer term perspective and value that perspective. The other side of the sword is change. Where change is not that frequent, change management skills are not muscles that are totally developed.

Our vision, quite simply, is to be Canada's leading food company. That's easy to say and far harder to do. There are five key

components that we need to satisfy: One, we need to have the most loyal and satisfied consumers. Two, we need to be number one in terms of customer service in the eyes of our customers. Three, we need to be the employer choice for our employees (and we realize that's a two-way street). Four, we need to be partner of choice for our suppliers. Historically, that's been more of a "buy" relationship than a partnering one. Finally, we need to be a business of choice in our communities. That means being more than just an economic contributor from a tax and jobs standpoint but also being a good social and environmental contributor as well.

That's what we aspire to be. How we get there, the strategies underneath the vision, are fourfold: One, to win with customers and consumers we have to become more of a market-facing organization than we've been historically. Two, to drive quality and innovation. Three, the notion of creating productivity enablers because it's an intensely competitive landscape. Four, are our people and the need to challenge ourselves to be better with a continuous-improvement mindset. In our core business we need to let go of the belief that we have nothing else to learn because we invented it. We need to adopt the notion of continuous improvement. No matter how good you are, you can always get better.

Where is the growth for us? We're focused on health and wellness. Certainly the greying of the Canadian landscape is an obvious trend. When you look at where growth is coming from within the Canadian landscape, it doesn't take long to figure it out that growth is largely, but not exclusively, driven by immigration. The world of new Canadians seems to be an opportunity if you ask yourself are we really servicing their needs well.

On differences...

The axiom that I generally use is that Canada is more similar to the US than most Canadians think and less similar than most Americans think. Americans think isn't it wonderful that we have a fifty-first state. Canadians tend to be at the other end of the continuum.

my ikonica

*What's ikonic to me are
Canadian values—
principally the sense
of collective responsibility.
That plays out in
many forms but not
the least of which is in the
health care agenda.
Is it really about
healthcare or is it about
a deeper-rooted belief
in responsibility for
the collective. There are
so many wonderful
things about the fabric
of Canada that should
be celebrated.*

Somewhere between those two points is reality. Americans need to understand that while on the surface things may look fairly similar, there are certainly cultural nuances and cultural values and beliefs that are different than in the States.

My experience is that companies that start in smaller markets and work their way out tend to be a bit more global in their perspective. In part, it's born out of necessity. I would like to say that it's this cultural sensitivity. In reality, it's just survival. Look at Nestlé in Switzerland. In smaller markets you've got to have broader expectations. The more you are reliant and dependent on looking outside for your success, the more pliable and resilient you are. If you start in a big country, it's just not as required. It's just the nature of the beast.

On social responsibility...
We should not be ashamed of the fact that businesses make money. What matters is how you want to make money. Having principles and making money are not oxymorons. If your principles resonate with that majority of the population then they'll have a magnetic pull for people. If you're vanilla, you're not going to have a real strong attraction with anyone. Corporate social responsibility is one and the same with how you do business; how you treat your employees, partners and communities. You won't believe the number of deals that are done here on a handshake even to this day. When we look each other in the eye and we say we are going to do this, we are.

On moving from good to great...
Our corporate values are reinforced in our performance reviews and our succession planning process. On the positive side, there is great teaming ability to work together. Everybody strives for results but you don't see the back-stabbing, hyper-aggressive attitudes of Wall Street. People are able to work with others because it's not "all about me."

On playing to your strengths...
Celebrate what you have. Focus on the things that define us, not what defines who we are not. Do not underestimate the magnet that running a Canadian company can serve as the attraction mechanism for highly talented employees. If Canadians have a choice between working for a multinational that is based in Canada and a company that is Canadian, there is somewhere deep in their hearts a desire to build the Canadian brand. That's an advantage in attracting some wonderful people.

Linda Haynes

Bloodlines: A former TV producer, Linda Haynes always has a lot on her plate—as author, entrepreneur and philanthropist. Before the rise of ACE Bakery as a commercial venture, Linda and her husband, Martin Connell, founded Calmeadow, a Canadian charity that supports the provision of credit and financial services to micro-entrepreneurs in developing countries. Over the years she's been active on the boards of various arts and child-centred agencies and is a past chair of Variety Village, North America's largest center for physically and mentally challenged children. Linda is the author of two successful ACE cookbooks as well. Her list of honours includes: Member of the Order of Canada (2007); International Association of Culinary Professionals (IACP) Humanitarian Award (2006); CESO Award for International Development (1997); Entrepreneur of the Year (Ernst and Young, Canadian Business Magazine) (1995), and Canadian Women Who Make a Difference (Business Category) (1994).

Field Notes: ACE Bakery is an "artisan" bakery that provides fresh and partially baked breads to hundreds of wholesale customers across Canada, New York State, the American Midwest and as far away as the Bahamas. The concept first took shape in Caledon, Ontario, when Martin set out to bake a great baguette in the family kitchen. Martin and Linda, herself an accomplished cook, visited bakeries throughout North America and Europe and continued to experiment with a wide repertoire of breads. ACE was incorporated in 2002. The story of ACE provides great food for thought about the potential of small, community-minded brands to thrive in niche markets.

On the genesis story...

The concept was to provide high-quality artisan bread to the downtown local market. At that time there was no local artisan bread provider, only local ethnic bakeries. The motivation for the bakery came from the idea we could transfer my husband's baking hobby into a small commercially sustainable bakery; one that would make high-quality artisan bread, sell it into the local market while generating adequate profits that would in part support our charitable organization, Calmeadow, engaged in micro-finance. The business opened to positive local media reviews and received critically important support and encouragement from a handful of high-profile restaurants and retailers. During the early years, the accompanying retail store/café was a popular local place for people from the food trade and food lovers alike.

As profile and popularity grew, our first major break came from Pusateri's and Loblaws. Encouraged by consumer demand, Loblaws began inviting us into their stores across Toronto. At the same time, more restaurants and independent retailers came on board. In early 2000, experimentation began in freezing bread that had been about eighty-five percent partially baked. It was clear that the real opportunity for growth lay in reaching out to different communities in Ontario. Transportation of fresh bread had its geographic limits, especially since freshness is a requirement. We do not use preservatives, so shelf life is short. By 2003, we had perfected the concept of par-baked frozen and commenced our sales strategy to take par-baked frozen bread by freezer truck to London, Ottawa, Hamilton and Kitchener. Over the next couple of years the program grew successfully and sales had more than

doubled. Our success caught the attention of a grocery chain executive in upstate New York. Soon, we were selling bread to TOPS, followed shortly by Meijer's in Michigan and the lower Great Lakes. More recently, we have started to serve A&P on the eastern seaboard. As of today, ACE breads can be found from upstate Michigan to New Orleans and even off shore in the Bahamas. We sell in Canada from Ontario to Nova Scotia. Today, ACE has approximately three hundred employees, one bakery with its own café and an offering of over twenty-five different types of artisan doughs. While we have grown, we remain committed to sustaining the quality of our bread.

On breads and brands...

ACE has a vision of providing a healthy and enjoyable eating experience to a growing number of people who desire quality, value and integrity of ingredients while leaving a positive impact on the community. Our logo, a wood cut, captures the handcrafted essence of our baking style. It gives recognition to handcrafting and the historical dimensions of artisan baking. These are age-old traditions. Even though large elements of our production are now automated, we adhere rigorously to the key elements of handcrafted artisan baking. Our materials, such as bags, convey commitment to natural or organic materials, the absence of preservatives, commitment to staff, to the community and quality baking methods including slow fermentation times. The simplicity of black on white speaks to cleanliness, directness, clear messaging and an uncomplicated story.

To succeed, keep it simple. Be transparent and straightforward with your brand promise. Stay with it, stay with the commitment to the best of natural or organic ingredients; keep the focus on the relationship with the consumer. Talk directly to them with your materials, and don't take shortcuts. Be innovative and responsive to the needs and wants of the consumer/customer. Be vigorous with the sampling program—our way of creating the ACE experience. Be visible where foodies congregate—gourmet shows, charitable events, etc. We support the

community that supports ACE by donating breads to local charities, maintaining a thoughtful, organized and relevant donations program. A generous portion of our pre-tax profits are donated to charities connected to nutrition programs, community kitchens, culinary scholarships, organic farming.

A strong brand is the corporate unifying theme. Without it we would be just another manufacturer of artisan bread. Our business would have been based on price, deals and traditional applications of advertising and marketing. The brand embodies pride of doing something that is an essential part of life with our commitment to quality excellence and customer service.

What are the important factors in building a brand?

}

Commitment to quality.
Commitment to quality.
Commitment to quality.
Commitment to customer service.
Commitment to employees and staff.
Commitment to community.
Commitment to innovation.
Commitment to financial success
Commitment to growth.
Commitment to making healthier breads.
Commitment to positive communications and outreach to our consumers through PR and media.

On engaging employees and social commitment...

We stress quality issues, from the bread, to production, to distribution, to plant efficiency and cleanliness. We reinforce that with workshops, training, visiting experts. Our sales and demo staff are trained and charged with the ACE culture and philosophy. From day one our social commitment has been one of the four pillars in our plan. The others being quality, customer service and employee satisfaction. With a large portion of pre-tax profits going to charity, it is definitely a significant part of our operating budget plan. It is a core belief of ours that by doing good in the community we derive benefits that enhance our brand profile, bring pride to our

There is no brand symbol more identified with Canada than the maple leaf. From our flag to the red maples of autumn, from the stitched-on patch emblem of our ubiquitous world travellers to maple syrup and the Toronto Maple Leafs, the maple leaf says it all. We are Canadians.

employees and help build a stronger and more enduring bond with our customers and consumers. As a cost centre, it is rigorously managed (we work closely with the Toronto Community Foundation to ensure maximum effectiveness and reach those opportunities in the community that we feel most strongly about). The program is tied closely to the operating plan and is reviewed annually. After fourteen years, we remain convinced that it is good for ACE.

On staying relevant…

We have yet to suffer any setback in brand relevance. By retaining our focus on quality and consumer satisfaction, and new product development, we are able to sustain interest and support for the brand. In Ontario, which is our largest and strongest market, our PR quotient per dollar of sales is probably off the charts and that the PR connection to the cookbooks and the ACE commitment have consistently re-enforced our local market presence. Our efforts in the Northeast quadrant of the US market have been undertaken without the profile we enjoy in Ontario. Notwithstanding our low level of awareness, we have consistently been able to use the ACE brand with our retailing partners. This, in the face of the persistent push by retailers to promote their house brand and only use co-packing partners. So far, we have been convincing in making our case for the ACE Brand proposition and promise, which includes our merchandising, in-store sampling and support of local charities. We consider each customer a partner and encourage a cross-pollination of sales and movement information.

Our strategy from day one was to be the highest quality artisan baker in our area. We wanted to please and delight our consumers. At the same time we realized that a supporting media was important, as was our commitment to the community. In fact, the former probably followed the latter. Because what we did was natural to us we came across as authentic. Therefore, there were no real surprises. We slowly gained awareness. We never changed our practice or approach to the market.

Without trying to sound precious, we remained true to our value proposition from the first day.

We started in Toronto and had our first major move to Ottawa. So, for those looking at the high-end food business, these are (excluding Montreal) the most important foodie cities in Eastern Canada. Toronto is over fifty percent foreign-born, which means our diversity brings with it wide ranges of sophistication and interests. There is also a well-educated and cultured community here that creates a ready appetite for high-end specialty foods. It is also highly competitive, which means differentiating oneself in the marketplace is important. Unless you have very deep pockets, start small, build credibility and grow on successful experience. We see no barriers to success.

On important lessons learned…

Our brand is our promise. Our promise to deliver and provide our consumers with breads that are consistently of high quality; our promise to be good corporate citizens in the way we work with our employees and support the community; our promise to use only the healthiest of ingredients, avoid additives and preservatives, offer new bread experiences, listen to our consumers and respond promptly to their concerns. We endeavour to be faithful and predictable to our commitments and never take a shortcut where there is a chance quality can be compromised. We stand behind the brand as guarantors that the brand promise will not be weakened.

ACE
BAKERY
Anniversary · Anniversaire
ACE
BAKERY
10
Anniversary · Anniversaire
ACE
BAKERY

David Goodman

Habitat: President and CEO of Goodman and Company, home of Dynamic Funds and about one year after this interview was promoted to President and Chief Executive Officer of DundeeWealth, the public company parent of Dynamic and Dundee Securities.

Bloodlines: Scion of the Goodman empire established by his father Ned, David Goodman has entrepreneurial credentials that were well burnished at Goodman & Company. A fourteen-year veteran, David helped steward the company from five-billion-dollar assets under management to $25 billion and accolades as Canada's best performing, fastest-growing investment management business—all in only six years. Much of that growth has been within Dynamic Funds. In 2007, David took up the reins of DundeeWealth. Before diving into the turbulent waters of investment, Goodman earned his stripes as a litigator. But perhaps the acumen that keeps David most buoyant is his quiet passion for performing stand-up comedy.

Field Notes: Our interview happened while Dynamic Funds was in the process of developing its "Invest with Advice" positioning. Bookshelves can offer useful insights into the preoccupations of executives. The roster of titles lining David Goodman's study ranged from management best practices and business strategy to autobiographies of political and business leaders. But what stood out on the shelves were five copies of a different kind of classic: *Green Eggs and Ham*.

On lessons from Dr. Seuss...
There was a time when I felt we were being treated like *Green Eggs and Ham* so I gave the book to wholesalers and investors at our annual meeting several years ago. At the time, the "Just say no" attitude was really strong. I wanted to get the message out, "Don't worry about those who have never tried us." Our company has gone through a lot of transitions. We're really in the sweet spot of our good times right now. But during our difficult times, we'd done everything we could to improve the quality of our business and our performance. Now, there's an element of time in any recipe—you just have to wait and let it settle. We have completed five years now and in that time we have seen ninety-nine percent of our assets in the top two quartiles. But people have long memories. There's a lot of inertia in changing behaviours or perceptions, especially in Canada. I talked

to a British portfolio manager who said that he specializes in buying Canadian stocks because, coming from a different jurisdiction, he sees changes before Canadian managers do. Trying to change people's perception of what your business is or what you stand for is really hard. Most people never get to the stage where they try it. So, I look to Dr. Seuss for my branding messages. He hasn't let me down yet.

On being focused...
We've been fortunate enough to attract some of the highest-quality investment thinkers on the continent, probably in the world. We started off with an investment performance mindset and we have not taken our eye off that ball. Once we started getting performance, we realized that we needed better relationships with financial advisors. So we started focusing on a customer-centric

WE'VE ALWAYS HAD A DAVID VS. GOLIATH MENTALITY. BUT WE ARE NOT THE DAVID ANYMORE. NOW, WE NEED TO SUPPORT ADVISORS AND CUSTOMERS AS THE DAVID AND STAND UP FOR THEIR NEEDS.

model, one that puts our customers in the centre of the universe. Yes, they want performance out of their funds, but they need a lot more things too. We would get rewarded in spades every time we delivered. Even with investment performance you can still have advisors that don't want to do business with you because you don't treat them properly, you don't service them well, you don't facilitate the growth of their business. We think our clients are involved in a noble pursuit of helping people navigate through the rough waters of the capital markets and helping them avoid knee-jerk reactions that can destroy wealth. That's what we believe in. We have to communicate that internally as well as externally and let it sink in so that it cuts through every fabric of the company. We've always had a David vs. Goliath mentality. But we are not the "David" anymore. Now, we need to support advisors and customers as the "Davids" and stand up for their needs. That's the power of "Invest with Advice."

On being leaders...
We went from being a company in difficulty to one that is leading the industry. But once you are leading the industry, where do you go next? I think it's much more difficult to take something that is successful and make it even more successful. It's a motivational challenge too. Too many people have gone to that school where the bar is set simply too low. To jump over it really isn't much of an achievement. We have to set the bar really high and we have to jump over that bar day in and day out.

I wrote a memo to the firm that reflected on Maslow's hierarchy of needs. I said that we are now at the point as a corporation where we have to start looking for self-actualization. What makes us tick? What are the principles by which we govern ourselves? You don't worry about that when you are scrambling. But as people mature, the need for fulfillment becomes much more complicated. You're not as worried about shelter and food; you're worried more about how you're going to make a difference in the world. You ask yourself, "Is what I am doing meaningful?"

If we can figure out how to lift this kind of personal introspection to a corporate level, we will take our company from very good to exceptional—not simply a Canadian success story but an internationally acclaimed company that really created a new business model. At the end of the day, we have to earn a profit to compensate people. Everyone needs to make a living in all this. The "what's in it for me?" question gets asked often in a high-performance organization. Increasingly the answer will be reflected in the success of the company itself.

On sustainability...
We think very long term. We're not thinking about quarterly earnings, we're thinking about building a great company over the next ten to twenty years. We've tried hard to make sure we have bench-strength with deep roots in the company; that underneath great leaders are emerging great leaders. That gives us the staying power but demands constant work. We're not there yet; perhaps, we're never going to be there. We're always going to be working on getting wherever "there" might be but remain focused on the journey as much as the destination. Businesses are typically valued as going concerns. By definition, a going concern isn't stopping. You're always at the beginning of the next five years.

On the importance of culture...
You've got to fight for culture. You've got to take a stand on certain things in a company. You have to say that's wrong and it's not going to happen in this company and it's over. You take a stand. Culture is one of those things that you have to protect with a type of zero-tolerance policy. We haven't been perfect but in our constant drive to improve our company one of the things we are much more focused on is the DNA of the culture and the value of every person that walks in this door. Changing from an organization that's an order-driven, command-central company to one that is inspired by teams of people requires consistent leadership and effective decision making. There's an old saying that

you've got to let the people that do the work tell you how to do the work. We've been doing a fair amount of that. The guys who are in the trenches know a lot of stuff about this company. They need to be empowered and respected and allowed to make their views known. We have saved millions of dollars listening to our employees. You can't have someone that is afraid to speak up. You need folks who are going to speak up with their suggestions—something like, "You know what we pay on our overnight money market rates? I think we can do it for x basis points lower if we get it here." For me, inspiring everyone in the company to think in that innovative way is huge.

On the value of brands...

Brands are always the most important thing. The problem is most people think of a brand as a logo. A brand's lasting value is captured in what your customers think of you. You know how good a business is by what the customers think of the business. If your customers are doing really poorly then you're going to do really poorly. If your customers are doing really well and like you because you're helping them, you're going to do well too. If a brand is a large part of what your customers associate you with then it can't be anything less than the most important thing. There are different stages in the life of a business. Sure, you can get by on other things for a little bit but to build a company, a brand, that's going to last fifty years or a hundred years, your customers need to easily understand the value of the relationship they enjoy with the brand. Often, you have to remind them.

Advice for other business leaders...

You should have a lot of patience in allowing your company to become what you want it to become. But you really should have no patience with anybody that is not respectful of people in your organization. Your culture has to be one that consistently fosters the goodwill of its employees and customers. If there are people in your organization who are not of that ilk, you don't want to waste too much time on them.

On defining success...

I always get the greatest sense of pride when I see people building their lives with our company. Young people that started out here as kids, married, having their third kid, having financial success, becoming responsible members of their communities and helping us deliver on the vision of the company. I think a key measure of a company's strength is both what its customers say about them but also the quality of life their employees can achieve working at the company. That's really important. You have to work for a company that you're proud of. Our employees talk about how we've made decisions that actually made us less money because it was the right thing to do, often for them. You've got to create an environment where your employees and your customers are allowed to make mistakes. If you're living in an environment where perfection is demanded, you'll achieve almost no return. My dad gave me a book many years ago called *Whoever Makes the Most Mistakes Wins*. You can't live with the fear of making mistakes. You've got to also be able to forgive others. There are not a lot of people who are easily willing to forgive nowadays but its one of the greatest investments you can make. Success also means having a nice profit margin—healthy, robust and fair. If you can do all that, that's a successful company.

my ikonica

My dad. He's a great entrepreneur who's fought for everything he has ever gotten. He started from nothing. And he's got great sons!

common ground

UNCOMMON TOUCH FOR THE COMMON GOOD

IN MANY YEARS of asking Canada's business leaders to rank the country's best-managed brands, we know there will never be much of a contest for the top tier slots; Tim Hortons and Canadian Tire inevitably take home the glory. When the Canadian Oxford Dictionary officially inducts "double double" into the national lexicon and Sandy McTire—the Scot who graces Canadian Tire's home-grown currency—is as instantly recognizable as Sir John A. Macdonald, you know you're in ikonic territory.

At first blush, it's hard to fathom how such inauspicious beginnings—a string of coffee 'n' donut shops or a place to get do-it-yourself car parts—could spawn such gold-rimmed success stories. In 2006, when Tim Hortons shares were first listed on the Toronto Stock Exchange, huge investor appetite pushed the chain's valuation to more than $5.5 billion! Canadian Tire's extensive retail network serves more than three million customers every week… a testament to the success of its "customers for life" strategy. Many an MBA student has studied under the hood of these high-performance operations to decipher exactly what drives their success. Certainly, highly disciplined operations are essential with such vast retail networks—table stakes for the big leagues. While the nature of their product selection may be polar opposites, both businesses share the kinship of dealer/franchisee cultures and a true genius for building culture and community. Each brand is deeply embedded in the weekly, often daily, routines of millions of Canadians.

Pull into the parking lot at Tim Hortons head office and you might find yourself checking the address to make sure you've come to the right spot. This is no brash, shiny, glass-and-steel HQ. It may be practical and understated on the outside but inside, the fresh coffee's served up with a warm, relaxed reception. In our interview, Paul House, the affable CEO who Ron Joist recruited to his team in 1985, paints a stark portrait of donut culture then and the challenge of creating an "always fresh" culture. House describes a management style that draws heavily on many of our *genius*

loci attributes: It's highly communitarian. His we-all-graze-in-the-same-pasture management style doesn't tolerate prima donnas or half measures. In the community, don't just sponsor a few individual hockey teams; sponsor every little kid that takes up the game. There's contrarian grit underneath it all. Where others see barriers, Tim Hortons sees opportunity. For House, adaptability means constantly "riding fences of where consumers let us play… don't become a prisoner to a given plan." The entrepreneurial culture is buoyed by its disciplined approach to getting the people part right: "You find good people with integrity and you work with them." With the business on such a roll, what keeps this CEO up at night? It's a skeptic's response: "I always say to our guys, we're not as good as everyone tells us we are, so don't get your head too full."

Michael Arnett, President of Canadian Tire Retail, attributes much of Canadian Tire's success to its unique product mix: automotive parts, accessories and service; sports and leisure products, and home products all under one roof. No other brand is so finely attuned to Canada's obsession with the rituals of spring, summer, fall and winter. First bikes, new barbeques, camping gear, garden tools, leaf-blowers, snow shovels, skates and holiday lights. Canadian Tire generates new items for our "must-have" shopping list with a steady stream of clever product ideas, from power washers to tents equipped with solar panels. When disaster strikes, the Canadian Tire network is quick to show its community stripes with practical assistance. House and Arnett represent two Canadian brands that endure and adapt by virtue of their extraordinarily rich and diverse community connections.

Paul House

Habitat: Chairman, CEO and President, Tim Hortons

Bloodlines: Food is home turf for Paul House. Raised on a farm in Stoney Creek, Ontario, House got his first taste of business running peach farms along the Niagara Peninsula. Armed with a B.A. in Economics from McMaster University, he joined Dairy Queen Canada, eventually rising to Vice-President of Canadian Operations. In 1985, when House made the leap to the Tim Hortons operation as Vice-President of Marketing there were just over 200 retail locations. (Today, the map of restaurants covers over 3,000 locations across Canada, the US and Ireland plus one outlet in Kandahar, Afghanistan.) In 1995, House became COO and President. He was also appointed Chairman of the Board. Despite the fact that under his leadership the Tim Hortons brand has achieved splendid growth and ikonic stature in Canada as well as a foothold in the US and Ireland, House maintains his "regular guy" style. He has earned numerous awards for his innovation, creativity and unique contributions to the foodservice and hospitality industry.

Field Notes: The genesis legend of the Tim Hortons brand is well known—famous hockey hero teams with entrepreneur Ron Joyce to create a chain of donut and coffee spots in 1964. The Canadian operation is ninety-five percent franchise owned and operated. North of the forty-ninth parallel, Tim Hortons has nearly twice the retail presence of McDonalds and dominates the baked goods and coffee markets. Nurturing close relationships with franchisees and their communities keeps the chain's reputation well burnished. Its we-fit-anywhere strategy has led to a number of non-traditional locations as diverse as gas stations and universities. After a decade as part of the Wendy's empire, in 2006 Tim Hortons rolled up its own rim to complete a sweetly successful $5.5 billion initial public offering.

Tim Hortons.

ikonica

110

On the early days...
My first day of work I went home and said, "My God, what have I done?" I had gone to our training store but nobody knew who I was; the restaurant wasn't clean. We had a company that was a dinosaur. As Ron described it when I joined, "We're the best of a bad bunch." And that's what we were. Coffee shops had a bad image at that time. There was the smoking. Ladies didn't want to go into them because the guys all sat at the counters—it wasn't a friendly atmosphere.

On culture...
I like to describe what we have here as an old-fashioned company. We start with the people and then we work from there. We treat people the way we want to be treated ourselves. The greatest pride I have in this company is when someone says, "Your people are incredible." Some businesses have lost sight of what part people play in a successful company. We don't take it for granted. You want to deal with a company that you feel proud of and that you feel cares about you. Whatever you can do to build that relationship is essential for building a great brand. It's a disciplined company. It's all the little things that are important. As a management group we always say, "If somebody says you can't do something, there's opportunity there." You've got to instill that culture within your organization.

On staying fresh...
People think we were an overnight success. I'd like to say we mapped out this wonderful strategic plan and followed it to the letter. Well, we're forty-three years working on an overnight success. When we took the

company through a complete conversion to "always fresh" baking system those were trying times. But for me, that was my greatest management moment. We met every Monday morning at 7:30; nobody could be absent from the room. I had a can-do team. Lots of people came in and gave us a whole bunch of reasons why we couldn't do something. We'd say, "This is the can—do room. You better come back with can do." If I had to teach one thing in business school, it's how to take a negative and create a positive. You generate so much energy. I believe in looking out eighteen months. Keep looking forward and don't become prisoner to a given plan. We've gradually changed the fences of where the consumer lets us play. If we had tried to do a breakfast sandwich fifteen years ago, it would have been an absolute failure. Who would have thought that we could sell yogurt? We're constantly riding those fences. We listen to the consumer but we aren't prisoners to them. The current customer may not want this but do we have enough of those current customers to keep the business alive long term? We haven't moved dramatically; we've just gradually moved the fences.

A five-year plan is nothing more than something to lay up in front of your bankers to keep them happy. I want to know what your two-year plan is because they're goals that you can see and keep your team focused on. Get a goal that's identifiable—it isn't going to take an eternity to get there—and drive the heck out of the organization to get there. If something is unattainable, you can switch gears pretty quickly, not disappoint a lot of people and keep the momentum.

Complacency is a disease in every organization. Nobody escapes it and we continue to fight against it. If you keep moving your brand, you keep it exciting, you keep it challenging, you don't let people get complacent with it. Analysts ask, "What keeps you awake at night?" Complacency is what keeps me awake. I always say to our team "We're not as good as everybody tells us we are, so don't get your head too full." We've got lots of room to improve our brand.

On quality...

We don't try to take advantage of the consumer. The best thing is when the consumer says you've got great value. We do have great value. I'm even shocked by it myself. I'll go in and buy for a group of guys and I'm amazed by the amount of food we have on the table for ten dollars. There's the essence of the brand. You can come here with your family and afford to come here often. Price and quality go hand-in-hand. You go to a restaurant where they know you by name and you've already built in a lot of forgiveness. I tell our team, "You've got to keep making those deposits." I get letters from customers noting that a particular store is not doing things right. They don't say, "I'm not coming back." They're asking me to fix it.

On community...

The success of our brand has been built on the community involvement of each and every one of our store owners. We're involved with kids but we don't sponsor one team, we sponsor the whole league. You want to sponsor every little kid that enters into hockey. Where do you find the new families in a community? They're at the entry level where sports are at their purest. Our commercials reinforce that the first goal is having fun. You build up trust with the consumer; they think, "Hey, they don't do everything just for money." The Tim Horton Children's Foundation proudly spends ninety cents of every dollar raised directly on the kids.

We're also now involved in a program to help coffee farmers directly. When we started talking about it I said, "If we're going to do something, don't do lip service, do it right." In addition to the dollars we're putting in, the people time is probably equal to that. We're not scared to do things other people won't do. Coffee is an integral part of what we do, and it's been a win-win for everybody.

On connections...

"I'll meet you at Tim's" has become a way of life for Canadians. People make jokes about how to get somewhere: "Go down to Tim Hortons and turn left and go another two miles." It plays on itself. We know that some of our commercials are going to be spoofed on *This Hour Has 22 Minutes*. We look forward to how they're going to do it. Where other companies might get upset about it, we're absolutely thrilled. Hey, make fun of us. That's great. It means you love us.

Tim Hortons is not strictly the cup of coffee. It's a friendly place to go. It's not pretentious; it's everyday Canadian. It is what we are, and what's wrong with that? We go across social boundaries. It's all the many things that we do that makes us different than anybody else and gives us the privilege of being a special brand in Canada. There's a Tim Hortons in everybody's town so people can relate to it. That is a big part of it. What did they want in Afghanistan? More than anything else from this country, they wanted Tim Hortons. How the hell do you say no to that? I had more volunteers than we had positions available.

I think the commercial "Proud Fathers," with the Japanese father and son, probably defines what this brand is all about. It cuts across culturally; it defines what Canadians are. I can tell you, the first time I watched it I was in tears. There were a lot of different meanings in that commercial. Everyone can take his or her own meaning away from it.

On working across borders...
There are differences but they are not as large as we like to make the public believe. If we get over this inferiority complex that Canadians have, I think that we'd recognize that. That's the biggest thing we find going to the US is that every hour you drive down the highway, you got a brand-new market that you got to fight and scrape and pay your dues to get into it; you don't get a market for free. You go down the road here for an hour and you get to Kitchener. It's not a lot different. But go from Buffalo to Rochester, it's like going to another world. In Greater Rochester, there are a million people. How many of those markets do we have in Canada? That's the beauty of it. You don't have to be a national player. That's why it's so exciting for us. We're not going to fail there. We've already got too many successes and twenty-year contracts.

On teamwork...
We built this company with a great team of people. Nobody, no one individual, is responsible for any company. People like to take credit but it's done by a team. We all graze in the same pasture. If you want to put fences around your piece of the pasture, then you don't play on our team. This is a company where every employee counts. In the early years, quite frankly, I probably leveraged the fear of Ron very well because I was the guy you could come and talk to. I teach our people, we've got to have trust in each other. My team here—I'd go to heaven or hell with them. We deserve to be where we are now as a publicly traded company on our own. We can make it happen. We won't be swayed by stock price or anything. We talk about long term, what's right for the company and what's right for everybody in it. But, hey, we are what we are. We are a pretty simple team. You know, individually, what are we? Collectively, we are brilliant. I'm proud of this group. I am the cheerleader; that's all I am.

First Person Singular

Michael Arnett

Habitat: President, Canadian Tire Retail

Bloodlines: Mike Arnett joined Canadian Tire in 1990 after eleven years with the grocery giant Loblaws, where he built his reputation in category management, advertising, real estate and store design as well as from turnaround initiatives. Arnett's retail marketing know-how has enabled him to implement significant changes to Canadian Tire's advertising, private label and product innovation programs. He was a driving force behind many of the retailer's key initiatives of recent years: its "Next Generation" store renewal; launching canadiantire.ca, the online shopping channel; integrating Mark's Work Wearhouse after the acquisition. In 2005, Arnett took on leadership of the Corporate Strategic Planning team. He served as Director of the Audit Bureau of Circulations, a group representing the interests of Canadian advertisers, for over seven years.

Field Notes: Canadian Tire Retail and its Associate Dealers together form one of Canada's best-known and most successful retail networks, with 468 stores from coast to coast serving more than three million customers every week. Canadian Tire's interrelated operations also include Canadian Tire Petroleum, PartSource, Mark's Work Wearhouse and Canadian Tire Financial Services. The corporation employs more than fifty thousand people. A national retailing juggernaut, the business is aiming for "sustainable" double-digit earnings growth in the next few years.

On staying fresh...
It's a delight to manage the Canadian Tire brand which is stronger now than it was fifteen years ago. I would like to think that the brand has not changed as much as the stores have. A lot has changed in terms of the size and quality of the store network while the brand attributes are much more stable. Canadian Tire continues to play a similar role for customers as it always has but we are doing a better job of representing the brand through the shopping experience now. There was clearly a need for Canadian Tire to be better than it was. As competitors have increased and customers needs intensified we have at least kept pace, maybe even been ahead of that.

On being unique...
Canadian Tire has always been about meeting Canadians' everyday basic needs.

We try to go above and beyond that and provide people with things they didn't know they needed. We want to inspire them to take on projects in their homes or with their car that they may not otherwise have done. We play a unique role in the world. There are other models that have similar attributes but there's nothing quite like it that we have ever seen. It starts at the very top. There is a unique mix of business under the Canadian Tire umbrella. From a retail perspective we have the branded stores of course. There are no corporate stores. They are all dealer operated; dealers have a loud and clear voice. We also have the credit card from the financial services division. They provide business support to each other in a unique way. We've done a lot of work of late to better understand those loyal customers who shop in all of our divisions. Retail's best customers have a credit card, fill up at our petroleum stations and

spend all their Canadian Tire money back in the stores. There's a virtuous circle that happens there that is unique. Within retail we have a unique mix of business that started way back as just automotive but grew into hardware, then repair maintenance products for the home that grew into sports and leisure. For the most part, we're a hard goods specialist that falls somewhere between where the discounters and the specialty stores play.

On providing value...

It's not a simple continuum but we are deep in a broad number of categories. What we have managed to do is to maintain critical mass, if not dominance, in a number of businesses. That puts us on the trip list for Saturday mornings—go to the grocery store, go wherever else, go to Canadian Tire, because they have these things that I need from light bulbs to golf balls or whatever else. We are still the place to go for all but really specialized shopping.

A third of our business is automotive. Strategically, it's important because most other large retailers just aren't there. It's a point of difference. For categories like car care and automotive accessories, most people couldn't think of another place to go. If you are a heavy-duty, do-it-yourselfer you would know places to go but in the car categories, we've maintained a level of credibility that people aren't drawn away. They don't need to go to a true specialty store to satisfy their needs.

On building trust...

We have ninety percent unaided awareness, which correlates highly with the level of trust for the brand. I think it is critical to the level of success of our brand. Obviously there is a burden of responsibility there when you have that level of trust with your customers. Customers are giving us permission to have a higher-value proposition—we absolutely have moved up—but we will never attempt to capture all the business in every category. It's just not possible.

The reality is that our customer mix has changed a lot. We are trying to appeal to the family much more. Our proportion of female customers has grown and it would exceed the proportions of male customers at certain times of the year; it varies seasonally. Clearly now, versus twenty or thirty years ago, there are not as many people who grew up with Canadian Tire—who remember their first trip, their first bike and all of those things. It is remarkable however, how many people who are new to Canada discover Canadian Tire and talk about us as if it is their own personal discovery—"I found the greatest store, it's not like anything else I've seen before." It's a difficult retail concept to describe but when they see it, they get it; it's not complex intellectually, they get it: "OK, I know what a role this store can play for me." We've done research with customers from other markets and they get it. It's unlike anything you would find in the United States. It would play a role that is not currently being filled in the United States.

On brand management...

I think dealers really appreciate the value of the brand. They certainly have operating guidelines to help them stay within boundaries; they're given directions on the use of logo and what's on side and what's not on side. For the most part I think they get it. We don't have brand police running around from store to store. I don't think that is a requirement in the business. It may not be one hundred percent consistent in terms of the executions store to store because of the differences between communities but that is a good thing. This is not out-of-control inconsistency; it is managed inconsistency to really do what's right in the marketplace.

What our dealers do is add to or complement what we do from a national communications perspective. They work on their local communities to build the brand at the grassroots level. It is one of the big advantages of our system and the dealer network. The dealers are, first of all, entrepreneurial and they tend to be pretty seasoned business people. They understand their role in the local community, whether it's chamber of commerce membership; sitting on the board of the hospital; coaching or sponsoring local sports teams; supporting the food banks, or whatever. Their cause of choice is delivering on our national charitable cause which is the Foundations for Families. The dealers are a big part of the delivery of those programs in our community.

For retail, you need to be good with people, have strong leadership skills and a focus on customer service. Merchant instincts are easier to identify in people who come from retail. People here go through a very vigorous screening process. We have a number of folks at home office that are part of the panel screening incoming applicants because they know what to look for.

On adaptability...

For Canadian Tire, we're always adjusting our business in order to maintain our position in the marketplace. Our business model may need to change, our stores may need to change but we are not changing to become something different. We're changing to keep pace with consumer expectations and requirements and we are doing that proactively. You have to work pretty hard to keep your place in the market because the market is always changing.

The uniqueness of our approach often comes down to the way we manage the business so that we have what people want. We have been investing heavily over the past few years at the product-innovation level. That's a big focus. You are what you sell. If you are the only place selling a particular product, it helps, not only customer loyalty but also the economics—the margins are better. This focus on product innovation is not new for us. We've been doing it for years— pressure washers and our camping tent with solar panels are good examples. That kind of innovation helps to shape our image and drive the business financially as well. We've given our private label brands a better, clearer identity. We used to position our house brands as lowest cost; now they have a distinct, value-added role.

On the Canadian market...

We are absolutely focused on this market. We aren't taking a successful model from some other place and adapting it to Canada. It was born and raised in Canada and has adapted over time to meet the changing needs of the Canadian customer. That's not to say that the model couldn't work elsewhere but we have no intentions of taking it elsewhere. We do tons of research to listen to our dealers and our customers. The fact is that the marketplace is changing. There are new competitors coming in all the time and that raises customer expectations on product, pricing, level of service and shopping environment. Therefore, we need to recognize that and continually renew our awareness and trust so we are top of mind.

In developing the character and personality of the brand over the years, our advertisements have had a bit of a smile associated with them based on insights that, if not uniquely Canadian, are certainly relevant to Canadians— like the weather. Canada is attuned to the four seasons more than almost any other market in the world. We would like to capitalize on that and help people make the transition from one season to the next. There are great stories around here about the heroics relating to storms where people worked through the night and weekends to get generators for their communities.

Understanding what makes a Canadian tick is very important. Lots of retailers in Canada learn the hard way. Canadians want good value for their money. Giving back to community is highly valued. We absolutely get held to a higher standard than other companies. However you describe what Canadian attributes are, they are the same for Canadian Tire.

my ikonica

Pierre Trudeau. There's a guy who created a brand for himself throughout his career in public life. It's now spilling over onto his kids. Whatever you think about his politics, he did a remarkable job of standing out and being clear about what he stood for.

movers and shapers

CANUCK COOL MEETS MONDO FLAIR

FEW NATIONS CAN CLAIM to be founded on the vagary of international fashion, but ever since beaver hats were all the rage in Europe, we've demonstrated a special genius for tapping the "swellegant" zeitgeist. Elizabeth Arden's creams and tonics spawned an international beauty empire. (Almost eighty years later, M•A•C, the cosmetics line founded by makeup artist/photographer Frank Toskan and Frank Angelo, a hair salon owner, brought even more "glam" to the category with the international success of its beauty products designed for "all ages, all races, all sexes.") Henry Birk designed "Blue Box" baubles that every style-conscious woman coveted; Bata brought fashion to the world's feet, while lululemon gave the world's yoga devotees downward dogs with style.

There's no question that on the collection runways of international fashion capitals, Canadian designers hold their own. It's ironic however, that it would be two US expats who would raise Canadiana itself into an international fashion ikon. Roots co-founders Michael Budman and Don Green have mined the popular myth of True North internationally better than any company since Hudson's Bay by tapping the rich ethos of vintage camp/cottage experiences. Robert Sarner acts as chief storyteller for the Roots saga— the website even has a "campfire" section. Adaptability is an essential survival trait in the fickle world of celebrity and fashion. While Roots is continuously reinventing itself (negative heel shoes are a distant memory) based on its keen cultural radar, the business hews consistently to its core values and lifestyle orientation.

Umbra is the yin of Roots retail yang. Both companies were the offspring of the 1970s, but while Roots makes hay from its maple leaf mystique, Umbra's global enterprise is rooted in a mondo-chic approach to housewares. In typical if-you-can't-find-it-build-it entrepreneurial style, co-founders Paul Roan and Les Mandelbaum forged the business out of a personal demand for affordable home accessories. But Umbra's cachet has everything to do with its international sensibility. Mandelbaum describes it as "a global kind of sensitivity. You can't quite nail it down. It isn't quite like the Americans. It isn't quite like the Italians, not quite like French or Asian, but it has all those influences. We take ourselves a little less seriously, which is part of our charm." Communitarian yet contrarian, it makes perfect sense that Umbra's first bestsellers were designer remakes of the lowly trash can: the colourful swing-top plastic model used as a template was Karim Rashid's Garbino Can, which is now in the permanent collection at the Museum of Modern Art.

Umbra marches to its own beat, taking inspiration from the likes of the Beatles and Miles Davis, artists who constantly reinvented their styles. Mandelbaum notes, "We took our time. We were turtle and the hare. We were fast moving in terms of design. From a business stance it's been twenty-six years. We took it one step at a time on purpose." That duality of ear-to-the-ground market awareness married to measured growth is part of the staying power that has kept Roots and Umbra at the top of their game for decades.

First Person Singular

Robert Sarner

Habitat: Director, Communication and Public Affairs, Roots Canada

Bloodlines: Robert Sarner's background in international journalism has served him well in his work at Roots. After beginning his career in Toronto, Sarner moved to France where he worked as a writer and founded Paris Passion, an English-language city magazine he edited for 10 years. (His partners were Roots co-founders Michael Budman and Don Green.) In 1990, Sarner moved to Israel, where he first worked at The Jerusalem Post as editor of its weekly magazine and later became a TV news reporter and anchor. In addition, he did various contract publishing projects in Israel, England, the US and Canada. In 2004, upon moving back to his hometown, Roots asked Sarner to take charge of its communications and public affairs work.

Field Notes: Starting with a tiny boutique in Toronto selling a "negative heel shoe" in 1973, Roots, selling leather goods, clothing and accessories, has left a retail footprint that now extends to more than 125 stores in North America and fifty-five locations in Asia. Michael Budman and Don Green built their fashion empire based on an ever-expanding suite of lifestyle must-haves: Roots Genuine Leather (shoes, jackets, bags and luggage); a full range of Roots Kids and Roots Baby (clothing); Roots Home (leather furniture, linens, towels and accessories); Roots Athletics (sportswear) and Roots Yoga (yoga wear and accessories), plus a selection of licencee products. In 1998, the trendsetter brand brought its athletic panache to the world stage as outfitter of the Canadian Olympic team and in subsequent games also outfitted the American and British teams. Since its inception thirty-five years ago, Roots has developed strong support links to many fields of endeavour including culture, entertainment, sports, health and wellness, community support and the environmental movement. A privately held company, Roots employs nearly two thousand people in Canada where it still manufactures many of its products.

On tracing his Roots roots...

I was in the original store on Yonge Street in Toronto in the late summer of 1973, not long after Roots opened for business in mid-August. I was an early customer and in early October 1973, after leaving Toronto to study in Paris, I must have been one of the few people in France wearing a pair of Roots. I recall that when I bought my pair of Roots shoes, it was Michael or Don who served me. There was a great vibe in that store, something very positive and alive. It was unlike any shoe store I had ever been to in my life.

On the roots of Roots...

While growing up in Detroit, Michael and Don both went to a Canadian summer camp called Tamakwa, a magical place in the wilderness of Algonquin Park in Ontario. Michael started coming in the 1950s. That's what first ignited his love for Canada. In the late '60s, Michael bought a summer cabin in Algonquin Park and was really attracted to Canada where he had a lot of friends from camp. He moved to Toronto in '69. Don first attended Tamakwa in 1961 and he too developed a tremendous affinity for Algonquin Park and Canada. He moved to Toronto in 1971. In 1972, they explored various ideas to go into business and

ultimately they were drawn to launching a crazy new kind of shoe in Canada. Little did they realize then where their entrepreneurial instincts would lead them.

On the upside of a negative experience...

In the early 1970s, a Scandinavian woman had come up with the concept of a negative heel shoe that was supposed to be good for your posture. She called them Earth shoes and they really took off in the States. Michael and Don went to New York to meet with the person who had the North American rights with the hope of snaring the Canadian franchise. After they could not work out a deal with him, they returned to Toronto and decided to do their own take on the shoe. They consulted the phone book for someone to make a prototype and ended up finding an immigrant family—a father and four sons—that had a small atelier downtown. It proved an auspicious hook-up. With input and direction from Michael and Don, Jan Kowalewski and his sons came up with a winning design for the soon-to-launch Roots shoes in 1973. Eventually, Roots bought their factory and it became part of the Roots constellation. To this day, two of the Kowalewski sons are running the leather factory and helping design the leather goods.

On tapping our Canadian roots...

Don and Michael are highly creative individuals with a tremendous love for Canada. Like many people who live in Canada, they were born and grew up elsewhere. As immigrants, they have an amazing exuberance and passion for their adopted country, more so than many native-born Canadians. From the outset, their appreciation of Canada has been an intrinsic part of Roots. It's as real as it gets and has proven a great source of inspiration for them and the rest of the company. Michael and Don are among the best ambassadors Canada has. They are crazy about Canada, and are quite articulate about it, both in their words and in how they've created and nurtured such a quintessential Canadian ikonic brand. Appropriately enough, the

Roots logo has always been a beaver. There's of course a certain irony in that it took two guys from the States to put Canada on the international map, from a style point of view.

On nourishing their Canadian roots...

When Roots was founded in 1973, among Michael and Don's early friends were performers from Second City, people like Gilda Radner, Dan Aykroyd, Marty Short and John Candy. In fact, they often visited the original store and even helped out serving customers when Michael and Don needed a hand. Michael and Don have always been involved with people in the arts and entertainment fields. They parlayed that involvement into getting celebrities to wear Roots clothes, which is always good for a brand. Michael and Don also have a tremendous love for sports and are both gifted athletes. They have supported many athletes over the years. There are certain sport analogies that can be applied to the Roots story and it's no accident that there's a great team orientation at Roots.

As part of their aesthetic sensibility, they've always had a high appreciation of design, architecture and high style. They also have a keen appreciation of communication and its importance to their business. Michael studied communications at Michigan State University. That is what he graduated in, and it's reflected in a lot of Roots literature, both in internal communication for staff and in external marketing for customers. In the beginning, their initial ad campaign and graphics were done by Heather Cooper and Robert Burns. Michael and Don have a knack for finding and attracting good people, which over the years has contributed hugely to the success of Roots.

On building the brand...

For a company to develop a good brand, it has to have a genuine story. It has to be real. It can't be fabricated. It can't be contrived or it will quickly wear thin. There has to be some kind of narrative—official or unofficial, formal or informal—to a brand in order to strike a chord among the public. It can evolve over time, but the essence has to be constant. The constant in the case of Roots are the two co-founders and their devotion and passion for excellence, their commitment to certain standards and values, their unwillingness to compromise or dilute the brand.

Behind a great brand, there must be a genuinely good story. Something that people can identify with. Here in Canada, it obviously helps if a company's logo, imagery, heritage, values and the product reflect something about the country. In the case of Roots, the co-founders are part of the product but they never put themselves first. Yes, they've earned a high profile, but they never lose sight of the fact it's always the company first, the brand and the products, not them. I would say their success is predicated mostly on their love for what they do, their acute understanding of the importance of details and their overriding concern for quality, style and integrity.

On selling Canada to the world...

You have to create the right environment at the retail level, the right imagery and tone in marketing and communication. The narrative has to be down to earth, credible and resonate with people. In Asia, the way people perceive Canada is not quite the same as what Canadians think of their country but Roots is seen as intrinsically part of a popular mythology and imagery of Canada. It is a proudly Canadian company and benefits from the affinity people abroad have for Canada and for the notion of roots. It's true that Roots may be perceived a bit differently when you are in Canada than when you are in China or Hong Kong or Taiwan or in the States, but it's still the same basic representation of Canada.

Regardless of where a brand originates, you can't just parachute it into a foreign country with a different language and different mentality and assume that whatever works in your country will work across the ocean. We're currently enjoying a fast-growing expansion in Asia but it would not have worked had we just gone in there blindly, and presumptuously thought, "Hey, we are successful in Canada and the States, and we are just going to

steamroll into Asia and people are going to be banging our doors down wanting to shop at Roots." That's one of the main reasons we went into partnership with a solid Asian company that has an excellent track record there. We had extended discussions to make sure that there was great compatibility and synergy between both sides but even then, like in any business venture, there's never any guarantee. Ideally, in any initiative abroad, you have good local people representing you and who understand, respect and relate to your brand and of course know well their own country, business landscape and compatriots.

On bringing the world to Canada...

If you are coming into Canada, you'd better have a good understanding of the Canadian sensibility and mentality. Whether you are European, American or Asian, you are bringing baggage no matter what. You are shaped by where you are from and some of it will work here and some of it won't. It is a different marketplace, the scale is different, the distances are different in terms of population concentration. The regional identities and sensibilities are different. Each people and country have their idiosyncrasies including the way they shop. You ignore them at your peril.

my ikonica

Ice hockey is definitely one of the defining Canadian experiences for me. It helped shape my youth. It made me connect strongly to winter. It led me to better understand the nature of sport and what team spirit and dynamics are all about. Playing hockey outdoors on a cold winter day is still very important to me. I'm fortunate to still be able to play. During the winter, I play on a team with Michael and Don several times a week, both on an outdoor rink and indoors. Working at Roots, Algonquin Park, the beaver and winter are unmistakable Canadian ikons for me.

Les Mandelbaum

Habitat: CEO and President, Umbra

Bloodlines: Since 1979, when boyhood friends Paul Rowan and Les Mandelbaum first joined forces, Umbra has transformed everyday products into award-winning objects of desire. Mandelbaum never set out to create a global design empire. His first career as a musician was the genesis of TCH, a company he founded to manufacture road case hardware for touring bands. When he needed design services to promote his gear, Mandelbaum approached Rowan. Rowan was looking for a partner for a few pet projects himself. So, Umbra was born.

Field Notes: "Umbra" means shade in Latin, a fitting tribute to the company's first commercial success, a stylish window shade. Umbra bills itself as the worldwide leader in casual, contemporary, affordable design for the home. Its distribution network of over 8,000 retailers in more than 70 countries makes a pretty convincing case for that honour. The company designs and manufactures products for every room, from picture frames to kitchenware and bathroom accessories. Umbra's award-winning design team—creatives from all over the world—remains the heart and soul of the company. Besides Canada, the business supports offices in the US, Hong Kong, China and Europe. Umbra's good-design-for-the-masses approach has been celebrated culturally and commercially. Its Garbino trash can, designed by Karim Rashid, landed a spot in the permanent collection at The Museum of Modern Art in New York. The company opened its first concept store in downtown Toronto on June 1, 2007.

On the upside of being unemployable...
Paul and I wanted to think of something we could do to have fun and enjoy ourselves because we viewed ourselves as a little bit unemployable. It took awhile to come up with our own idea. I was a musician. When I came back from the States, where I went to school, I had these instrument road cases and everybody wanted them. They didn't want my bass playing but they all wanted these cases. Paul was a friend from high school. He became a graphic designer and he did my first catalogue and logo. He had the idea for consumer products and I had a business in place. I was good at organizing and motivating and had the energy and confidence to do that sort of thing. So I started that business and Paul came up with this idea for design products.

On recognizing opportunities...
I had to move quickly into a new place and the first thing I had to do was cover my windows. There was a window place down the street along Yorkville in Toronto. I said, "I just want some simple, solid drapery and drapery rods that look okay." They did have some architectural-like drapery rods but they told me they would be special order and so would the curtains. I said, "I just want something simple, you know?" Their response: "Sorry. Then go to Canadian Tire." In Canadian Tire, yes, you could pick up drapery rods, but they had no style. And anything you wanted to buy that was cash-and-carry from a place like Fabricland was god-awful. I said to myself, "I can't cover my windows tonight but, on the other hand, I see a huge business opportunity." Our biggest item now came out of that experience. We were the first to put architectural finials onto

metal telescoping drapery rods and put them in a box. Our first customer was Pottery Barn. We were also the first to do plain-colour, tab-top drapery panels in a bag and stick them on the shelf. The first customer was Pottery Barn. I think the second was Bed, Bath and Beyond—they are still a large customer. We opened up that whole category. We didn't do a market study. We didn't talk to customers. It just came from personal experience and recognizing that businesses had ignored this opportunity.

On being international…

For a good ten years when I started this business, I was on a plane twice a week so I have some perspective on what Canadians are and it's fairly consistent to what Umbra is. In the early days Canadians would walk into our New York booth at a trade show and say, "Oh we want to buy directly from the US company. We don't want to deal with the Canadian company." We'd say, "You are dealing with head office if you're dealing with Toronto." You know, with the name Umbra, they think we're Italian or American.
In terms of our industry, there's a dearth of brands that cover multiple categories in the contemporary casual home accessories. I can't think of any in-home accessory companies that cover as many categories as we do and have a real brand. There are brands for certain departments or products but not the breadth of products that we have with an identifiable aesthetic. I'm not just talking in Canada, I mean in the world. There are store brands like Ikea but there're not really any manufacturing and design companies like we are. We're kind of unique in that regard.

Our products were originally very niche oriented. The thing about Canada is—if you're selling any sort of niche goods—the market here is too small and you've got this huge market right next door. You're forced to think outward whereas Americans think inward. Americans typically, because they have such a fat market and such a strong, identifiable culture, tend not to be looking outward as Canadians do. I knew the States so I went to New York and knocked on doors. Then we showed at the Chicago Housewares Show

and that was really our launch. Within three years, most of our sales were in the US.

On the Canadian consumer…

I would say the Canadian consumer is more contemporary than the average American consumer, more quality-conscious and generally, less price-driven. I can speak with some authority because we have Canadian and American businesses. We're conservative in the way we react to business styles, but not in terms of design. Canadians don't like over-flashy businesses, businesses that are too trendy. Relative to European businesses coming here, we're more American than a lot of European markets. To the Americans we seem more European so it depends where you're coming from.

On Umbra's design esthetic…

You can't quite nail it down. It isn't quite like the Americans. It isn't quite like the Italians, not quite like French or Asian, but it has all those influences. If you visited our offices and walked into our design studio, you would see designers from Europe, from China, from Mexico, from the US all working here together. We're very international. We're also adapting to other markets, other cultures, which Americans aren't. We're good at understanding other cultures. That's why I think we've been successful at creating a mini-international brand, a mini-multinational corporation. We do sell throughout the world. And I credit Canada for this ability. If I was sitting in America, it probably wouldn't have happened like this. It's really hard to easily define what a Canadian brand is and what Canadian culture is. But we're certainly very influenced by being so close to such a major power in the world, the US.

On the importance of design…

You can't just think locally when you're competing with the rest of the world. You certainly can't just compete on price and the cost of labour, particularly in the US. So, the added value and the advantage that we can bring to the market place is design. So far, I'd say ninety percent of the goods in our

my ikonica

*Oscar Peterson.
He was well respected
internationally and
he did it from here.
I think it's great.
Bruce Cockburn...
wonderful.
Izzy Sharp at
Four Seasons has
done a remarkable
job too.*

industry are coming in from China or similar countries. They tend not to understand the subtleties of the culture. Even though you think that would be the easiest way to communicate, it's actually the hardest way to communicate. What is the right blue? You think, well, blue, that should be fairly easy, but trying to describe the perfect blue is impossible. It's something you either know or you don't know—what is the blue that women want in their home today or in six months. So, design is key and it comes with understanding your market, your culture. The companies that are failing are the ones that didn't take design seriously. If you read the papers today, the biggest manufacturers, the biggest businesses in the West were the car companies... General Motors and Ford and the others. They just went with the volume and didn't pay enough attention to design.

We define ourselves relatively. I would say the Europeans—the Italians and the French—take their design more seriously. We're buffered by Americans in the sense that we have a more democratic approach. We take ourselves a little less seriously which is part of our charm. We've let our products speak for themselves. We haven't done a lot of advertising—probably couldn't afford it in the early days. Americans do make a lot of noise about their brands. Ralph Lauren has a huge brand, the biggest brand in the world, and I say, "Where's the beef?" What are the great ikon products of Ralph Lauren? What has he done to earn this great brand? We do hundreds of new products a year and thousands over the years—that's our brand. We've been consistent with the sort of aesthetic and creativity and affordability. That's typically Canadian I would say.

When you sell millions of a product, it sort of changes the category. That certainly was the tipping point. The first product was a swing-top plastic trash can. The one-two punch was Karim Rashid's Garbino can. Europeans take themselves more seriously when it comes to design. They're less likely to apply their top designers to something as low as a trash can. So the fact that we picked a trash can is very Canadian and that we built

the brand on it, too. And we did it from grassroots by selling, I don't know, ten million, twenty million, whatever it's been. We did it twice because we went on to the picture frames and changed the whole photo frame industry. Again, millions of those were sold. That was the tipping point. We were able to self-finance. We didn't have to sell out. We didn't have to get investors, which happens to a lot of Canadian companies.

On future growth...

We don't have to become Coca-Cola but I'd like the world to know more of what we do. People know the trashcan or the picture frame but very few know the thousands of products that we create. I'd like greater awareness of all the things we do. We have the foundation for an international brand. I'd like to raise that whole profile. I don't necessarily think that we have to be that much larger a company. We're growing organically quite nicely. It's not about getting richer but certainly I'd like to see our whole team share in some of the recognition and success for what the whole team has done here. I'd like to do that without having to do the typical things like go public or sell. I'd like to let the others in the team share in the success by growing and strengthening the brand. That would make me very happy.

On why brands matter...

Your brand is your reputation. A reputation is a huge asset and a brand is a huge asset. When we go calling customers like retail chains for the first time if we said, "This is our great new drapery rod," we probably wouldn't get past the front door. But now we say, "We're Umbra and we have a great new drapery rod." They say, "Sure, we'll see you right away. We love Umbra." Your brand, like your reputation, is something that you actually can trade on without having to buy and sell anything. I think it's something you've got to protect at all costs. In the end, it's your biggest asset. Anyone can copy your product and mimic what you do and sell it cheaper, but they can't mimic who you are.

storytellers

TAKING THE CULTURAL PULSE

"**THE TRUTH ABOUT STORIES** is that's all we are." It's a refrain woven throughout writer Thomas King's 2003 CBC Massey Lecture series. Stories, King reminds us, are wondrous yet dangerous things because the stories we tell ourselves and each other have such a profound impact on our world view. They can be powerful exempla of meaning and purpose or fundamentally challenge our self-image.

Arguably, given our size, Canada's particular genius for storytelling is disproportionately well represented in the world. The international success of CanLit stars as well as artists and expats in film, television, music, performance and the arts is certainly one tangible measure of success. Nevertheless, the business of contemporary culture is always a precarious one in this country, as our three interviewees can attest. While all three hail from Toronto, the lessons of entrepreneurial cultural organizations with international reach are applicable across the nation.

William Boyle, CEO of Harbourfront Centre in Toronto, describes how the world-renowned, ten-acre creative district rebounded from a near-death experience with an extraordinary show of support from its diverse community constituencies. Harbourfront Centre's international outreach and confluence of multidisciplinary explorations has made it a wellspring of innovative cultural cross-currents. Boyle warns, however, that we can't become complacent about the story of Canada's role in the world—we have to live our own brand of authenticity.

Commerce, culture and community all get starring roles at the Toronto International Film Festival Group, where Piers Handling, Director and CEO, is stewarding the next evolution in the group's ambitious mission to transform the way people see the world through the medium of film. Handling explores how international ties have shaped the organization, which is in the process of shifting gears from ten days of annual festival frenzy to a year-round cultural destination.

First Person Singular

William Boyle

Habitat: CEO, Harbourfront Centre

Bloodlines: In 2004, William J.S. Boyle was made a Member of the Order of Canada in recognition of his tireless work to champion Canadian and international culture at home and abroad. His career with Toronto's Harbourfront Centre spans more than twenty years. In that period, Boyle has positioned Harbourfront Centre as what is arguably one of the world's most diverse cultural centres and the model for numerous international cultural redevelopment projects.

Boyle was the Founding Director of The Power Plant Contemporary Art Gallery at Harbourfront from 1983–1989. He took on the role of Director of Public Programmes at Harbourfront in 1986. In 1991, Boyle was appointed the General Manager and CEO when Harbourfront Centre was reconstituted as an independent, non-profit charitable organization.

Field Notes: Harbourfront Centre's reputation for breakthrough programming is rooted in its signature festivals and events including: World Stage international theatre festival, International Children's Festival of the Arts, International Festival of Authors, Contemporary Dance series, an eclectic line-up of community and ethno-cultural festivals, national and international exhibitions at The Power Plant and York Quay galleries, the Craft Studio program as well as a series of unique, monumental celebrations: Today's Japan (1995), the largest exposition of contemporary Japanese culture ever presented in North America; World Leaders: A Festival of Creative Genius (2001), highlighting the transformative legacy of fourteen of the world's cultural ikons; and SUPERDANISH: Newfangled Danish Culture (2004), an extensive investigation into contemporary Danish culture. But success has not come easily. Harbourfront Centre has threaded its way through perilous funding challenges on route to becoming one of Canada's most innovative cultural institutions. Navigating Canada's brandscape takes real chutzpah and vigilance, as Boyle will attest.

⊙ **Harbourfront centre**

On authenticity…

What is interesting about Harbourfront Centre is that the essential brand was established thirty years ago. It was an upstart, starting from nothing. It was determined that we should provide things culturally to the public that don't happen anywhere else. Anything that we do should be new. Right off the bat, this was really visionary for its time. And we decided to start working with all of the culturally diverse communities—make them feel at home here, ensure that they are respected, celebrate what they are about. It has been absolutely core to the values of the organization and core to the brand. Also, what we should be doing, unlike other arts institutions, is celebrating new, emerging,

avant-garde, leading-edge arts. No dead artists! That was our mantra. Those founding principles, unwittingly, are actually what shaped the brand. And then all of the community and arts organizations that partnered with us organically shaped the brand into all the different meanings that it has today. It grew organically out of what we did, and what we did became the brand. That is where the persona, or the personality, has been authenticated.

Harbourfront Centre has a very different personality than the Royal Ontario Museum, or the Canadian Opera Company, or the Art Gallery of Ontario. The brand comes out of, or is reflected by, the personality of the place… the way it operates, the speed with

which it operates, the values that it actually has, not just the ones that are written on paper, the way we really conduct business. There is hardly any place like it in the country, or in North America. Here you have working studios, architecture and design, exhibitions, with theatre, dance, and a huge literature program. I can find few places in the world that put all those under one umbrella. That is really a determining factor of what makes the place different. The other thing that we talk about all the time is how important the geography is. The fact that this institution owns ten acres of the central district of the city and it is driven by a cultural agenda is unique.

There was one really galvanizing moment when the place was threatened to be shut down by the Government of Canada and the institution fought to the death and won. It was absolutely seminal to the personality of the organization, its relationship to the city and the public. That was 1995. The government was overwhelmed by the public response. There were rallies, editorials, there was front page coverage for weeks. People came out in droves and said, "Wait a second! You cannot take this away from us!" We actually changed our tagline and our brand after that because people always referred to it as "our place." That was the term that kept coming up over and over again… "How dare you? This is our place!" To me that was an absolute symbol of the sense of ownership people had for the place. I had several colleagues in the cultural field say, "Geez, that would never happen with our institution!" I bring it up to staff over and over again. We need to make sure that people always feel that there is a sense of ownership for the place. It re-affirmed the value of the organization to itself but it also really galvanized the sort of street fighting part of the brand. That is not a way that a lot of organizations think of themselves.

On branding and the arts…
The idea of brand is absolutely relevant to arts organizations except it used to be anathema to call it a brand, in the same way you should not talk about cultural things as a product. Only in the last five to ten years have we started thinking about the fact that we have a brand. We talk branding to corporate people in order to get them to sponsor something. It's inevitable that it rubs off. If you're talking to a beer company or a bank about how their brand is going to be reflected at your site, you start thinking, "Wait a second, what is my brand?"

The challenging thing for cultural institutions is that branding can be very superficial. That is a real danger. It's one thing to have a logo, but that does not necessarily mean that you have the depth of thinking that drives the content of the institution. That's what worries me about branding. The way that people often talk about branding is very superficial, a gloss over the top of things. People don't sit and think, "What is the essence of this place? What are we really committed to?" Half the time it's just clichéd talk about mission statements and value statements. A lot of them are interchangeable. They all sound alike. What is the real essence of your brand? Brand is a worrisome word. It tries to capture in one thing, everything about the organization—the philosophy, the reason you're doing business, the ethics, all of it in one thing. Can you really distill it into that?

On the changing role of the arts…
The most prominent change is the multiplicity of voices that is happening now. In the next twenty years here the art production is going to be completely different. It already is. It's trans-disciplinary. What is exciting to me is all of the fusions that are happening. That is probably where we think differently. We do all our programs for their intrinsic, cultural significance. We approach everything from a curatorial perspective. It's a missionary kind of zeal about things that we think are significant for the public to know; things that will create greater understanding, greater respect among people, probing things of human significance. That's the non-profit mentality. It's not, "Oh gee, we are doing this to attract three million new people." In the world of high culture internationally, there is a lot of respect for Canada in serious arts, much more than we

my ikonica

*Northrop Frye.
He was the first person
who really outlined what
he thought made Canada
distinct. Frye was a seminal
thinker about Canada,
analyzing it through its
cultural output, which is an
interesting way to look at it.*

would ever know. What I hear from abroad is they see Canadians as having a very distinct view of the world. They see Canadian artists putting forth a transnational view of the world. For example, one of the projects we brought here during the SUPERDANISH event was the most prominent Danish composer's opera of Margaret Atwood's *The Handmaid's Tale*.

On the heroes and myths...

We in Canada are not big on creating Canadian cultural heroes. It's the polar opposite of the "Living Treasure" syndrome in Japan where Japan designates major artists as Living Treasures. You do not have to be 150 years old for this. When you are designated a Living Treasure you are like an ikon of the country. It's in all disciplines. I can't see that ever happening in Canada. By the way, that is probably our strongest non-American trait. Americans celebrate their cultural heroes and ikons and everything else. Canadians do the exact opposite.

The Canadian myth is that we believe that we are the most diverse, accepting, international country in the world. We've started to believe our own publicity that this has become the mosaic and that we are the model for the future. But Canada may be slipping into complacency on that issue. We think that it is all just going to happen, that it has happened organically and naturally. To a certain extent it has, which is great. But we all have to put our minds to the fact that if that is going to be (Canada's) brand, which I think that we have accepted that it is, then we are really going to have to work on it, on a daily basis, to make sure that it survives as a brand... that it is actually true, that it's not just a "mission statement" that isn't in fact

happening. Most Canadians that you talk to would think that there is very little racism, that everybody is accepted equally. They all believe that but it is not true. I think that we're way ahead of many places but we have a long way to go in order to create this cohesive society that is made up of people from all around the world, which is what we really believe in. That is different from fifteen years ago. Now the peacekeeping nature of Canada is gone out the window. That was an ikonic thing for us. We were the peacekeepers, the neutral Swiss of North America that could always be respected. That is a deeply held belief in Canada. There is a lot of work to be done on the "cultural mosaic" because a mosaic implies that most of the parts are equal and that is not necessarily the case.

Piers Handling

Habitat: Director and CEO, Toronto International Film Festival Group (TIFFG)

Bloodlines: Piers Handling's first taste of the Toronto International Film Festival came as a member of the audience during its inaugural season. A few years later, in 1982, he joined the organization as a programmer and a dozen years later he was named Festival Director and CEO. In his decades at the helm of the Festival, Handling has mounted numerous programs including major retrospectives of Canadian, Latin American and European cinemas and directors, and co-founded Perspective Canada. Prior to his film festival life, Handling worked at the Canadian Film Institute (CFI) for a decade, attaining the position of Deputy Director. He has also taught Canadian Cinema at Carleton University in Ottawa and Queen's University in Kingston, and published extensively on Canadian cinema.

Field Notes: The Toronto International Film Festival Group's mission is to transform the way people see the world. Its vision: to lead the world in creative and cultural discovery through the moving image. In 1976, it debuted as the Festival of Festivals, today TIFFG is now powered by more than 100 full-time staff, 500 part-time staff and the largesse of thousands of volunteers. The Toronto International Film Festival generates an annual economic impact of $67 million (2002 figure). That number is estimated to grow considerably when its permanent home, dubbed Bell Lightbox, opens in Toronto. The Group has expanded far beyond its star-studded annual film festival to include: Cinematheque Ontario, its year round program of film classics; Sprockets Toronto International Film Festival for Children; Film Circuit, a community-driven initiative providing Canadian and international films to under-serviced communities across Canada; The Film Reference Library; Reel Talk, a popular subscription series, Canada's Top Ten awards and Industry Initiatives, which presents specialized industry programming.

TORONTO INTERNATIONAL FILM FESTIVAL GROUP
tiffg.ca

ikonica

138

On the benefits of geography...

There are three major European film events—Cannes, Berlin and Venice. There was a need for a major North American counterpart, and Toronto is neutral ground, almost mid-Atlantic. People comment on the fact that the festival isn't aggressive or edgy, it doesn't make you nervous. The stars that come are more relaxed and prepared to mix with the public. Our guests always compliment the cosmopolitan offerings of Toronto and our accepting and casual atmosphere. They can't believe the public support. We are the largest public film festival in the world and value the diversity of Canada. Today, Toronto is seen to be one of the top two film festivals in the world, there are few other Canadian initiatives with that kind of global reach and awareness.

On international connections...

We were never satisfied to be a festival just based in Toronto and we were really keen on stretching the boundaries of festival programming. The Festival has always been a blend of different kinds of cinema—the avant-garde, hardcore art cinema—and the commercial. The nature of an international film festival means you're showing films from around the world. At the very beginning, the Festival paid great attention to English language cinema and we very consciously made the decision to cover the globe. We were very aggressive in terms of sending our programming team around the world and it's taken us twenty years of conscious strategic planning to become an international event. You can't just sit in Toronto and proclaim yourself an international event; we travelled to Asia, Latin America and then Africa and brought the filmmakers to Toronto. Actors and producers, then buyers, sellers and the media began to follow and then things took

TORONTO INTERNATIONAL FILM FESTIVAL GROUP presents

TORONTO INTERNATIONAL
FILM FESTIVAL®
SEPT 7-16

06

off. You have to travel, be on the ground listening to the filmmaker's concerns; profile their films; give their work key positions in the festival when it's appropriate, provide publicity and marketing support and persuade their film institutions to support the travel of the filmmakers. The same kind of work has gone into our other activities: Cinematheque Ontario, Sprockets, The Film Circuit; they all have significant international profile.

On domestic growth...
We realized that the ten-day festival was not enough, over the last two decades; we evolved into a 365-day organization with on-going activities. We have a library, an archive and a year-round screening program. We have a lot of ambition in the area of film learning, and hope Bell Lightbox turns into a destination for all film lovers. To date, there are very few buildings in the world which concentrate on film as an art form and cultural expression. We'll show films from the hundred years of the art form, as well as new films that don't get large distribution. There will be exhibits and programs in Bell Lightbox that will contextualize the films: objects, memorabilia, displays, costumes and lectures. It's designed to be a living, breathing, active film center, creating dialog, where the international film industry—filmmakers, producers, actors—will be flowing through its doors, talking to audiences but also talking to the Canadian film industry. We're totally committed to the Canadian film industry and we're contributing to the positioning of Toronto as a film production centre, a place with an abundance of creativity. That's definitely part of our mandate.

On lessons from abroad...
The Americans are absolute marketing geniuses. Sundance has a very strong brand. It's a vertical brand, unlike our own. They changed the name of the United States Film Festival to the Sundance Film Festival about fourteen years ago because of the association with Redford and the film. It was a brilliant name change. The festival is in Park City; Sundance is actually about an hour's drive

away. It's kind of like a virtual space but I guess it's what brands are. Because Festivals are limited to ten days, they (Cannes, Berlin, Sundance) are starting to think about year-round programming and global impact—sending their material out into the world. That's the future for us very definitely... we're there.

On managing brands...
We're a multitude of brands. After establishing the Toronto International Film Festival, we added Cinematheque Ontario and the Film Reference Library; then The Film Circuit and Sprockets: Toronto's International Children's Film Festival. Suddenly, we realized we had all these names but no overall brand. The Toronto International Film Festival is still the biggest brand we have, it opened doors domestically and internationally and created a huge profile but people aren't really aware of all our activities and initiatives. Bell Lightbox is our vessel in which we will strengthen and highlight all our initiatives, achieve our goals and bring together our brands under one roof. We have a very strong mission statement: Transforming the way people see the world. That statement reflects our organization: the desire to be curious, the desire to be youthful, to be fresh and to be innovative. The Festival represents excitement, energy, glamour, star power, with a unique exploration of cinema, and our year-round screening programmes are about creating serious debate and learning around film culture in a way that often festivals can't address. We struggle to balance and promote the year round initiatives with the Festival. We're trying to grapple with putting these two parts together. The tension is really interesting—we may never want it resolved. I thought a lot about this—it may be healthy for the festival to have a counterpart that forces it to be serious. It's like complementary personalities. Our identity and authenticity lies in this tension and will be there in the brand as well... always questioning what exactly we are as an institution.

On the Canadian narrative...
The Canadian narrative used to be about how you survive in a rough, tough, hostile

BELL LIGHTBOX

The new home of the Toronto International Film Festival Group

environment. Is there a new one? I don't think it's yet defined. It's probably more about coexistence and diversity. Canadian culture has always being more community-oriented, we value the collective. Canada is predominantly urban now and multi-cultural. We have our own cultural identity. It's one of diversity where people are coexisting safely and happily with each other, in a community that works. This is a compelling idea when you see such tribal, ethnic and religious strife in the world. Something's working here. Taking care of each other and respecting other people—those are core values in this country. It's always been a very safe culture that way. We take care of everybody but, at the same time, sometimes we make it hard for the high-achievers. This may explain part of the reason why there are lots of brands that are not really known. I don't think we have this self-confidence yet.

On conditions for success...

You have to have a very clear mission and vision in terms of what you're trying to accomplish and remain honest and true to that. I would always stress the international. Whatever we're doing, the objective is not to be best in Canada; it's to be the best to the world. Be committed. It's a long-term strategy as opposed to quick answers and quick successes and you can't give up. If you are determined, just hanging in sends huge signals—it pays off. Reciprocating is important. Deliver on your promises. Delivering on expectations is really important—be very clear and honest with people about what you've created so that you don't hype them into expecting another experience. That's a big lesson a lot of people learned in the early days of the film festival. Never, ever rest in on your laurels; always be aware of the environment around you. Never be afraid of taking ideas from elsewhere. I get so many of the best of my ideas when I get out of the office. Relentless self-searching is key. At the end of every event we do a postmortem and target the challenges. There are always things to pay attention to. That self-questioning and self-searching is really important.

Early Film Festival poster image by Jayme Odgers.

CANADA from the air

fellow travellers

NAVIGATING BRAND BUILDING ROUTES

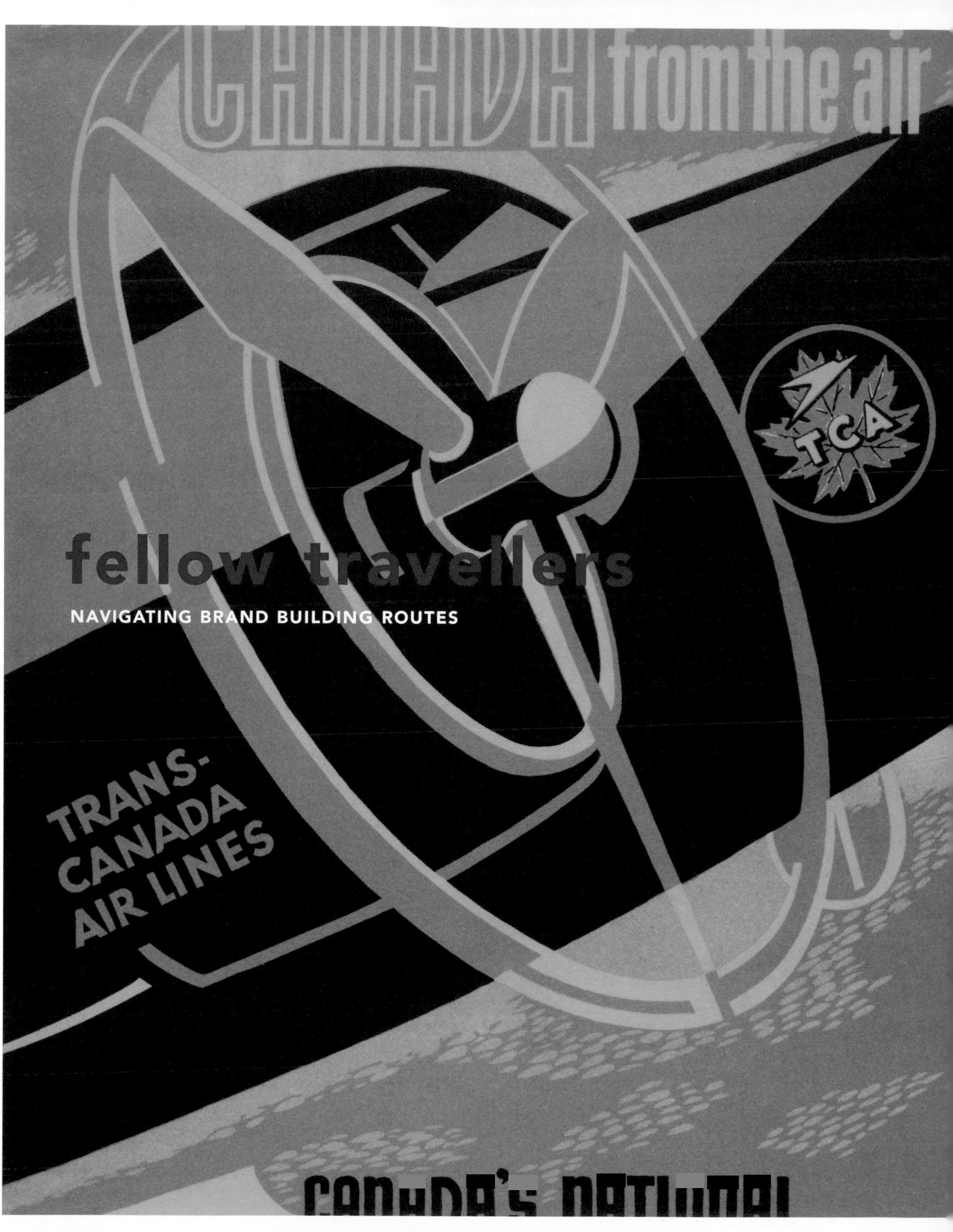

TRANS-
CANADA
AIR LINES

TCA

CANADA's NATIONAL

CANADIANS ARE PASSIONATE travellers, motivated in part by weather—the annual "Snowbird" exodus—and our lust for experience. Younger Canadians especially view themselves as citizens of the world. Knowing the "it" spots in emerging tourism destinations or recounting adventures of biking/hiking/kayaking hidden byways have valuable social currency. It's not surprising that Canada has such a genius for great travel, adventure and hospitality brands: Four Seasons Hotels and Resorts, Fairmont Hotels, Butterfield and Robinsons, Mountain Equipment Co-op and Tilley Endurables.

Four Seasons' founder Isadore Sharp is a great study in how ikonic Canadian attributes and values mold a successful organization. Sharp's first foray into hospitality—a motor lodge on Jarvis Street in Toronto that opened in 1961—began modestly with room rates at nine dollars per night. In *No Guts, No Glory: How Canada's Greatest CEOs Built their Empires*, author David Olive describes Sharp as, "an entrepreneur in a trade that was dominated by corporate bureaucrats. His outward appearance as an urbane, low-key family man belied a gambler's heart… More than Sharp cared to admit, Four Seasons was an extension of his personality. And his contrarian instincts." Born of Sharp's vision, entrepreneurial, experiential and international are clearly strong suits for the Four Seasons brand. Contrarian and skeptical go hand in hand as well; skeptics aren't bound by conventional wisdom.

Four Seasons' phenomenal international growth is highly dependent on the ability to transplant its unique service culture to diverse locales—from Boston to Beijing. The company takes extraordinary pains to recruit people based on their service attitude, sometimes requiring up to five interviews to assess the cultural fit with prospective hires. At one of the New York hotels there were thirty thousand job applicants; three thousand were considered and only four hundred chosen.

Sharp is quoted in an April, 2007 *Report on Business Magazine* profile saying: "A culture cannot be copied, it cannot be imitated. It has to grow from within over a very long time, based on the consistent action of senior management. That is the barrier to entry for other hotels trying to compete against us." That kind of long-term vision is also manifested in the persistence with which Four Seasons pursues opportunities. It took almost two decades for Four Seasons to find the right opportunity in Mumbai. That kind of patience, "is the hallmark of Sharp's management style," *Report on Business* author Derek DeCloet notes, "probably the biggest reason Four Seasons has succeeded in global expansion where so many other Canadian businesses have failed." From cruises and exotic tented camp adventures to a growing network of shared ownership Residence Clubs and Private Residences, Four Seasons brand is prime example of creating a seamless fusion of culture and commerce that can thrive in diverse communities around the world.

Elsewhere in the travel sector, as commercial siblings Air Canada and Aeroplan provide a unique opportunity to explore different brand building strategies from the same organizational roots. Both businesses share lineage that traces back to ACE Aviation. Aeroplan was established in 1984 as an incentive program for Air Canada's frequent flyers. In 2002, Aeroplan became a wholly owned limited partnership of Air Canada, with its own dedicated management team that took the company public in 2005. The transaction raised $287.5 million, earning Aeroplan an initial valuation of $2 billion, one of the largest business income trusts in the country at the time.

In the turbulent world of air travel, Air Canada and Aeroplan survive through adaptability. Robert Milton recounts the trials of bringing Air Canada back from the brink after 9/11 and SARS. In contrast, it's instructive to hear how Rupert Duchesne and his team negotiated the delicate matter of reinventing Aeroplan's brand, internally as well as with customers, keeping the best of its Air Canada heritage while carefully off-loading old baggage that could weigh it down.

First Person Singular

Robert Milton

Habitat: Chairman, Air Canada; Chairman, President and CEO of ACE Aviation Holdings Inc.

Bloodlines: As the head of ACE Aviation Holdings, a role he took on in 2004, Robert Milton oversees a vast network of air travel services. ACE is the parent holding company that spawned the reorganized Air Canada and its many siblings, all separate legal entities: Aeroplan, Jazz, ACTS and Touram (Air Canada Vacations). A graduate of Georgia Institute of Technology, Milton lived and worked in many countries before 1992 when he began working with Air Canada as an aviation consultant. In 1999, when he took control as CEO, Milton's flight plan encountered more that its share of turbulence. Within days of being appointed, the airline was facing a hostile takeover bid from Onex and American Airlines. Then came an economic downturn, later compounded by the aftermath of 9/11 and SARS—a tough set of body blows for Canada's travel industry. At the same time, Milton was marshalling a major restructuring to position the carrier more competitively. The plan worked and Air Canada celebrated its Seventieth Anniversary in 2007 in fine fiscal health complemented by many new service innovations.

Field Notes: Canada's flag carrier is the fourteenth largest commercial airline in the world, carrying more than 30 million customers annually to over 150 destinations around the world. Air Canada's predecessor, Trans-Canada Air Lines (TCA), first got its wings in 1937. The fifty-minute flight between Vancouver and Seattle may have included only two passengers and mail bags but by the mid-60s, TCA had landed a new moniker, Air Canada, as our national carrier. Privatized in 1989, Air Canada acquired its arch-rival, Canadian Airlines, in 2000. In recent years, the carrier has racked up numerous industry kudos including: "Best Airline in North America" (Skytrax, 2006–2007); Airline Industry Achievement Award for Market Leadership (*Air Transport World*, 2007); "Best Airline in North America" (*Global Traveler Magazine*, 2007). In time for its anniversary, the airline also launched Project XM. The "extreme makeover" is the largest cabin refurbishment project in the company's history.

AIR CANADA

ikonica

144

On being Canada's national carrier...
It's about providing safe and reliable service to any community that can viably support it. We get into some localized debate, especially in smaller communities, on why Air Canada doesn't serve more places or offer bigger airplanes. Sometimes they're pressing for service where it's just not economically viable. Most airlines in the world just wouldn't worry or think about it. But there are some unique aspects to Canada, including the vast geography with many small communities and the overall small population. Some people point to the low fares available on other airlines. We have moved to where we match the low fares but when these other airlines— any airline you can think of—basically just serve the biggest markets and don't have the

quote "burden" of serving smaller, less exciting, less economically robust, less profitable markets, they have an obvious advantage right from the get-go.

On turning disasters into opportunities...
We have been hit particularly hard because we're the only airline in the world that both had its air space shut down after 9/11 and had SARS at home. When you're in a situation like SARS where nobody wants to come to your country, it doesn't matter what your brand is, it doesn't matter how safe you are, it doesn't matter what kind of service you provide... if nobody is going, nobody is going. That led to an opportunity for us to deal with how we go about changing the company, which meant cost structure and

how we sold our product. We've learned a lot. Air Canada meant to the travelling public what they remembered from thirty years ago—you wear a tie and you get served baked Alaska on the airplane. Since there has been some deregulation of this industry in North America, it's become a lowest-common-denominator kind of game. Lower fares are what consumers ultimately want, but it's meant less and less service because all through the periods of deregulation, wage rates and labour costs kept going up and fares kept coming down. The only things that could give were all the amenities provided. The recollections were still there but the reality was no longer part of the way we were operating. People would say, "I want the Baked Alaska, and I want the pillows" but they wouldn't pay anything for them.

On amenities a la carte...

The advent of the Internet has meant that low-cost airlines around the world could sell tickets, in real time, at much lower prices, without any competitive distribution disadvantage. In the old days, they had to go through travel agents but now they can just sell right on the Internet. All the advantages of distribution that the legacy airlines had, disappeared. Along came these low-cost airlines with very low prices because they had low-labour costs and they offered no amenities.

Where I really had a revelation was back in around 2002, after 9/11, as we tried to stabilize the airline in this lower-revenue environment. We actually painted some airplanes purple, didn't serve any food and took business class out. You could buy food, you could buy a seat assignment, you could buy all sorts of things, but you paid for them as you went. There was nothing but the bare-bones commodity price of a seat. When we had about a dozen Tango airplanes flying, we had Air Canada flight attendants, Air Canada pilots, Air Canada check-in agents... the exact same employees as Air Canada. In those two years, we carried about 3 million passengers on Tango and I can honestly say we never received one customer complaint. What that

told me was that the halo around low-cost airlines is largely because people think, "Hey, I'm paying bottom-dollar, I don't have expectations on service. As long as you get me there, I'm happy." But on Air Canada they would expect a pillow, a blanket, an amenity kit, a meal. And if anything isn't delivered, even if it was the exact same $99 flight fare, they would be upset with Air Canada. On Tango, with the same airplane, same employees, same facilities, they weren't upset.

It told us that we had to go to optionality. What you want, you pay for. Whatever you pay for is going to be completely competitive with the low-cost carriers. We had to move to a complete value outcome for customers. Over time, they will get over their expectations that somehow there was going to be caviar and candlelight dinners. I think a lot of that has been about our brand... managing expectations of what we are today which, thankfully, is working pretty well. Now we're offering all sorts of flexibility and different features. Now we're offering passes. On our website you can buy ten or twenty passes to sun destinations; you can buy ten or twenty tickets to get you to work and back. You manage that yourself, on the Internet. What we really want to get to is the notion of subscription. People buy whatever they want; it's always their choice and value. My hope is that we get to a point where people say, "You know what? That was good value. I got exactly what I wanted, exactly what I paid for, and I got to fly with good, experienced, competent aviation people at Air Canada."

On managing change internally...

A critical success factor for us was buying Canadian Airlines. From an airline that couldn't really offer you Asia or South America or parts of Europe, all of a sudden, Air Canada could offer everywhere in the world. And that's made an enormous difference in terms of the proposition that we offer. The years after 9/11 with the crisis in the industry meant there was really no ability to invest. So, as we came out of the restructuring in 2004, one of things we wanted to do was really reinvest in our fleet, get the most modern, efficient airplanes around and invest in product onboard the aircraft: new lay-flat seats in business class; personal televisions for everybody, the best standard of equipment available. That was an expense but with that was the ability—with employees in particular—to say, "We're turning the page." As that ad says, "This is not your father's Oldsmobile." This is a new Air Canada. Okay, we'd been through holy hell. This airline has been essentially bankrupt since the day it was privatized in 1988. Since October, 2004, we've fixed the balance sheet and the cost structure. We're investing in the future. We told our people, "You're a part of it and we're going to change the way we look. Whether it's the way the airplanes look, or the way the uniforms look, or the logo looks, this is where we're going and this is the turning point, right now."

On how to measure success...
When you see awards saying Air Canada is the Best Airline in North America and in Canada you've got to say, "Okay, we're making some progress here. This is good." In terms of the profitability of the airline, which is something that historically has not been there, our share price and how the market is reacting to it all, you say "This is good, it's working." In our history, the airplanes have never been this full and we're a bigger airline then we've ever been. A lot of people do want to come back and fly on us over and over and over again.

On carrying the Canadian flag abroad...
It is a big positive because, as harsh as Canadians are on themselves, and as hard as the country is on itself, or as hard as the country may be on Air Canada domestically, internationally what Canada connotes is very positive in terms of big, wide-open free space, fresh air, cleanliness and, to a degree, neutrality. It's a big, peaceful place—an enormous Switzerland. In terms of what international travellers want, those attributes—clean, safe, open, fresh—are all things that you'd like to be selling, and you'd like to be selling as an airline. So we get the

benefit of that. And because Canada is such a popular tourist destination, you'll see that for much of the year, around the world, the overwhelming traffic on the aircraft is actually foreigners coming to Canada.

On the importance of branding...
There's a fascination with our industry that I think is greater than most. It's probably rooted in the fact that flying is unnatural for humans. Beyond that, in our case, we've got over three hundred flying billboards whizzing around every day. So visibility-wise, there's a lot of visibility. How the airplanes look in terms of the paint job, in terms of the being clean, is also important. So it really is a 24/7 branding exercise worldwide. There's a piece of that that gives you non-stop presence. For sure, the most effective marketing an airline can do is just prices—old fashioned, barebones, bare-knuckle stuff. But you know, you can do these hazy pictures of the fancy meals and all the rest of it, but in reality, all people care about is price. So you advertise the price. If you've got the right brand image and the right advertising support, it hangs together.

On Canadian-ness...
I remember years ago when I was in high school a professor in economics was talking about how Nestlé was another evil American corporation. I got in trouble for correcting him. In large measure, a lot of the world thinks everything is American if it's big. But I do find, very clearly, that the anxiousness with which people look at Americans around the world definitely does not follow for Canadians. As we look at investment opportunities we've had this issue come up. People are looking more favorably at us because we're Canadian.

One of the things that I always find comforting and positive is when Canadians say, "I was travelling in some exotic part of the world, or I was away from an airport for a week and I got to that airport and saw that Air Canada airplane, I saw that maple leaf on the tail and I felt good. When I got on that airplane I was home." I hear it so often but it always makes you feel good.

my ikonica

I grew up with Bob and Doug MacKenzie. Those are the guys who were my first exposure to Canada well before I moved here. Another interesting aspect of Canada is the extent to which artists, whether they're in writing or music or film, punch way above their weight class on the global stage. With the size of the population, look at the number of big stars from this country. It's really quite amazing.

GREAT WHITE NORTH

brand experience atlas

149

Rupert Duchesne

Habitat: CEO and President, Aeroplan

Bloodlines: Duchesne immigrated to Canada from the UK to head up Mercer Human Resource Consulting's global aviation practice. He joined Air Canada in 1996 and was part of the executive team that defeated the ONEX take-over bid. His next big task was overseeing the merger of Canadian Airlines with Air Canada. Duchesne took over the reins of Aeroplan, Air Canada's loyalty program, in August 2000.

Field Notes: Aeroplan now has more than five million active members collecting Aeroplan Miles through over sixty commercial partners, representing over one hundred brands. We asked Duchesne to talk about reconstituting brand loyalty for a business with its own unique baggage.

On the heart of loyalty...

It was very clear that Aeroplan was something we could build as a separate entity that already had, in the consumer's mind, its own space. Was it very, very closely allied with Air Canada? Of course, but did it mean something different to them from Air Canada? Absolutely. In 2005, Aeroplan went public with a valuation of $2 billion. As of this morning, it was worth about $3.5 billion. Think of the airline's IPO late last year; it's now worth about $2 billion. It's very bizarre that this marketing scheme attached to the airline—and it's a damn good airline, very efficient and well-run now—is worth more than the entity.

It goes back, in my view, to the fact that Aeroplan as a proposition is somewhere else in the consumer's mind than the airline. They loved it so much they often hated it. When Aeroplan disappointed them they got passionately angry. We represented

something that really mattered to them and we weren't delivering. It seems that the place that Aeroplan operates in their lives is—and it sounds very hackneyed—the place that allows them to escape from the mundane to the pleasurable; allows them to spoil themselves in a way they may not be able to justify if they were paying with real dollars. It's all about bringing out this sort of joie de vivre. That's why people accumulate Aeroplan miles. At the back of their mind they have something that they know they can spoil themselves with. When you get a brand to that point, it's a hugely valuable place to be.

One of the key piss-off factors for our members was being told no. The real break is to say, "Yes, you can have a seat, but you, the member, have to choose whether you're willing to pay this price by booking ahead, or if you want to leave last minute, then it costs you twice as much." We engineered the profitability of the business to be constant per

WE'VE PUT THE CUSTOMER'S DECISION
IN THEIR OWN HANDS SO THAT JOIE
DE VIVRE SPACE—I'M GOING TO SPOIL
MYSELF, TREAT MYSELF TO PLEASURE
AWAY FROM THE MUNDANE—WORKS.

mile redeemed so we've put the customer's decision in their own hands so that joie de vivre space—I'm going to spoil myself, treat myself to pleasure away from the mundane—works.

On the role of identity...

We had a really fundamental debate about should we change the way the company looked and then do all of this work so we'd catch up? Or, should we try and fix everything and then launch the new brand? We fixed all of the mechanics to the ninety percent level and came out with the new tangerine branding. The tangerine branding was meant to say a couple of things: Firstly, Aeroplan is distinct and different than Air Canada. Secondly, the Aeroplan you know is still there. It's evolved. And thirdly, Aeroplan is something palatable, whatever business you're in. People were very, very split about Air Canada. They weren't about Aeroplan. If we wanted to grow into a broader demographic, we needed to neutralize the "I hate Air Canada" group. The most effective way to do that: change logo, change colour. A new identity showed very, very clearly an evolution.

On emotional connections...

The experience that we've created with Aeroplan is a proposition that you see less often in what I would call a more linear economy, whether that's American or German. It's a little bit more Latin in its flavour than what I call Anglo-branding. We said the only place that it makes sense to be a brand is in that emotional space—go for broke in that area. Aeroplan, whether by luck or by judgment, has captured that diffuseness of attachment that I think is peculiarly Canadian. If you ask Canadians, "What is being Canadian?" it's defined by what it's not, as opposed to what it is. But it's a deeply emotional belief, a very fundamental belief in not only being Canadian but in Canada's role in the world. Our charity program, "Beyond the Miles," is almost unique in the corporate sector in Canada, let alone in the world. We've handpicked a group of charities that we think are taking the best of what's

Canadian and doing very, very valuable stuff, principally overseas: Engineers Without Borders, Stephen Lewis Foundation, Médecins Sans Frontières, Schools Without Borders, Vets Without Borders and the Canadian Executive Service Organization. Veterinarians Without Borders didn't exist before we created our program. We wrote to the Vet Association of Canada and said "Do you do overseas development?" They said "No, but it's a great idea." We've put money in, as in miles, and we also have members put money in, in terms of miles. I think to date we're roughly at thirty million miles that have been donated by our members. If I'd done this in England, Germany or the US, it wouldn't have had any appeal at all because it wasn't a linear cause and effect like the Heart and Stroke Foundation. Yet, it's absolutely on brand for Aeroplan.

On value and values...

The Aeroplan brand is all about intrinsic values. There's no statement of values on our website. It's all in the mind of the member. If it isn't, we'd never get anywhere. The top thirty-five percent of income in the country are our members. The fact that they often choose to use Aeroplan as the vehicle to buy what they otherwise could with cash is a testament to a very, very emotionally engaged brand. These are consumers who, normally, you would not expect to drive out of their way to get Aeroplan miles. But when we introduce a new partner, forty-six percent of our members will actually change where they buy that commodity product from in order to accumulate Aeroplan miles, which is an extraordinary statistic. The real value of the twenty miles you earn is almost irrelevant. But the fact that every twenty miles you earn goes towards that spoil yourself opportunity or that aspirational opportunity is fundamental.

On employee loyalty...

There's two different parts. First of all, our call centre agents, about eight hundred full time equivalents, are still Air Canada employees but they're permanently seconded to us. They were brutally airlined in 2000: they were Air

my ikonica

Skating on the Rideau Canal. It's crowded; it's crappy ice; there's no other circumstance in which you'd eat a beaver tail. But it is such a quintessentially Canadian experience. And everybody's incredibly polite if they bump into you.

Yousuf Karsh. I'm passionately interested in photography. Look at his portraits of Canadians, or, indeed, of Winston Churchill or Pablo Casals. Those are the definitive portraits of those people. He came here with almost nothing and put himself on the world stage in an intrinsically Canadian and humble way.

What defines Canada in terms of "place" are the downtown cores of the three big cities. That is the best experiment yet in social engineering I think the world will see.

Canada Red or Canadian Blue and, boy, they didn't want to be part of this stupid idea called the loyalty company. They get some very attractive things from the CAW but they were treated really poorly because seniority in the union is very important. Suddenly, they became very important people to Aeroplan. We created a working environment where they were treated not as a union workforce but as employees of the company. When you hold people accountable for what they're doing, they realize that they're part of an organization that cares about performance, that cares about its customers. We've seen extraordinary statistics come out of the call centres since we've done that. Productivity five years ago was fifty-three percent. It's now in the low eighties. That's the active work time versus paid time. You don't get that through people being ordered what to do. You get it by persuading them this is a good thing to do.

We completely changed the working environment so that people saw that it was something different. We did non-stop communications. We introduced merit awards. We had annual off-sites for the whole management of the company, all two hundred people. I would say we spent half a million dollars a year whereas previously we spent nothing on employee-based branding activities. By branding, I mean "Big B" Branding right across every aspect of what we did… We toured the country to every Aeroplan location and spoke to every employee about the Aeroplan brand, about breaking the mold and doing things differently. We really over-invested in taking those brand attributes into the employee pool. We did the same thing with our industrial partners as well to really embed an understanding of where the brand was heading. They quickly learned that the Aeroplan culture was different. The management style is very consensual. Everybody was equal, whatever their title and whatever they were getting paid. For the first two or three years we ran on the classic "skunk works" model because we were doing all sorts of stuff that you couldn't see the results of it until two or three years later.

On brand building…

I think we've done a better than average job of obeying the rules as to what a brand is. It has to be distinct; it has to have clear attributes, it has to have practical benefits and emotional benefits. Frankly, I think it's much harder to create a brand from something that's broken than it is to take a good small brand and make it a good big brand. There have been plenty of examples in Canada where brands that weren't in particular trouble like Eaton's got themselves into trouble by not obeying the brand rules and the brand book carefully and not listening to their members in the right kind of way. It's quite clear what the brand is to our members. It's a lot harder to define what it is to the employees and, to a certain extent, to our industrial partners to really make decisions on the basis of your core brand proposition. What does that mean in terms of the employment experience or the recruitment experience? Those things, particularly when you have a highly emotional brand, as opposed to a product brand, are hellishly difficult to tie down. We've struggled to define the brand internally as crisply as it's defined externally.

On advice for other brands…

The obvious one is do your homework. When I went through the first brand evolution at Air Canada in '97, I put together the CEOs and the chief creative at each of Air Canada's agencies, about twenty agencies all together. We spent almost three months in very, very intensive homework about what it meant to be a Canadian brand. The Canadian brandscape is quite subtle, it's intrinsic, it's humble, but it's very passionate when you scratch the surface. If you don't do your homework right, you'll get it completely wrong—essentially just a slightly pickier version of American, which is very, very off where we really are. Talk to the consumers or participants in your industry on a qualitative, non-focus-group basis… something where people don't just give you a ranking of attributes, but give you opinions and hopes and aspirations and desires.

Lesson 1: Work from the inside out

Working from the inside out means looking at everyone within the company and making sure they have a role to play in the experience of the brand. Great brands begin by looking at how the experience is delivered throughout all touch points. If there's a gap, try to close it. We provide experiences, events and education that give employees opportunities to actually touch and feel the brand so they know how it impacts our members and partners. Work cross-functionally so you get new ideas and greater buy-in. Branding also impacts training, hiring and other touch points that create the ninety percent of the iceberg that you don't see. Living the brand doesn't mean adding more work; it's about doing things from a different angle.

Lesson 2: Get your leadership on side

Executive leadership is by far the most important success factor. If our executives were not behind the brand, we'd have a major challenge. You need a catalyst for change. In our case, we need to move the mindset internally and externally—that we are not just a frequent flyer program, but a true loyalty program. The brand can't be seen as just a marketing function. Brand and business strategy are almost one and the same. Alignment with HR is vital. Having executive support gives you carte blanche to deliver constant improvement to grow the business. But you have to demonstrate change and be accountable.

Lesson 3: Make it personal

We're trying to bring the member experience and partner perspective inside Aeroplan. We call it "brand relevancy." Understanding the whole picture allows all employees to contribute to growth and deliver on competitive differentiation. Putting employees into the shoes of our stakeholders and competitors is essential. We are constantly sharing the good and the bad, trying to learn from successes and roadblocks. For instance, we've been doing monthly action meetings with our key ambassadors on how we engage all employees. Our brand is tied to everyone's personal performance review because the delivery is not one individual's responsibility—it is everyone's.

Lesson 4: Tell great stories

Stories are keys to making our currency real. We had a gentleman from Vancouver who had more than a million miles. One of his dreams was to go to Italy to learn to cook. But he couldn't because of a heart condition. He contacted us explaining his situation. So we had an Italian chef flown to cook for him and six of his friends. That experience was great but the impact of sharing the story, and a multitude of others stories, makes all employees become more engaged in delivering a unique experience. It shines a light on how your day-to-day makes an impact on people's lives.

Lesson 5: Connect with the community

I think Canadian companies have to step up to the plate on sponsorships and corporate charitable giving. It's not just about sponsoring for the sake of sponsoring; it's about actually helping change and shape culture inside and out. There is huge potential for Canada to be part of the global landscape. Of course sponsorships and donation programs need to be aligned with a companies business lens but they can symbolize Canadiana to the world. Creating a significant footprint can influence other countries perception of our values, economy, interests and so forth. For me, being able to drive growth, connecting and differentiating Canada on the world stage is very exciting.

wealth wonks

COMPARING A WEALTH OF ALTERNATIVES FOR CREATING VALUE

THEY DOMINATE OUR SKYLINES and our daily lives. They are party to many of our biggest rites of passage: schooling, first job, new car, new house, retirement and beyond. Though relatively few in number, our financial institutions live large on Canada's brandscape. We take it for granted that our banking system is one of the safest and most efficient in the world. We never suffered the trials of bank failures during the Great Depression. We call them banks but it would be more appropriate to call the "Big Five" that dominate the industry here financial conglomerates—many-headed hydras of wealth creation—with reach that extends far beyond our borders.

Differentiation is challenging in a small gene pool but each financial institution is shaped by a unique alchemy of commercial, cultural and community forces. The payoff of our three profiles is hearing first-hand perspectives on how different organizations interpret the idea of customer and community wealth.

RBC Financial Group, Royal Bank of Canada's master brand, encompasses 70,000 employees serving fifteen million clients through offices in North America and thirty-four countries. The distinction of being Canada's most international bank goes to Scotiabank. With close to 57,000 employees, Scotiabank Group and its affiliates serve approximately twelve million customers in some fifty countries around the world. Wealth stewards are typically risk averse. Vancity, Canada's largest financial co-op, plays against type. It aspires to be, "disruptive banking revolutionaries." Sloan Dinning's profile of the "un-cola" of banking in Canada illustrates how profoundly different a community-centric banking experience can be. Vancity's "change the way your money works" community activism ties directly to its communitarian roots but also appeals to what Dinning describes as "cultural creatives."

Like Vancity, Scotiabank and RBC have both invested heavily in community connection, though in very different ways. Barbara Stymiest's profile of RBC addresses the challenges of finding common ground within a diverse internal culture. RBC's "customer first" positioning builds on key relationship moments—of service, of truth and of intimacy. RBC ties its corporate responsibility priorities of environment and diversity to community leadership.

Scotiabank draws on its own non-conformist, non-establishment roots for inspiration. John Doig discusses how Scotiabank's "You're richer than you think" positioning has opened up new ways of defining personal wealth beyond economic status. From its involvement in major public arts—the Giller literary prize and art happening Nuit Blanche, for example—to film and hockey sponsorships, Scotiabank is reshaping its community engagement in provocative ways.

As Stymiest said in a 2007 speech to the Canadian Club, "to be successful in a lasting way, we need to understand well where we come from and where in the world we want to grow."

Sloan Dinning

Habitat: Director, Brand and Marketing Communications, Vancity

Bloodlines: Sloan Dinning spent the first dozen years of his career with some of Canada's leading advertising agencies developing marketing programs for brands in diverse industries—from telecommunications to packaged goods. In 2004, Dinning joined Vancity where he oversees the credit union's brand management and marketing communications.

Field Notes: Vancity is Canada's largest credit union. Its roots go back to 1946 when postwar challenges created the need for a more community-centric financial institution. The co-op has come a long way from those days: $12.3 billion in assets, more than 381,000 members and fifty-seven branches throughout Greater Vancouver, the Fraser Valley and Victoria.

Vancity

On being risk-averse averse…
The genesis was basically that banks were very stingy about where geographically in Vancouver they lent money in terms of mortgages. And so, just after the war, about a dozen people pooled together the money to form Vancouver City Savings Credit Union, which has been truncated along the way to Vancity. Today any bank will fund a mortgage on any house as long as it's at the right rate. But that wasn't the case back then. East of Cambie Street, the banks weren't interested in funding because of the nature of the neighbourhood. They felt it was too risky or the value of the house wasn't there. Vancity was the first organization to issue mortgages east of Cambie. We were also the first organization, at least within the Lower Mainland of B.C., to offer loans to women without a male co-signer. We'll make decisions based on credit and risk and all that, but there's also a human element, where a branch manager is empowered to say "you know we need to be financially judicious, but at some point, people are people and we'll treat them as such."

On sharing the wealth…
We have a mandate to be very profitable so that our members make money, but board members are not bankers; they're people from the community. Their mandate is not just to run a highly profitable bank, it's to make as much profit as we can get and make sure that it goes back to the membership and back to the community and things that are important to them. Thirty percent of all of our annual profits are given back to either members or the community—that's enormous! Last year about seven or eight million dollars went back to the members and seven million dollars back to community grants. "Community Leadership" is how we refer to it. We don't call it "corporate social responsibility." The mandate for community leadership is about three things: First is the environment—and

that's been a focus for ten to twelve years. The second is financial accessibility. And the third is strengthening non-profit organizations.

On taking the mandate to heart...

Here's a great story of building relationships: An older lady was having some financial difficulty and had come to take out her last twenty dollars to pay her hydro bill and the branch at the same time was having a contest —like put in a dollar for a chance to win a hundred dollars. And so the teller who helped this woman felt really bad for her and gave her the twenty dollars and said "Why don't you take a dollar and put it into the contest?" The employees pooled their money and called up the lady and said that she'd won the contest.

On learning to walk the walk...

Dave or a board member goes to every staff orientation session and you're introduced to the Vancity story. You're taught where the credit union came from and the history of Vancity. When I started, what blew me away was how, working in the marketing department, you get random calls from members who get put through to marketing for whatever reason. I was astounded by the way in which my staff and other staff wouldn't just say, "You've got the wrong number, call..." They would go out of their way to answer the question if they could or find the right person for them. In other organizations I think they can easily just blow them off and say, "Call the main switchboard," and they'll do it. You're helping but you're not really helping. That's the culture. So I had to change my behaviour to say I need to be helpful to this person, to go out of my way to be helpful.

On building that into the brand...

As a brand manager, how do you make that accessible to the public? We've done a lot of work to say how can we make those strategies clear and those things that we're

my ikonica

A person:
Mike Weir, the golfer.
He looks Canadian.
He's understated.
He's a better golfer than we
give him credit for.
He strikes me as the typical
Canadian as opposed to
Tiger Woods—he'll get
very emotional, he'll swear
and he'll throw his club.
This is not Mike Weir, he'll
just look disappointed.

having an impact on relevant today. From a brand management perspective, it's a big challenge. We're not all about low cost. It's about how you can profit, the environment can profit and the community can profit. Last year we landed on this notion of, "Bring your money to Vancity and change the way your money works." which we thought was strategically brilliant. You could personally benefit by good products and great rates but it also works differently because it goes back to the community.

On the challenge to stay true to the brand...

From a brand perspective for me, the challenge is convincing the organization that this is the story that we need to tell. It's breaking out of conventions. How does Vancity advertise? They'll say in January and February, it's RSPs. In May, it's the mortgage campaign. We're trying to break those conventions, the ones that are worth breaking. That is probably more of an internal challenge. When things get tough, people really go back to, "Shouldn't we just be talking about getting a mortgage at Vancity?" So, from a brand perspective, how do we stay ahead of this? I think it's understanding the other two pillars of the community leadership strategy. What do they mean? What role do they play in our brand strategy? Right now they're not drawn a lot into our brand work. We're trying to seize the moment, with the environment being the hot topic. Right now, it's not hard to convince somebody that the environment is his or her problem. But helping the homeless, or the unbankable is more difficult to sell, so we're going to sort that out. One thing we're talking about doing is re-engaging the membership to determine what are their priorities because it's member driven, it's a cooperative. What are the issues that you want to see us tackling?

For me, our board and our Community Leadership department are the big drivers of the brand. Between those two groups they craft the community strategy. The goal now is to immerse it more fully into the business. For me that is the key driver of our differentiation. We've collaborated with them over the years

to create the Clean Air Auto Loan, or the Bright Ideas home renovation loan where we'll give you a discount on your renovation loan if you follow standards on how to improve energy efficiency. Marketing and Community Leadership collaborate.

On standing by your brand...

As a company, we're hugely courageous. A few years ago we came out and publicly supported the gay and lesbian community in our external, mainstream advertising. And four years ago there wasn't a lot of that happening. At the time, we were running youth credit unions in a number of schools around town. A few of those schools were run by the Catholic Church, who took great exception and, basically, threw us out of their schools. It made national news but we stuck to our guns. Did we lose some members? Absolutely. But we have, by far, gained more than we lost. We now run around forty youth credit unions. We buddy them up with a local branch and the branch basically sets up youth credit unions for the kids, from grade six and up. Someone's the president; someone's the treasurer; they bring their money; they make deposits, and the branch people take it back. It started maybe four or five years ago. Together, those kids have saved a million dollars… fifty cents at a time.

On competing with financial elephants...

I'd argue that statements that describe us could describe a lot of Canadians: unpretentious, pioneering, clever, honest, a bit self-deprecating. The other one I would add, being a credit union albeit a big one— although we're so much smaller than all the big banks—is that we're a little bit feisty, which Canadians think of as Canada's relationship with America. We're the small guy that can fly under the radar a bit. We're disruptive banking revolutionaries—that's aspirational. Does our branding deliver on that in some way? Does it deliver on the descriptive points? Is it clever, honest, pioneering, unpretentious? At the top of the brand blueprint is our vision, which is to get people inspired. For banking, that's very disruptive. To be inspired by your bank? That's a lofty order.

First Person Singular

Barbara Stymiest

Habitat: COO, RBC

Bloodlines: Her role as COO puts Barbara Stymiest squarely on the hot seat of directing enterprise strategy as well as all corporate functions including risk management, finance, human resources and treasury. She is one of eight leaders responsible for setting the overall strategic direction for the whole organization. Stymiest brought an impressive resume to her RBC role, including a stint as CEO of the TSX Group where she stewarded operations and strategic development of both the senior capital market—Toronto Stock Exchange and its junior market—TSX Venture Exchange. Before TSX, she had been Executive Vice-President and Chief Financial Officer for Bank of Montreal's investment banking division. Despite her demanding schedule, Stymiest serves as a director of Research in Motion Ltd., Symcor Inc., the Canadian Institute for Advanced Research, the Royal Ontario Museum and Toronto Rehabilitation Institute Foundation as well as volunteering with a number of charitable organizations.

Field Notes: Royal Bank of Canada and its subsidiaries operate under the master brand of RBC. Measured by assets and market capitalization, RBC is not only Canada's largest bank but also a North American heavyweight in the diversified financial services category. RBC's "first" campaign not only refers to the company's customer service philosophy but also its own standings on many corporate measures including: 2007 Best 50 Corporate Citizens in Canada (*Corporate Knights* magazine) and Global 100 Greenest Companies (*Newsweek* magazine).

On differentiation...

We look at our brand as a leadership brand. In some regards, RBC is a quintessential Canadian organization—like peace, order and good government. A lot of our culture is focused on integrity, discipline and doing the right thing—those core Canadian traits. All financial services firms have had the trust and integrity elements, all the good solid banking attributes. But consumers expect more than just a trusted institution. In the Canadian retail context, there is not a huge amount of differentiation amongst our competitors. I am not sure that most consumers, when asked, can differentiate significantly between their experiences at various banks. So, what are the other levers we have to be differentiated? If it's about leadership, what kind of leadership? What's the character? What's that voice? We're hoping we can get to empathy and

passion without clients and get it more right than our competition.

We try to achieve differentiation in moments of service, moments of truth, and moments of intimacy. It's difficult to create too much differentiation in moments of service—you open an account, help someone deposit a cheque, or do an effective transaction for them. Moments of intimacy are when we've got a high-value client relationship and we can invite them to special events and the like. We've been particularly focused on moments of truth—those life-changing experiences when kids go off to school, when people are switching jobs, when they have a family, when they hit retirement. That is when clients are looking for expert advice to help them make the right financial decisions. Those kinds of moments, especially problem resolution, are important opportunities.

my ikonica

I think of the Rockies and ice wine. When I think about symbols, I think about the maple leaf. When I think about large corporations, I think about our company.

On being first…

The embodiment in our brand is "client first"—always earn the right to be the clients first choice. It's the modus operandi of the entire organization. With our size and scale it's easy to become more focused on the internal workings. We are not one homogenous organization but "client first" works very well across all of our platforms including the roughly one-third of our employees who are not in client-facing roles. It puts that filter on everything we do. From an HR perspective we've identified behaviours to ensure that we bring all the capabilities of the organization to bear for the benefit of the client. If we don't get it right with our employees—make sure they're educated, engaged and trained—then we're not going to be able to execute it with our clients.

We all recognize that clients have high expectations and want all sorts of control. A lot has been written in the last while about how the Internet and other factors have empowered our clients. It comes back to the "client first" concept—we must demonstrate that we really are working around their needs instead of expecting them to fit into our working model. If we don't, clients are going to start saying, "That's not acceptable!" In the era that we live in, clients expect something in return for their loyalty. Financial services are a bit later to the game but we'll continue to try to excel in that field. Today, you might get free chequing if you have two or three of our products but I think that the sophistication around the bundling of different offers is going to continue to grow.

In a financial institution where very few of the employees are from a background in branding and marketing, we're continually trying to make the impact of the brand on the business clear to everyone. This is not Nike or McDonald's or other organizations with more of a brand focus so we've had to make education a more important part of our work.

On being international…

The "client first" positioning works inside and outside Canada. Our customer loyalty scores are much the same in all those business where we touch individuals. On the wholesale side, we keep score by league tables; the amount of business that we're awarded is a strong feedback mechanism on how well you are received by your client because they award you mandates or they don't. In global private banking we're in over twenty countries. We'd be a top twenty player. In some of our businesses, it is helpful not to be American, in Europe especially. In the US specifically, stating that we're Canadian is neutral but the attributes that are often associated with Canada—being reliable, operating with integrity, having a forward-looking orientation—those things come up in research.

From a financial services lens, Canada is a very different landscape. The US has been a very fragmented industry. It wasn't that long ago that they had ten thousand banks. It's been consolidated but they still have thousands. In Canada, people can get ticked off, they may purchase one of our products or services but they're unlikely to move. Poaching existing customers of other institutions is very hard to do. Foreign entrants have found that here. They've come and gone in the various waves of deregulation.

On social responsibility…

In terms of corporate social responsibility, we have applied a framework that was developed by Roger Martin from the University of Toronto. The framework helps us prioritize doing okay, doing well or doing distinctively. There are certain things that we will do as well as everybody else. They're the table stakes like basic consumer education and privacy issues. There are things that we'll do well. And then there are things we'll do distinctively.

The greatest opportunity for us is to create business value through distinctive corporate responsibility initiatives. We have chosen to focus on the environmental sustainability and employment issues relating to diversity. With employment, we drilled down into the issues to address immigrant diversity as it relates to inclusion and prosperity. So, in terms of access to financial services, banking the unbankable, disability, we'll do it as well as everybody else. Our distinctive focus will be visible minorities and women.

Diversity is a strong fit because it connects to the Canadian cultural identity. It impacts how we operate the business internally and it also makes great sense from a domestic business perspective recognizing how the demographic landscape is changing here. It is a good example of how the pieces fit.

On brand-building challenges...

In Canada our challenge is to be differentiated in our execution of our brand promise around the client experience at the moments of truth. I recognize that's also an aspiration of our competition, which just makes it harder. In our US and international businesses, we're still tackling the challenge of brand awareness. RBC itself was only created about six years ago as a way to bring the pieces of business together. We now see people associating themselves as being part of RBC much more than a few years ago. Down the road, we're looking for even stronger, more consistent views from within the business that we're all part of RBC.

Now, there's alignment and commitment to have far more focus on the master brand, which is part of what we've been talking about with embodying "client first" through the brand elements of RBC. Remember that for most large Canadian financial institutions, deregulation only happened in 1987 so it's only been a phenomenon of the last twenty years. These things take time. I think success will be when someone stops saying that "I come from the investment bank" or "I come from Royal Trust" and they all talk and walk as RBC-ers.

On the Canadian values...

There is a real sense of fair play I think. There's a limit to what people are willing to accept, there's a sense of play by the rules. You want to be a competitor but not in a disparaging way. You never win by putting your competition down. Canadians tend to recoil a bit from anything considered dirty tricks. It just shows that there are cultural

norms that exist in Canada that need to be reflected by the businesses and the way they operate. At the same time, we need to make sure that we are as competitive as we can be because ours, like every other industry, is getting even more competitive so we need to find the right balance.

RBC Moments...

1864: The Merchants Bank of Halifax was founded by a close-knit group of Haligonian merchants.

1898: Bankers hauled a 4.5-ton safe by horse and pulleys over the mountains from Skagway, Alaska, to Atlin, B.C., to open a branch during the Klondike gold rush.

1901: The old Merchants' Bank of Halifax name is shed in favour of The Royal Bank of Canada.

1907: Symbolizing the bank's coming of age, its head office moves to Montreal.

1961: Royal Bank was the first Canadian bank to install a computer—an IBM 1401.

First Person Singular

John Doig

Habitat: Senior Vice-President, Marketing, Domestic Personal Banking

Bloodlines: John Doig joined the ranks of Scotiabankers in 1998. Before taking on the lead marketing role for personal banking domestically, Doig's responsibilities included managing Scotiabank's national network of Private Client Group Centres that provide the well-heeled with customized financial solutions. Doig attended the University of Toronto and the University of Western Ontario, Richard Ivey School of Business Executive Management Program. He is also a Board Member for Toronto's Ronald McDonald House.

Field Notes: The Bank of Nova Scotia opened its doors in 1832 in Halifax during the thriving trans-Atlantic trade between Britain, North America and the West Indies. In 1889, the Bank opened a branch in Kingston, Jamaica, to expedite trade in sugar, rum and fish. It became the foundation of a thriving network throughout the Caribbean and Central America that's made Scotiabank the biggest player in the region. The Scotiabank Story, a corporate history published to celebrate the institution's 150th birthday, provides a fascinating insight into the bank's character: "The tradition of the Bank of Nova Scotia is non-conformist and non-establishment. From the beginning the Bank had to fight the colonial establishment in the shape of the Halifax Banking Company, just to obtain a charter and then to stay alive… The same thread is apparent in the Bank's entry into Scotia Plan, which cut the borrowing for individual consumers considerably but was regarded as an inappropriate, or indeed an improper, kind of business for a bank by some bankers… As a non-member of the establishment… the Bank of Nova Scotia has had to scurry for a living." In 2007, Scotiabank celebrated its 175 anniversary, still non-conformist after all these years.

Scotiabank®

On the "you're richer than you think" positioning…

It's about richness of life as much as how much you have in your bank account. We are building the brand to stand for richness broadly defined. It works extremely well. We have a wonderful brand platform that talks to the rational approach of looking for financial security that is a common need of everybody as well as the emotional side of it. We're a bank that's being optimistic on both sides. I think that gives us a lot of running room.

We started with our mission statement: help our customers become financially better off. That's something that every employee in this company knows backwards and forwards. That's why we come to work everyday. We truly, truly believe that we can help our customers become financially better off. It's not about products; it's about really taking a look at their financial situation and providing

true help. For most Canadians, that's helping them save, getting them into a home; planning for retirement. What it says to our staff is, "I am going to do what's right for my customer. I am not going to sell our product just because the bank says I need to get these sales numbers. I am going to do what's right for the client." It makes your job really rewarding.

There were big ahas when we talked to Canadians about their financial security and getting ahead financially. Nobody talked about product. Consumers don't think about products. They think about fundamental needs. We need to explain products but under the umbrella of enabling their lifestyle, what people believe is important in their life.

On community engagement…

We have had the pressures of any major marketer in the country because our conventional media are not working very well.

They helped Canada grow

J.A.D. McCurdy and his associates

John McCurdy had worked with Alexander Graham Bell, inventor of the telephone, Glen Curtiss, and others. Their aim: to develop an improved type of airplane.

An exciting day—Feb. 23, 1909! McCurdy takes the Silver Dart 60 feet off the ice at Baddeck, Nova Scotia in a ¼-mile history-making flight. He is the first within the British Empire to fly a heavier-than-air craft.

McCurdy in 1910 is first to receive and send wireless messages while flying. He also sets a new overwater record—Key West to Havana—a flight of 96 miles.

Canadian business firms pioneer in commercial aviation, opening up new mining territories and all the rich natural resources of Canada.

McCurdy becomes a leader in commercial aviation. The aircraft industry grows—the pace of Canadian development quickens. Airways become vital arteries.

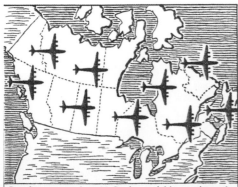

Canada owes much to McCurdy—and his associates, the men who financed his achievements. Their historic work laid the foundations of Canada's present air might, a might both commercial and military.

The initiative of men like J. A. D. McCurdy has made our country strong. But their work depends on all-important associates—the far sighted lending institutions and banks of Canada... whose funds are the invested savings of Canadians like you.

When you deposit your savings or do business with your Bank, you add to the financial power helping to develop your country. You enter into your Bank's partnership with the men who are making Canada an enviable place to live and work. See your Bank of Nova Scotia manager. If *your* initiative needs financial advice or merits help, you'll find him a good man to know.

Your Partner in Helping Canada Grow

We should be looking at other ways to reach consumers. You just can't buy CTV and CBC and hope you can reach Canadians in any way that really engages them, especially in this category that's not very engaging anyway. The richer life aspect has directed us to embrace the right kinds of sponsorships and make sure that we are in them in a meaningful way. Some of the things that we identified are sponsorships that make a richer life for everybody. It's not about the elite. We really want to touch everyday Canadians.

That's a very powerful filter from the marketing standpoint when we look at sponsorships, whether it's arts and culture events from the Contact Photography Festival to Nuit Blanche. Scene is a perfect example. It touches a whole lot of people in Canada who go to the movies. There are 65 million visitors to Cineplex annually. For us, that says something about Canadian culture. How do we become a part of that experience in a way that's relevant? Can we do it in a way that gives something to the movie going customer? It takes a big commitment on the part of an organization to launch a loyalty program like Scene for young people because they aren't the most profitable segment. It's great for the future but these programs are tremendously costly. It may take a long period of time before we reap benefits.

The Giller Prize celebrates wonderful literature in Canada; it's totally accessible to all Canadians too. We take the Scotiabank Giller program to libraries and to schools. Then there are a lot of other people that will be caught up with the passion of hockey. So, we are also very involved with teams like the Ottawa Senators. When we get involved with a NHL or CFL team, it's about what we do in the communities, in the schools, how we interact with the team. What fundraising programs are we going to do? How are we going to cheer on with the fans in the local market? The message across our organization is that we want to be involved in the communities where we live and work; we want to be relevant in those communities. We do it from a corporate standpoint, picking the right sponsorships, but also from a grass roots approach. We have programs that allow staff members to do things in their communities too.

On corporate culture...

I've spent time at other places as many of us have. Here, everyone makes coffee. You can be sitting in the CEO's office and he'll get up to make the coffee. There is no sense of entitlement and hierarchy. The "One Team. One Goal." theme is fitting. In meetings you can have very wholesome debates no matter what your level is. Senior executives will relate to you with respect and integrity. That fits into that whole lack of hierarchy and entitlement. If you have good ideas, you can go forward, and there's not going to be any sacred cows. Good ideas don't get turned away. We are also culture that is driven very, very much by recognition. I don't know of any other institution that gives out over half a million recognition certificates in a year to 28,000 employees. That's a lot of "thank you's" across the organization. It's powerful and genuine.

We're always leading with our culture first. Get that right and then the other pieces fall into place.

When you drive in diversity internally, you can get it externally. I think there has been a huge push and a real committed effort on the part of management in terms of diversity. Approachability and real accessibility, understanding, respect, commitment—those things are part of our key values. People are skeptical. We're very empathetic. A really key way to get across that empathy is to have the insight of, "We understand where you are." We demonstrate in our advertising. Those TV spots are based on real insights about how people feel when they deal with their bank. We want to get across the humanity. They are also a little bit self-deprecating. We aren't talking about us being "first" in things. We are talking about you and what's important in your life. I think that it's really critical to be tremendously customer-centric. It's amazing that many of these things port over quite nicely internationally. Some of the ads that are out of here are being run in other countries. We benefit from insights coming the other way as well.

my ikonica

*The stubby beer bottle.
Water and mountains.
When Peter MacKay takes
Condoleezza Rice out for
breakfast and they swing
over to Tim Hortons…
I don't know if that's
what I would have
picked, but wow.*

On stability…

Compared to other organizations, there's not a massive amount of turnover in the executive ranks. Stability and the culture are important. When there is a change at the top, there's not a purging of those who didn't get it. Very often the case in other organizations is there's a camp A and camp B. Camp A wins and camp B goes and works for the competition. That hasn't happened here in the last four transitions. I think it speaks a lot to the culture and how those things are handled. You are not going to have massive shifts in philosophy and how we are going to do things tomorrow. Change is good and change will happen but change is not always easy to sell to the front lines and that's where we make a difference every day with customers. We have retention numbers that are measured. When we compare ourselves to best-in-class, we are in the top tier of those share-of-wallet numbers. We have probably the lowest number of customers in total but of the ones we have, we are very, very entrenched.

On being international…

With the international side of the business, you have an opportunity to learn how you can manage in different countries, different cultures, different languages whether be Caribbean or Central South America or in Asia. Everyone jokes about this but we were in Jamaica before we were in Toronto. In Mexico we are looking to have some two thousand branches by 2010 so that they will have a bigger network certainly. International as a whole is producing in a very similar level as Scotia Bank Canadian operations, which is a great sign of doing the right things in the right countries.

We take a really committed approach. We have got into countries such as Latin America, Caribbean and elsewhere early on and stayed the course through really bad political periods. Scotiabank started very small in Mexico and now it's a huge player there. It's not quarter-to-quarter looking at our revenue. It's really a long-term strategy of where we're going. You'll see that with the kind of expansion that we have right now.

On advice to others about the Canadian market…

What you'll find in Halifax versus what you find in Victoria is that there are a lot of similarities, but many differences. Those subtle differences are what you need to understand. Those kinds of insights you won't find doing focus groups in Toronto. When you are up in Saskatchewan, it looks a hell of a lot different than Victoria or Vancouver or Calgary or Edmonton. Canadians are pretty conservative and they are actually fairly content. Don't presume that they need what you are providing. They've got great radar about being patronized. While they are very friendly and open their arms to people and encourage them very well, they also look at what's important to them, what's important to their community. Often, a lot of those are values as opposed to things. That's where it sometimes gets very hard for companies coming in here—it seems below the surface.

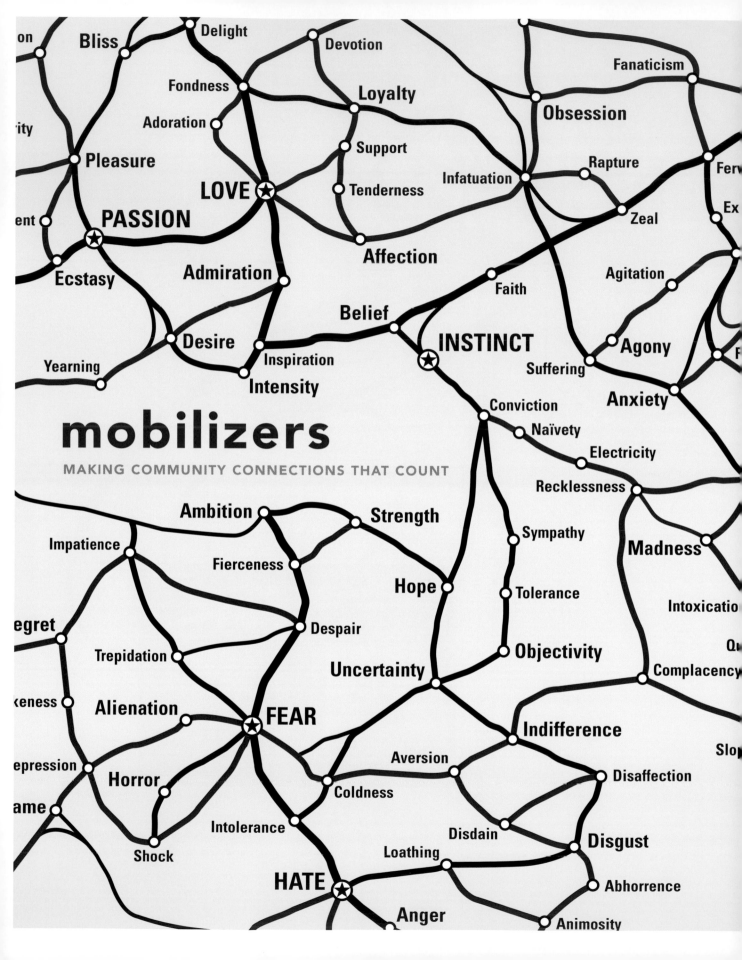

IN MANY RESPECTS, the social sector is a model for business. Charities, NGOs, arts organizations, social activist and cause-related organizations of all kinds—like Canada—must punch above their weight. What they have in their arsenal that many commercial enterprises envy is a huge surplus of meaning and authenticity, the active agents that create engagement, passion, loyalty and community —and powerful brands.

There are so many practical challenges for social sector organizations to address—hospital beds to pay for, new professors to hire, grants to chase, equipment to finance—that the crowd of competing needs seems to grate relentlessly against the stark confines of limited people, funds and time. But vision, meaning and connections are abundant, renewable resources with no limits to growth. The power of not-for-profit brands—sometimes realized, sometimes latent—is their ability to connect culture and community with dialogue, insight and action. NGOs are often the voice of those who can't speak out for themselves in the collective conversation about the things we value and the society we want. The piece of the puzzle that often eludes social activists is knowing how to demonstrate the value of their connections for commerce. Judith John and Russ Kisby are two stellar examples of social activists who understand what it takes.

In John's role as a connections catalyst for Harbourfront Centre, Toronto's United Way and Mount Sinai Hospital, there's no such thing as status quo once she brings her infectious passion to a cause. "Charities act as arteries into the community," she states. In her interview, John describes how the Toronto chapter of the United Way reconstituted its role as, "a force in the city. We have the best understanding of what's going on. Beyond just funding charities what we aimed to do was to take a role in educating and gently being advocates."

Russ Kisby's story of ParticipACTION is an object lesson in making common ground between culture, community and commerce pay big dividends for all. Kisby chronicles the impact of an advertisement that compared the fitness of a sixty-year-old Swede to a thirty-year-old Canadian, a campaign that galvanized generations of people to jog to the back of the bus, walk around the block, take the stairs and, in myriad other ways, take control of their health and wellness. Armed with only a handful of staff but legions of volunteers, ParticipACTION mobilized millions of people in communities across the country with its energizing fusion of wit, intelligence and possibility.

Kisby talks of the ParticipACTION City Challenge Day as an exercise in nation building. We've found that what's true for not-for-profits and social activists is also true for communities that aspire to redefine themselves. Places—towns, cities, regions, even countries—are the latest adopters of brand models in an attempt to identify their *genii loci*. The business magazine *Fast Company* noted in its annual ranking of great places to work that, "For all the challenges cities face… they are still where jobs and youth gather, where energy begets even greater energy, where talent masses and collides… The race to attract the brightest and the best of Canada's highly mobile youth, as well as highly skilled immigrants from abroad and capital investment, is forcing places to band together to create definitive answers to the fundamental question, "What makes this place special?"

Place brand consultant Malcolm Allen coined a new grammatical tense, "future authentic," to describe the nature of the storytelling places need to develop. Rather than jingoist slogans, meaningful place branding requires collective dialogue about what is the distinct character and interplay of culture and commerce that the community aspires to create. Ric Young, in his address to Toronto's City Summit Alliance stated, "The relationship between place and identity is profoundly important. Meaning-making and future-making go hand in hand." The stories that Kisby and John tell illuminate how the few, whether they are social activists or community boosters, can inspire the many to act by tapping deep reservoirs of collective meaning that lie hidden beneath our brandscape.

Russ Kisby

Habitat: Former President, ParticipACTION

Bloodlines: ParticipACTION, Canada's movement for personal fitness, pioneered the use of social marketing and health communication techniques to spread its message of healthy, active living. Created in 1971 to battle growing inactivity and the resulting health care fallout, ParticipACTION relied on government funding, donations and media sponsorship to get its message out. The organization was widely regarded for its quirky, clever marketing and is considered a global pioneer in fitness promotion. Run as a non-profit company, its most famous TV spot declared that the average sixty-year-old Swede was in the same physical shape as a thirty-year-old Canadian. The commercial was only shown six times but it sparked a national debate about fitness and provoked many people into action. The group also championed unique participatory events such as ParticipACTION City Challenge Day, a program eventually adopted by one thousand communities in thirty-five countries and involved some fifty million people. Throughout its first three decades, Russ Kisby was ParticipACTION's driving force, transforming it into one of the country's best-known and most-trusted brands.

Field Notes: Despite its popularity and success, ParticipACTION was put to rest in 2001 after federal funds were cut off. In late 2006, the federal government announced $5 million in funding to bring the get-active crusade back to life. The new ParticipACTION is governed by a national, volunteer board of directors. A small professional staff team provides leadership in collaboration and communications to foster a "movement" that inspires and supports Canadians to be more active. As a brand phoenix, it has secured support from numerous physical activity promoting organizations: public health, labour, education, media, corporations and governments. In its new form, ParticipACTION will try to capitalize on its legacy brand and support the many existing health-promotion organizations across the country.

On overcoming skeptics...

The rationale for ParticipACTION was a fair amount of research in the late 1960s showing an increasing trend towards inactivity, resulting in many health-related issues. The Federal government was concerned. Philippe de Gaspé Beaubien, who had been the general manager of Expo 67 and then started his own media company, Telemedia, was asked to head it up. He proposed creating a marketing agency to see if we could promote lifestyle or behaviour change using some of the same strategies as commercial marketing. Today, we refer to this approach as social marketing. There was a huge amount of skepticism within the health and physical activity field

whether health and lifestyle could be promoted like toothpaste or beer. A number of my colleagues essentially called me a traitor. It took about two years before the health and physical activity field started to realize that the public were indeed responding. From then on they were amongst our biggest supporters.

Within the field of physical activity, Americans have the President's Council on Physical Fitness. One of the major differences is that the head and the board of directors from the President's Council typically have been pro athletes. That immediately said winning medals is what it's all about. The program they put out in their first decade was

the true

north st~~strong~~ SOFT

and free.

Run, walk, swim, jog but let's get Canada moving.

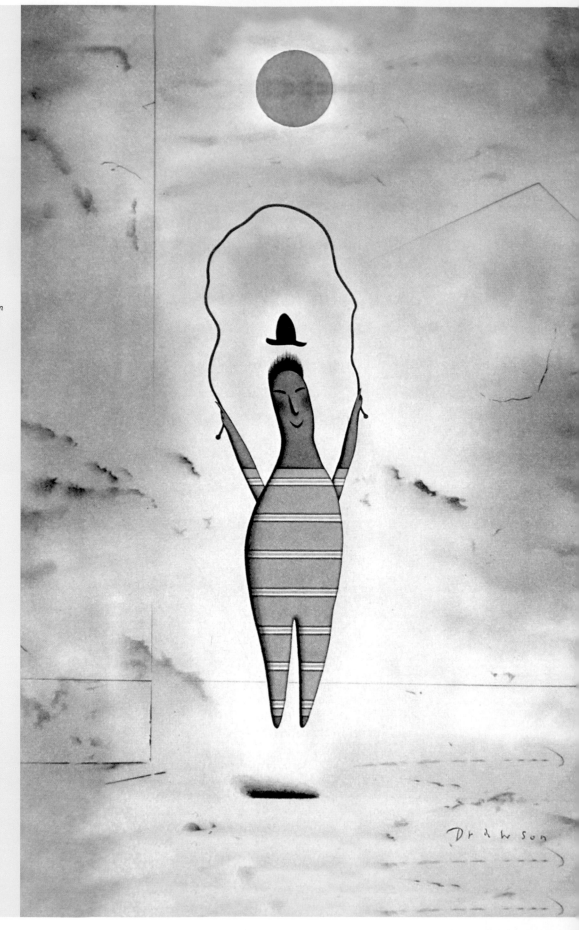

From "Fitness Now and How" campaign.
Illustrator: Blair Drawson

always for what I would call the super-fit. If they were doing a demonstration in a mall, it was always a woman in a leotard who could turn her body into a figure eight. Our approach in Canada was to work with ordinary people, the bottom twenty-five percent of the population. The President's Council's advertising featured top athletes, super-fit, and inevitably, television personalities. We really avoided the whole celebrity, super-fit kind of an approach.

On the value of brands...

The brand is the organization. I wish we could say we were brilliant and sorted it all out at the start but as we continued it became more and more evident what was working. We kept the messages very positive. Any advice that we provided was simple and very practical. Humour was absolutely critical. It said that while this message is important, we the message provider don't take ourselves too seriously. We avoided preaching this is what thou shalt do or must do. We thought we'd use humour to catch attention and it did. But it also created a personality that appealed to media outlets. We decided right from the beginning that we were going to do highly sophisticated, very professional advertising. The stations really appreciated that. Stations would say, "If it comes with ParticipACTION on it, we'll play it." At the time [1970s], we were unique in terms of production quality and therefore the volume of the exposure that we were able to generate.

By the early 1980s through to about 1995, we were generating about $15 million a year in measured exposure but we never paid one penny for advertising time or space. At the thirty-year mark we did an analysis of the value of the media exposure during that period. It was about $280 million—one hundred percent donated. By the '80s, we were able to show the federal government that for every dollar of public funding they gave us, we were generating about $15 in media exposure value. In addition, for every dollar they gave us we'd get close to $2 in real cash from the private sector and other governments. From about the late 1970s to

about '95, aided awareness was around eighty-five to eighty-nine percent. That was really consistent for almost a twenty-year period. Of the aware group, around fifty-five to sixty percent would say, "Oh, definitely, it's influenced me," or they knew someone they thought the campaign had directly influenced.

On creating impact...

The truth of the sixty-year-old Swede is that I happened to be looking at a textbook and there were actually some sixty-year-old Swedes who were getting the same scores as thirty-year-old Canadians. Looking at it now, it's got to be the cheesiest, most simple little ad you ever saw. It was a fifteen-second TV spot, which was unheard of in those days. It only ran six times on Canadian Football League games. It was one of those magic things that caught the public's imagination. In 2000, the advertising council came out with their list of the one hundred most effective ads of the last one hundred years and we were in that list.

We ceased operation January 2001. The government had cut back and cut back and the board decided we're not going to be operational anymore, however it agreed to continue to exist in order to legally protect the organization's charitable status and, most important, ownership of its valuable brand, ParticipACTION. In 2004, we got funding from the federal government to do a feasibility study on whether to reintroduce ParticipACTION. We had two studies done in 2004 and 2005 that found that in the thirty-plus age group there was still a seventy-five percent awareness of ParticipACTION and most thought it was worthwhile.

Did anybody actually become more active? What studies have shown is that from about '80 to '95, when ParticipACTION was the strongest, there was about a one percent increase each year in the number of Canadians who were regularly physically active. That was defined as active enough to be getting health benefits. The first surveys [early '70s] found that about ten percent of the population was regularly active. By mid-'90s, the number was up to about thirty-five percent, a significant improvement. However, it's virtually impossible to say that's all due to ParticipACTION because during that same period all kinds of organizations and governments were getting on the fitness bandwagon. I'd say the cumulative effect of all those efforts resulted in that positive change. We got a lot of credit for it because it was so high profile but there's no doubt in my mind that it was a combined effort. Around '94–'95, when our funding started to be reduced, the amount of advertising we were able to put out started to get cut back significantly. The research found the number of active people started to drop. With young people, the situation today is worse than it was ten to fifteen years ago. The very time ParticipACTION cut way back on its promotion also matches the time when a decline in the amount of physical activity was also evident. Whether there's a direct relation or that's coincidental, I just don't know.

On community…

Canadians are community oriented. Volunteerism is a big thing in our country. Whenever you can do something that isn't just for my own good or my family's good, but will also contribute to our community and give pride to our community. That is really important for us. I did a Masters in community development and became fascinated with how you create social change from the ground up. One of our fundamental ParticipACTION strategies was making sure the local volunteers and leaders were the heroes. We went out of our way to find opportunities to give them exposure and credit.

One of the biggest innovations that we did was called the ParticipACTION City Challenge Day. Sponsored by Crown Life Insurance Company, it was a one-day competition to see which city could be the most physically active. It ran for about thirteen years. All sectors of the community came together to make sure their community would win. It was nation building across Canada. Over ten years, we had the active support of over five hundred communities participating each year! Those communities annually donated something like eight hundred paid staff members for

approximately a one-month period. Each year we had over twenty-two thousand community volunteers. This whole event was organized nationally by two staff members. Period. All the rest of it was done at the community level. We provided the tools, the posters where they could personalize it. But everything was done at the local level and no paid media exposure. We later introduced that program to the international community. It still continues in many countries. They call it "Challenge Day." It is estimated that over fifty million people participate in Challenge Day in many countries each year. That's one of our real successes—a Canadian success story!

Quite separate from what we were doing, we were occasionally asked by the Government of Canada to take on a major national role in terms of mobilizing communities. One was for the '88 Calgary Winter Olympics Torch Relay where we worked closely with Petro-Canada. The other one was in '92, which was the 125th anniversary of Canada. Then again in the year 2000 we assisted the Trans Canada Trail Foundation and the Relay 2000. The feedback from the Government was, "ParticipACTION is the only organization we know that can actually do this." As soon as you walk in and you're with ParticipACTION, there was no questioning what you are all about. People trusted us and were delighted to be involved.

(Author's note: A few weeks after approving the transcript of this interview, Russ Kisby died after a long battle with cancer that he navigated with extraordinarily positive grace. In his career, Kisby had an incredible influence on the well-being of all Canadians. For those that had the privilege of working with him, he will always remain a great mentor.—JH)

From "Fitness Now and How" campaign.
Illustrator: Anita Kuntz

First Person Singular

Judith John

Habitat: Senior Vice-President, Communications and Marketing for Mount Sinai Hospital in Toronto and its Mount Sinai Hospital Foundation, Auxiliary and Samuel Lunenfeld Research Institute.

Field Notes: In our interview, John talks about the challenges and opportunities for not-for-profit organizations to leverage their strengths more effectively. During her dozen years at United Way of Greater Toronto, Canada's largest annual fundraiser and allocator of funds for human and social services, John helped generate more the $10 million in editorial and promotional media, ten times previous support levels. At Mount Sinai, ranked as one of the top teaching hospitals in North America and one of the most respected research institutes in the world, John led the process of renewing the hospital's image under the banner of "Bright Minds. Big Hearts. The Best Medicine."

Bloodlines: Judith John's service record reads like an encyclopedia of major arts, culture, health and social service agencies in this country. In the three decades since she immigrated to Canada from the US, John has applied her marketing, communications and branding acumen to the Art Gallery of Ontario, Harbourfront Centre, National Gallery of Canada, Toronto International Music Festival and the United Way before joining the leadership team at Mount Sinai Hospital in 2004. At the hospital John has created what many aspire to but few—especially not-for-profits—achieve: a coherent integration of communications, public relations, publishing, marketing and branding, all within tight budget constraints. When she's not acting as organizational change agent, John finds time to write articles for *The Globe and Mail* and other major publications, as well as teach and lecture regularly. She currently sits on the Board of ABC Canada Literacy, its Marketing Committee and the Marketing Advisory Board for the University of Toronto's Rotman School of Management.

On resource challenges...

The challenge facing the not-for-profit sector is always dominated by resource limitations. Marketing and communications are often seen as "nice to have," but not as fundamental as some of the programming, political initiatives or hardcore operations. This can both drive and limit what you can do in terms of marketing, and restrict the function to tactical rather than strategic.

United Way is very linked to the community by the work it does and the way it works. It's a great barometer of change. The old norm was very: "Take my money and use it well. See you next year." Now, donors are more involved, more interested in tracking results, more aware and more directive. That defines how you build your relationship with them.

United Way's public positioning is fundamental to its success. Corporate donations are flat or going down; there are fewer individual donors giving more money— it's the reality across North America. At United Way, we had a policy not to spend donor money on advertising. That board-approved guideline enabled us to present United Way as the community charity and ask for donated editorial space. When I started in 1992, the donated space, including editorial, was about $900,000 worth of value. By the time I left, the donated and editorial space was well over $12 million. Regarding pro bono advertising, I just kept fearlessly asking for more. I had nothing to lose and the community had everything to gain! It was possible to position it as, "this is the community charity" and I think sometimes the media also looked on it as a way to withstand the onslaught of other requests.

On connecting with community...

The United Way funded charities are like arteries into the community. Beyond just being a clearing house funding charities, we aimed to be a community connector with a real role in education, community leadership and being advocates. Our Board was very anxious when we first proposed advocacy because it was concerned that United Way has to appeal to all segments and affiliations; it should not risk taking a stand that might alienate the unions, business, different population segments or the government. But we positioned this kind of soft advocacy as fact-based, solutions-oriented education. We began, in the '90s, to create research-based reports on social issues related to our mandate. We proclaimed that United Way was going to watch what's happening in society in order to galvanize people to make positive differences in that society. One of the real advantages of the organization and its leadership is that it's a binding influence: able to bring people and organizations together to have a real impact. That set the stage for all the community consultations, the various reports that were so well received like "Decade of Decline" or "Poverty by Postal Code," and often the task forces that came from that work.

On building brand on the strengths of your institution...

We were able to take internal tools—the research done to help us make the right decisions in terms of funding—and make them public statements of the organization's mission, mandate, expertise. Those were very conscious efforts to say, "United Way is more than just a good charity. It's a force in the city. We have the best understanding of what's going on. We are apolitical. We bring communities together. We can actually influence the influencers to make a difference." It was very deliberate to position United Way as an organization that isn't just a conduit to drop your funds, but one that would use the funds to make a difference. It sounds so high falutin'—unless you can demonstrate results. United Way is on the

ground with intimate knowledge of other charities and social trends; it has the experience, tools and mandate to assess the situation and act for good. It brings all kinds of disparate groups together with a common cause. Not many organizations can bring together a corporate CEO, the head of the unions, the school board and government and be that non-biased, impartial advocate. It's a potent opportunity. We would do presentations at United Way conferences in the States because they had never seen this kind of work. We didn't single-handedly transform homelessness, but we elevated the issue, brought people to the table, proposed solutions. People trusted that United Way would work to make that difference.

In terms of marketing, to capture the essence of the organization, it came down to one word "empowerment"—empowering the individual to make a change in his or her life; empowering the donor to make a real difference. Then we created a tag line to express that and engage the public; a line that would be all encompassing and embracing, simple and memorable, flexible and strong. Not much to ask of a few words! In the end, the value of United Way is that it makes people part of something—they don't need to feel helpless, they can make a difference. When we developed "Without you there would be no way" I knew this was it! It's a strong statement at the bottom of an ad, as part of a speech; it resonates with our volunteers, agencies, donors, staff, the public. It was an accurate reflection of everything—and everyone—that create United Way.

On selling the importance of branding...

Like United Way, Mount Sinai Hospital is a generalist. When I arrived in 2004, it was evident that the reputation of the brand was strong, but had not been publicly expressed or refreshed for some time. It was ill-defined, inconsistently presented, and in a period of transition. Right now we're in a period of renewal at Mount Sinai—everything from capital redevelopment to the senior leadership team and our operational and organizational model. Our strategic plan is focused on:

patient- and family-centred care; academic and research excellence, and our community-based partnerships. Our hospital has a strong history and very ambitious goals, and we live in an intensely competitive, dramatically changing environment. It's dynamic, and it's challenging.

The idea of reconsidering our brand was cynically received initially (to put it mildly!). In an organization dedicated to patient care first and foremost, we all feel the complexity of our work and the consistent financial constraints. Some of my colleagues thought, "Why are we bothering with this? We don't need to do it; we can't afford to do it, and do it right. It's just window dressing. We're not like the American hospitals who advertise to compete for patients—we certainly aren't looking to fill beds!" In Canada, we're not competing for patients and market share. Here, our goal is to position Mount Sinai, to create a broad, knowledgeable halo of support from the broad community, including government and donors.

On building brand ownership from the inside out...

Branding is far more than a logo or an ad—it's about the authentic truth behind the image, the promise of performance, the consistency of experience. All effective branding happens from the inside out. We did extensive focus groups and research with all our stakeholders—everyone; including nursing, finance, medicine, administration, volunteers, sectoral leaders and colleagues, educators, donors to patients and their families. We got enthusiastic buy-in for the themes and brand attributes; we rolled out applications and got endorsement. We broadly tested theme lines, graphic images, key messages and positioning.

We developed a new graphic design, with standards and guidelines. The goal was to visually represent Mount Sinai—distinctively and memorably. With dynamism and openness, the image also reflects and respects our history. We felt that the open star also has a modernity and flexibility that we could use throughout our organization. We wanted it to reflect our unique attributes and instill pride in our Mount Sinai community and it has.

Before taking the branding to the board for approval, we consulted, tested and got backing from many staff teams, because it is essential that they feel part of this effort. I've made more than fifty presentations about the brand to staff and volunteer groups large and small because our most powerful tool for making a brand real and living is our own team. The work has to connect and resonate with them. We got commitment from our sub brands, the Foundation, Research Institute and Auxiliary, so now, for the first time ever we look like members of the Mount Sinai family. We tested and presented the positioning line—"Bright Minds. Big Hearts. The Best Medicine"—and people across the organization love it. Like the United Way's "Without you, there would be no way," this tag line is authentic and involving; it speaks to everyone from the housekeeping staff to scientists to clinicians to volunteers to donors. Everyone is among our Bright Minds and Big Hearts, and they have a role in ensuring that Mount Sinai can fulfill its mission to provide The Best Medicine.

On making your brand an individual responsibility...

When you explain that branding doesn't belong to the marketing department, it belongs to the all the stakeholders, especially staff—they need to own it, that they are the ambassadors—people really respond. In a service organization like Mount Sinai, ultimately the most important thing we can do to ensure brand loyalty is to provide great service. That is in fact what our caregivers do. And everyone has a role to play in ensuring that level of patient- and family-centred care.

All good communications comes down to storytelling. The brand is the truth behind the image, delivering content with credibility, content, authenticity and emotion—and it's exciting to see such a positive response to and ownership of our Bright Minds. Big Hearts. The Best Medicine.

my ikonica

Trite as it must sound, I'd have to say Tim Hortons. Everything about it is Canadian, from its consistency, its comforting dependability, its unremarkable utilitarian décor (brown and beige—how unoffensive can one get?). It's not going to dazzle, it's not going to offend, it's going to be there for me. I am a real fan of Tim's coffee (and love making that announcement in a group of more gourmet coffee addicts), and when I go into Tim Hortons I am assured of a reliable experience, good value and the hot drink I expect and want.

cultural connectors

BRANDS AS CHANGE AGENTS

ONE OF THE KEY ENABLERS of globalization is technology. With our huge land mass, relatively small population and strong ties to international trade, communication and transportation infrastructure loom large in Canada's history.

Managing global brands is a two-way street lined with conundrums. Canadian brands moving abroad have certain advantages including relatively light cultural "baggage" and a chameleon-like ability to blend into the local scene or adopt a nomadic internationalism. But analysts argue that too few home-team businesses are willing to take the plunge off shore. Major brands from "away" typically thrive in Canada. We're cultural omnivores, anxious to sample the best the world has to offer. Nevertheless, establishing strong community bona fides here can elude some organizations, despite generations of co-existence.

In terms of global/local issues we found it instructive to compare the experiences of two different brand-builders: Dirk Miller of Siemens had only recently arrived in Canada when we first met in 2006, but he was certainly not new to the world of brands. Miller had spent the previous five years as one of the major architects of Siemens global brand strategy. One of the world's largest companies, the conglomerate's six divisions are highly diversified. Today, Siemens is involved in everything from generating our electricity, to phone and transportation systems, to medical technologies. At the heart of the Siemens brand is the concept of being "the architect of the global modern society." It creates a lofty sense of purpose but the idea, according to Miller, "has been more challenging to adapt regionally than we originally anticipated." For someone who spent years at head office creating what

is arguably one of the world's most sophisticated brand-management models, supported by an everything-under-the-sun array of on-line resources for Siemens communicators, it has been a sobering experience to endure the day-to-day realities of local adaptation. As Miller has discovered, it can be hard sledding here.

Canadian Steve Graham returned home, after a number of years in the US, with a suitcase full of brand-builder trophies. Graham wears the stripes he earned during various major marketing clashes—the cola wars, the beer challenges, the telecom rumbles, battles of the banks—with pride. Today, he's leading the charge in the convergence minefields for Rogers. For Graham, to be relevant in a marketplace, organizations must focus on the cultural differences in the psyche of various markets. The challenges for Rogers are regional, not global, but the principles are much the same.

Both men share the challenges of working in the quicksilver world of technology where nimble competitors can strike from out of the blue and redefining relevance is a never-ending story that demands tons of local learning.

Dirk Miller

Habitat: Director of Corporate Communications, Siemens Canada Ltd.

Bloodlines: A native of Germany, Dirk Miller has the unique perspective of being one of the lead architects of the Siemens global brand during his long tenure at the company's head office as well as being responsible for its implementation in Canada where he was posted in July of 2006.

Field Notes: Siemens was founded in 1847 by Werner von Siemens, the inventor of the first pointer telegraph—the equivalent of SMS today—that could communicate over a distance of fifty kilometers. Early orders from the Russian military gave the business its first taste of success. Werner's brother soon opened an office in London to capitalize on international opportunities. Today, Siemens operates in more than 190 countries. Its Canadian roots go deep. In 1874, Siemens connected Europe to Canada with the first trans-Atlantic cable laid by the Cableship Faraday, designed by Werner and his brother. Siemens Town in Londonderry, Nova Scotia, the site of Siemens first involvement with manufacturing in Canada, opened in 1876. Siemens Company of Canada was formally established by federal charter in Montreal in 1912. Today, Siemens Canada continues its innovation tradition in a wide array of markets including information and communications, automation and control, power, transportation, medical and lighting. We talked to Dirk Miller during his first six months in Canada. He provides a frank testament to the challenges of making global brands effective on a regional level—a cautionary tale for brand managers where comprehensive systems are no substitute for cultural insight and local know-how.

SIEMENS

On business to business brands...

There are many challenges being a global brand, especially in the business-to-business environment. We are quite a diversified company—we're in the automotive industry, medical solutions, power supply and more. Covering all these different businesses under one brand is sometimes quite a challenge. We always say we are a "branded house" not a "house of brands" like Procter and Gamble. It may sound easy because we just have to handle one brand only but in reality it's even more complex than having fifty or one hundred brands. If you have different brands you can really segment your businesses, segment your target groups, brand promises and work on the brand in very specific markets. This is not the case for Siemens. This has a lot of impact on how we understand brand management. Centrally, we define brand values and "the look" but

then we hand over this to our different regions and business groups and they have to translate this into a value proposition for specific markets. In addition, it is still a challenge convincing executive management that we have to invest in our brand on a continuous basis. In Canada, for example, we have approximately one hundred energy suppliers in the utility market. We know all of them. Why do we need a brand? There are a lot of good reasons: building trust, creating a price premium, increasing margins if you do it right and so on. But it's hard to sell internally.

On defining a global brand...

When I was at head office, for five years we did a lot of interviews with customers and employees all over the world. We defined our brand core, brand values and the personality attributes. These elements describe the DNA of our company—something that's long term

and doesn't change every day. We created a brand fact book to talk about who we are and what we stand for. It was a long process. We had to get internal buy-in and convince executives that a brand is an asset not to be taken for granted. We defined a very sophisticated corporate design platform: treatment of the logo, corporate colours and so on. We introduced a Siemens typeface, provided formats for print ads and brochures. We even produced audio examples of how Siemens sounds. To be honest, these guidelines were very well received by our brand managers and agencies, although they haven't been very effective in terms of a consistent regional implementation. I was surprised when I arrived in Canada because we had to fight simple things like using the right colour for the logo. It's also reality in other regions. One reason is that regional communications departments don't have the requested expertise in managing brands, but more importantly it becomes a question as to understanding, appreciation and support of the regional executive management—which translates into investment.

On competing images...
Having one brand on a global scale doesn't automatically mean that you have one brand perception. In fact, we are perceived as very different companies in different countries and business segments. We have a few common denominators like the logo but how we talk to people and our target audiences are quite different in different regions. For example, a few years ago we were active in the cell phone market. That group decided that the cell phone brand had to be trendy, fresh and innovative—an emotional "love brand." Being in the consumer market, they spent a lot of money, approximately forty percent of our overall communications budget on a worldwide scale. They shaped the brand so much that in some countries we are just seen as a cell phone company. For their market quite a success, but this wasn't very useful in our infrastructure business when we are competing for long-term projects like power plants or hospitals. In this environment, the

last thing we want is to be trendy. For sure, we discussed creating a new brand for the mobile phones but we decided to communicate under one brand. The rationale was it will only open the door for a lot of other brands. Today, we don't have any cell phones; we sold that business to a Taiwanese company. We're back to being a business-to-business infrastructure company. In Canada, as many of my regional colleagues, I have the challenge of harmonizing the brand again.

Although Siemens is German based, only nineteen percent of our sales were generated in Germany last year. Almost seventy percent of our workforce is outside Germany. The core idea of the Siemens brand is "the architect of the global modern society." And global megatrends—such as urbanization and demographic change—are key drivers for our defining our strategies. (The global megatrends concept of urbanization and demographic change were identified and defined in a recent worldwide research study sponsored by Siemens.) However, each region has had to create an adaptation of this value proposition. It's a very sophisticated concept that has been more challenging to adapt regionally than we originally anticipated. Siemens in Canada has to drill down to how it can be relevant for target audiences here. We have to take into account cultural differences and differences in values. For example, innovation scores high in some European markets and even in some Asian markets. But in China, for example, innovation is also perceived as scary because their perception is that innovative products are not tested or fully reliable and are more expensive. Fortunately, The Siemens brand is very well perceived in China because we've been there for more than one hundred years. The sound of Siemens in Chinese translates wonderfully into, "the friend who comes to the door of the East."

In Canada, people still mistake us for a mattress company or a beer brand despite the fact that we have been here for almost one hundred years. We've achieved a lot of firsts in Canada. We have 7,500 employees and sales of $2.3 billion Canadian last year. We are active in a lot of communities but we

my ikonica

I'm quite impressed by how well Tim Hortons is connected to the Canadian consumer. From the very first day, I recognized that Tim Hortons does a great job in touching Canadians life on a day-to-day basis, across all generations—just thinking of the almost legendary Tim Hortons coffee and the phenomenally successful Timbit, today available in over thirty-five different varieties.

are still not seen as a Canadian company. Inside Siemens, Canada is sometimes seen as just another part of North America. From a market point of view, my colleagues always look at the US first because the market value is ten times bigger than Canada. Because of our global reach, we then focus on China, India and Russia because these are emerging markets right now. This is unfortunate for Canada because Canada has so much potential in terms of resources and business projects. So internally we are facing the challenge to put Canada on the map in order to get appropriate support and resources from our colleagues at headquarters. This is really a wonderful opportunity to be part of growing the business of Siemens in Canada. One of the first things I learned here is that you cannot treat Canada and the US the same. They are different culturally, in business behaviours, in values. This has to be reflected in the communications as well. Sometimes we just get communications material from the US that we can't use here. The language is often too bold and marketing driven. Canadians want to see the real value behind the product and the actual benefit to them.

Europeans are used to adapting quickly to differences. This might be an advantage for me in terms of finding the right tonality for the brand reputation programs for Siemens in Canada.

Stephen Graham

Habitat: Executive Vice President, Corporate Marketing and Convergence, Rogers Communications Inc. (RCI)

Bloodlines: Stephen Graham is a man who's made a career of being at the right place at the right time in terms of fertile brand territory: Procter and Gamble in the heyday of packaged goods; Coca-Cola during the cola wars. In his thirties, he headed agency-side to champion Labatt against archrival Molson. But the beverage battles paled in comparison to his next market skirmishes. AT&T's siren call lured Graham south of the border. The largest single brand-advertising spender in the US at the time, AT&T made Graham responsible for marketing communications worldwide. Graham's "rainmaker" reputation was crowned by a bevy of citations including Global Marketer of the Year and *AdAge*'s Top Multi-national Marketer. When CIBC offered him Executive Vice President of Retail Banking and also the Chief Marketing Officer role Graham was attracted to the scale of the opportunity to shake up another category. But never one to pass up a market challenge, he took on the leadership of Corporate Marketing and Convergence for RCI in January 2006.

Field Notes: Graham's experiences across sectors, national boundaries and diverse organizations gives him unique perspectives into the ongoing challenges of being meaningful in the lives of customers. For RCI that means helping the Rogers brand be relevant to over eight million customers across a "triple play" of divisions: Rogers Wireless Communications Inc. (wireless voice, data and paging); Rogers Cable and Telecom (cable, high speed internet and Rogers Video stores), and Rogers Media Inc. (ranging from radio and TV stations to Rogers Publishing and Rogers Sports Entertainment, home to the Toronto Blue Jays and the Rogers Centre).

On the brand challenge...
A brand is simply what people think when they hear a name like Coca-Cola, Rogers or AT&T. It's what you stand for in customers' minds—how you can make their lives better. You need to be relevant emotionally as well as rationally. People don't dream about getting a big mortgage. They dream about a new home. In any large company, it's easy to lose sight of that customer benefit perspective. Great brand companies like Procter and Gamble are continually improving their offerings and communications to stay in touch with what's relevant and meaningful in the lives of their customers. A brand really is about that level of trust and reputation. Whether you like it or not, people form

impressions based not just on what you say or how you market or communicate but, more importantly, how you deliver for them. Are you really clear about the role you play in their lives? Do you care about what they care about?

On cultural context...
The way you're successful, the way you build the brand, the way you build a strong and enduring culture in the company are the same in most countries. Certainly the US and Canadian marketplace are not different in that. But to be relevant in a marketplace you really have to understand the cultural differences of what makes up the psyche of that market, the unique situation/competitive

environment of the particular market you compete in. The competitive situation for Rogers is different in Ontario than it is in the West; it's different in Quebec and different in the East. So you really have to understand the things that will make you most relevant to helping people and doing it continually better than the competition.

In Canada, we tend to be more conservative, a little less extroverted and competitive than the US. Having said that, we're actually more adventuresome and worldly and open-minded, just because of the diverse culture of Canada. Canada is a country that's been created through a melting pot. And right now over fifty percent of the population of our major cities wasn't born here. That cultural difference is really important to understand. You need to understand not just who Canadians are, but who South-Asian Canadians are, who Italian Canadians are and how it all fits together. What are the common shared values and how can you be most relevant to them all? If you have a global brand, a lot of things can be the same strategically across cultures, but the local execution may be very different to really drive tight relevance. We had a big partnership with FIFA World Cup last year at Rogers and it was a great hit because we have so many first-generation Canadians who grew up on the sport.

On employee engagement...

The brand is critically important to your consumers but it's also critically important to your employees because it's the pride of who they work for. A great brand creates an aligned internal culture. As you get larger, you need to keep renewing your heritage; your role in your customers' lives as well as what you're there to uniquely provide as an employer. Rogers is in a category that is absolutely critical to people and businesses in terms of how they operate. Employees need to understand how we serve a core human need to connect and how important that is in our customers' lives. It's both a privilege and a responsibility.

On giving back...

I think it's important for people to feel that the large companies in their area—whether it's in their city, province or country—are giving back. From a Rogers perspective, we do a lot in the form of community programming. It's part of our core TV and cable business and we give back a lot by covering community events, being part of those community events, sponsoring those community events in every market in which we operate and taking a real interest in those communities. We're very involved in a whole litany of causes that help us give back. I think it's really important that people see that you are giving back because they want to care about a company and it doesn't matter what kind of organization it is. It helps the individual do a character test on a company. A brand is something you want to associate with, not just something you buy. People feel better about brands and companies that give back. In our TV and cable business, it's not just what we do in the core business of providing that information and those signals to everybody but also the community programming commitment we have.

On the importance of your reputation...

With any company I think you measure success through what people think of you. Reputation and perceptions are a good indicator of whether or not you are in a good position to be a provider of product and services in the future. Are people continuing to buy more from you and are you profitable? Often your market price or share price will reflect this. Share price is an indicator of two things: people's perceptions that you're going to be stronger and that's often both business-based and brand-based. You also need to ask yourself are you a place where people want to work? The answer will be yes if you're a company that's doing things for the right reasons—and winning.

On competitiveness...

I think there's no question that Ted, and Rogers, has represented a real Canadian success story. Sometimes I think Canadians can be a little self-effacing. It's not surprising when you sit on the doorstep of the most powerful economy over the last hundred-plus years. But everywhere in the world a great idea, hard work and inspiration wins. You see that with companies like Rogers and RIM— Canadian success stories that have done exceptionally well by any world standard. Do something great and don't be afraid to take the risk. To try to do something great, to create something new. Whoever does that with conviction and hard work wins. It's becoming less and less relevant where you do that. It doesn't matter who creates the best thing, the world will beat a path to your doorstep. Increasingly, you have a greater opportunity to do that today when there's a greater flow of capital and an easier flow of ideas in the digital world.

I've always believed we are the test market of this world, of how people from diverse cultures can live together. As Canadians we are given incredible gifts and we should strive to be the best in the world at whatever we do.

my ikonica

Ted Rogers is a great example of a Canadian leader and entrepreneur who has combined vision, risk taking and hard work in equal measure to succeed. I also always admired Pierre Elliott Trudeau. You can agree or not with his politics but he had courage, was a strong leader who had personality and wasn't afraid to stand on the world stage.

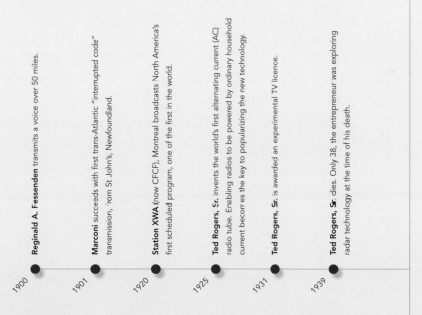

Reginald A. Fessenden transmits a voice over 50 miles.

Marconi succeeds with first trans-Atlantic "interrupted code" transmission, from St John's, Newfoundland.

Station XWA (now CFCF), Montreal broadcasts North America's first scheduled program, one of the first in the world.

Ted Rogers, Sr. invents the world's first alternating current (AC) radio tube. Enabling radios to be powered by ordinary household current becomes the key to popularizing the new technology.

Ted Rogers, Sr. is awarded an experimental TV licence.

Ted Rogers, Sr. dies. Only 38, the entrepreneur was exploring radar technology at the time of his death.

1900　1901　1920　1925　1931　1939

Canada was an early pioneer in telecommunications and the Rogers family was one of the moving forces in the burgeoning new industry. Since 1962 when he pioneered stereo FM broadcasting with CHFI and launched CFTR–AM in Toronto, Edward S. ("Ted") Rogers has carried on a legacy his father started near the dawn of the radio dial.

leading roles

LESSONS IN LEADERSHIP

THE SINGLE MOST PRECIOUS RESOURCE in an organization is that performance-enhancing elixir of worklife—belief bonded to trust. Like air and water, the two are the fundamental preconditions of a thriving enterprise. Pollute them, denigrate them, and it takes Herculean effort over years to restore the balance. The majority of CEOs aren't brought in simply to act as stewards of a robust, thriving culture. The "rainmakers" are tasked with boosting value and performance but astute leaders understand that care and feeding starts with the roots.

Charismatic leaders can be invaluable in kick-starting a sense of possibility but they can only take an organization so far. Especially in Canada, skepticism alloyed with endurance often breeds a this-too-shall-pass inertia in enterprises. Chaviva Hošek provides a leader's primer on successful organizations and communities based on insights from research teams at the Canadian Institute for Advanced Research (CIFAR) where she is President and CEO. The Institute's acronym may be cheeky (see far) but their findings should be fodder for competitiveness and leadership dialogues in boardrooms across the country. By quantifying the economic and social impacts of high-trust culture and community, CIFAR moves the focus of trust and belief from nice-to-have into necessary-to-compete.

William Thorsell's discussion of the role of leadership in transforming the Royal Ontario Museum, a venerable but then-moribund institution, into a twenty-first century hub of culture and community underscores the persistence and vigilance that culture change requires. Time tempers vision. Leaders must keep fanning the flames to build steely resolve within the organization to stay the course through the unavoidable periods of evolutionary stress.

In founding WestJet, Clive Beddoe and his team had the benefit of a model for success to emulate. But WestJet hasn't been content to be slavish copycats. They've deliberately upped the ante on their "owners care" culture to great effect. Beddoe chides business schools for missing the real meaning of corporate culture and values. His lessons in leadership came from lack of engagement in previous work experiences. "I absolutely know everybody in this world could put out ten percent more without even thinking about it, probably twenty percent. They can, but they don't. They are not induced to; they are not inspired to," Beddoe asserts.

Cirque du Soleil is such a highly polished gem on the international scene that it's easy to be blinded by its high-wire élan. But even the most prosaic of operations has much to learn from Cirque's genius for synthesizing diverse influences, managing organic growth, nurturing diversity and investing in quality. Every organization can exploit the power of passion, character and storytelling as well; it's what Cirque du Soleil calls, "Inspired by life and emotions… being one of a kind."

The common threads that link this eclectic ensemble of leaders is their focus on empowering culture and community as essential fuel for commerce. Clive Beddoe sees huge untapped potential for the country as a whole in these core lessons: "Look at what we've achieved with so little and imagine what would happen if you could take the whole Canadian economy and achieve the same with it. I think it could be done, I really do. The principles we've pursued are not that difficult."

First Person Singular

Chaviva Hošek

Habitat: President and CEO, Canadian Institute for Advanced Research (CIFAR)

Bloodlines: Vivacious, fiercely intelligent and an omnivore of ideas, Chaviva Hošek's leadership pedigree was established long before she took up the reins of CIFAR in 2001. Her political resume includes stints as Director of Policy and Research (1993–2000) for Prime Minister Jean Chrétien and as Ontario's Minister of Housing. A Harvard PhD, Dr. Hošek's life as an academic included thirteen years as Professor of English Literature at the University of Toronto. As President of the National Action Committee on the Status of Women, she tackled many significant social issues. Hošek's accomplishments have generated considerable recognition: Public Policy Forum's Outstanding Performance Award in 2003; the Queen's Golden Jubilee Medal; honorary degrees from the University of Ottawa and the University of Waterloo, and Officer of the Order of Canada.

Field Notes: CIFAR brings together teams of elite scholars from around the world to tackle complex, provocative questions as profound as: What makes societies successful? What is the nature of the universe? How can we build a quantum computer? As an institution, CIFAR's research approach is also a compelling model of how small, resource-challenged Canadian organizations can collaborate effectively, on an international scale. Its literature describes CIFAR as, "intensely Canadian and intensely international… an exciting intellectual community that connects Canada's researchers with their peers around the world." CIFAR's "Social Interactions, Identity and Well-Being" program challenges fundamental assumptions of traditional economics. Researchers are exploring how strong social networks (family, friends and communities), good health, good government and trustworthy employers play a major role in a person's sense of well-being. One of their findings (CEO's take note!) is that the standard practice of providing bonuses and penalties for performance in the workplace can be less effective than ensuring that employees identify with their job, and with their employer.

Canadian Institute for
Advanced Research

On collaboration…

It's very Canadian to know we're not the centre of the universe. If we're going to be the best in the world, we have to play with the world. That conditions us in a lot of what we do… not just to be open to the rest of the world but to be eager to connect to the rest of the world. Another theme that is very Canadian is the desire to patch together our strengths to be more than the sum of our parts. Our resources aren't infinite so we need to be intelligent about creating critical mass.

[For CIFAR] collaboration is important on two fronts: first, it matters in terms of our size and scope. The other point—which has been

our mantra for twenty-five years—is that the questions that are out there for the human race to solve are increasingly complex. Therefore, people can't just stay in their silos and work with the tools they already have. If we can create safe places where people can take risks; if we put together the strongest people we have in terms of being imaginative and gutsy; together, we can go places we couldn't otherwise go. It's a great advantage for Canada in terms of taking risks together in order to get a better result.

The irony is that there are people who believe that one of the reasons [CIFAR] has made the kind of progress we have is

because we haven't had as much money. In other countries, there is so much money that researchers can spend their entire careers going deeper and deeper in the same space. They may be making progress but insofar as what we really need to learn, there hasn't been the need or necessity to go beyond where they are to the "white spaces" in between because there has been enough money to keep going where they are. You need a certain number of intrepid explorers who are willing to go into the white spaces. If certain parts of researchers' endeavors are so highly funded that they can have their whole career in one spot, why would they bother? It's not that we don't all learn. The problem is that we haven't learned what we need to learn. We don't connect all the pieces. So despite vast amounts of work by various researchers and the many breakthroughs, there are other huge areas of knowledge we need to address.

Another thing about CIFAR that is very Canadian is its combination of aspiration and modesty. On the one hand, we really want to make the world a better place by supporting people so they can tackle the big questions—supporting them not only with money but with cultural affirmation. We create an atmosphere where it's a matter of pride to take risks. We trust that they are incredibly brilliant and passionately committed to what they do. We try to be helpful to them rather than try to control them.

I think Canadians have a sense of both hope and unease. Things can be going well and yet we acknowledge much anxiety. And that's part of what drives us. There's an anxiety—we're not sure we're good enough. I think that's a good thing. There are two kinds of "good enough." There's good enough in comparison with the best in the world. And there's good enough in comparison with what you really need to change the world. We use our anxiety to drive us towards ever-higher levels of excellence.

On health and well-being...
CIFAR programs cover a variety of physical and natural sciences, but many people getting to know the organization identify most quickly with our programs dealing with health and well-being. We closed down our highly successful and influential programs in "Population Health" and in "Human Development" because they had succeeded so well and it was time to get a new approach. We had made enormous progress on the whole question of social divisions in society and their correlation with health and well-being but it was time to take the next logical step. The next and harder question is "What is it about how societies organize themselves and their institutions that has impact on health and well-being?" Thus was born a new CIFAR program, "Successful Societies."

In a related project we are finding out that after a certain income level, more income

" ...FOR LEADERSHIP TO FUNCTION WELL, BOTH LEADERS AND FOLLOWERS MUST BE BOUND BY A SHARED IDENTITY AND BY THE QUEST TO USE THAT IDENTITY AS A BLUEPRINT FOR ACTION."

John Helliwell and George Akerlof, Canadian Institute for Advanced Research 06/07 Annual Report

does not make the difference on whether people are happy or not. Other things, like trusting your neighbours and the time you spend with family and friends, have more to do with whether you assess yourself as happy or not. This program is trying to think about well-being more broadly. The other factor they consider is the question of sociological identity. People's sense of who they are is not a singular thing. It may be a combination of gender, ethnicity, religion, social status, education, you name it. Some things are more important than others and some can be in conflict with each other. But, what they do with their identity is say, "A person like me should do X." Sometimes their economic druthers can be in conflict with their relationship druthers. The program's social goal is to describe a more nuanced way of explaining why people make the decisions they do. We also need to get people out of thinking that the only measure of a successful society is the economic measure. Some of the Americans in this program say we're the only people who would let them come here to work together on this set of questions.

When you poll them, Canadians will tell you that if the choice is between income per capita and quality of life, we choose quality of life. It speaks to the fact that Canadians work fewer hours than Americans. They take longer holidays. Canadians live the trade off between more money and more time.

On changing behaviours...
Ann Swidler in her new research compares the AIDS fight in Africa in Botswana and Uganda. In Botswana, the HIV/AIDS fight was personalized and individualized. People were told all about the illness and told to get tested—all the usual rational things. However, a woman walking into an AIDS clinic to get tested was already admitting her guilt. Uganda ran their AIDS program as a grassroots organizing effort: "We Ugandans will not allow ourselves to die of this disease! Together we will conquer it!" It became a communal force in the form of grassroots organizing.

You'll probably remember that when AIDS was first identified as a dread disease

particularly affecting the male homosexual community, part of what the gay community did was say, "We're not going to let ourselves get killed by this!" That became an organizing tool, not for individuals as individuals but for the community as a community. That's what changed behaviours. The notion of organizing for the common good of a community versus the individual, rational, be careful, do-the-right-thing approach—especially in an area connected to something as powerful as sex drive—turns out to be very interesting.

On the value of trust...
In John Helliwell's work, he has done multiple studies which show that the most important thing for people's personal happiness is trust in their community and their neighbourhood. However, people spend more than half their life at work so trust in management at the workplace is also an important ingredient for personal happiness and well-being. In fact, if you measure it against pay, through regression analysis you can show that a one-point improvement [on a ten point scale] in trust in the workplace is worth more than a thirty percent increase in salary! What does it mean to trust management? Genuine trust has to be mutual. In order to build trust with your workforce you've got to actually trust them. People who work in organizations where they feel management can be trusted, where there is real mutual trust, are qualifiably happier than people who don't.

There is an assumption by many that the only way to motivate people is by paying them more. Not true. The way to motivate people is to have a set of shared goals they really want to achieve together. It's not that you can get away without paying them properly but the real marginal difference is not more money. It's a shared sense of the enterprise, of wanting to accomplish something together and feeling trust in, and from, management.

my ikonica

My favourite Canadian ikon is the Cirque du Soleil because it has reinvented an extremely old art form. Because of its artistic and craft excellence and its inventiveness, it has seen itself as deeply international from the start. My only disappointment is that only Canadians know that it is Canadian.

William Thorsell

Habitat:
CEO, Royal Ontario Museum

Bloodlines: *The Globe and Mail*, Chairman of the Editorial Board, Editor-in-Chief for ten years. *Edmonton Journal*, Associate Editor. Assistant Dean of the Woodrow Wilson School of Public and International Affairs at Princeton University.

Field Notes: Appointed CEO in 2000, Thorsell has been a force of nature, spearheading the renaissance of one of Canada's premiere cultural institutions. The $250 million project features a signature architectural makeover by superstar architect Daniel Leibskind. But behind the crystalline facade, Thorsell is nurturing a deeper renewal of vision and purpose. We asked him to talk about the brand transformation process at the ROM and relevant lessons for other business leaders.

Royal Ontario Museum

On getting to "yes"…

When I first got here, the museum had done some market research as to how it was perceived. People saw it as a grey old lady—dusty, dark, confusing. It was this great thing you were taken to as a kid and never went back. It was behind the times, virtuous but sidelined. No longer relevant to people's interests, particularly adults. I think it was branded by the school buses. It presented to the city, as I said to the board when I came here, like a moat on Bloor Steet and a rather ugly cliff on Queens Park.

Back in 2000, when the architects first came here to see the place, I would take them to the corner of Bloor and Avenue Road and turn them back to look at the building. From that corner I said, "This place looks just like a big 'No!' And I want you to turn that into a big 'Yes!' " We want to make the city create ROM and the ROM create the city in return. Engagement, transparency, drama—that's the kind of daring that we were looking

for. We probably have the best piece of property in urban Canada in terms of attracting attention. But there was absolutely no sense of that. This place could have been out by the Don Valley Parkway.

On brand as experience…

When you get people into the building, you have to think about what the experience is going to be like. And so this whole planning process began—thinking through what it's going to be like for a visitor. We started with the galleries, the comprehensibility of the place and the emphasis on the collections. This is not a storytelling museum or a theme-based museum. To a large degree, it's a collection of spaces. So, our comparative advantage is stuff. That's why the approach to the content of the museum is very object centered. There's lots of density of material to see, presented in a beautiful and interesting way, in beautiful spaces. It's about objects, it's natural history, it's paintings, it's

A NEW AGE IS DAWNING

music, it's cuisine, it's lectures, it's films. There has to be a change in substance and a change in how we present the substance of the experience to be credible in the market place.

We are making two big assumptions: First, that we have great stuff. Second, that the people of Canada or Toronto or the visitors that come here are curious, educated and smart enough to appreciate good stuff. Then we add in all the other aspects—the amenities of shopping, retail and restaurants, the creature comforts, as well as programming for different communities, different demographics.

What are you buying here? You're buying experience. That's all we can offer. Part of it's intellectual; part of it's esthetic; part of it's social, and part of it's just plain pleasure. Thus, the creation of this new position called Director of Visitor Experience. We're trying to develop something called the gold key standard, which comes right out of Four Seasons. This includes new outfits for everyone and identifies them more elegantly. We will have sessions on dealing with different kinds of communities. We have a whole task force on accessibility, for people who are not only physically disabled but for sight and hearing. You take it step by step. There is no short cut to experience.

On making transformation real internally...
The thing about branding is that it's very hard to take a deep, broadly entrenched section of something like the ROM and change it through incremental actions. That's very hard to do. Staff are busy. They're not going to see what they have to change. Part of our strategy in choosing our architect was to do something shockingly different. We have to back it up with content and behaviour, but we're not going to take a chance in spending $250 million and have people not realize there's a change. The project itself has to be so visible and conspicuous, and so noted already internationally, that there is no doubt something very significant is happening.

Second is working with the world's best exhibit builders and designers, and then developing our exhibition program where we are not just a roadhouse but we now have three or four significant collaborations underway for major exhibitions that we can generate ourselves. I think the ROM has tremendous depth intellectually and a lot of that has been eroding for years because of financial pressures and maybe various styles of leadership, but it is all there, just under the surface. Now that the resources are starting to come in we can start doing some really credible things on our own or with other people. The first step is just producing permanent galleries of first rank internationally like the China, Japan, Korea and Canadian First People's galleries.

I think the biggest surprise has been how receptive everyone was to all this change. We've been in a very fortunate period. We presented the goals. We were given the mandate. Then we executed the mandate without interference from the boards or the Government of Ontario. We've had far more autonomy and latitude than many other places. The culture within the museum has also been much more receptive than people warned me it would be when I first came here. It's been a much smoother process than I thought it would be. The staff, which has been very responsive. I assumed there would be more static.

On the role of the CEO...
You, as the driver, have to be on the frontlines with all those people, explaining the change, defending it, building a faith in it, getting through the periods where nothing much seems to be happening. If you can't do that, you shouldn't be there.

First of all, you have to have a very clear vision that's exciting. People can be doubtful about it, make it sound unrealistic and maybe even be cynical, but you have to be there for a reason that you can explain. You have to lay out something that is quite focused, quite comprehensible. Fundamentally, it must speak to the aspirations of people in their deepest, darkest hearts, even the most cynical. If you don't have that you're soon going to lose your audience.

At the beginning you have to spend a huge amount of time one-on-one with your own constituencies. You can't do it by email; you can't do it by town hall meetings, you can't do it by speeches. They have to know who you are. I learned to do that at *The Globe.* You have to start inside. Build a sense that everybody knows why you're doing what you're proposing to do and where it is that you're going. Even if they doubt it or disagree with it, there will be no loss of understanding. Then, you use the same process for external constituencies. You have to go around and make the same case. And then you have to start over again. You have to keep people bringing into the project as you go along.

When I came here in the summer of 2000, by September we had set up staff meetings. I think we had fifteen meetings of fifteen people or something, over about six weeks. Everybody from every department—cleaners, security guards, every ticket taker—was in these meetings and I had a whole presentation on why am I here? Where are we right now as an institution? Where should we be going and why? And here's how we are going to approach it.

It's very hard to keep people up to date through our weekly bulletins, emails and town halls. One day, two years ago, when the building was starting to be built, I organized a series of hard-hat tours again, fifteen people at a time. Every staff member and many volunteers were able to go out there and get the whole picture. The updating and refreshing of the reality of your vision is something that has to be done throughout the process and it's best done by CEO.

Don't pull your punches. When I came here and proposed that I needed $200 million on a project, some members of the board said, "we'll never raise $200 million! That's just way beyond the capacity for something like this." My answer to that was, we can raise it if we do something really daring. When in doubt, push, go for it, don't pull back! Several other cultural projects in Toronto didn't pass that test. They were too worried about raising money or too worried about community opposition that they pulled back rather than pushed out. I think they underestimated the community.

You have to be very bold these days in any market place. Market places are used to boldness. We're not going to pay a lot of attention to a variation on any norm when we are used to that norm. So if it's going to be new, it's got to be an iPod, not a version of the Walkman. It's got to be something that really takes a leap. The idea that you can do this through market research and focus groups is false. A focus group never comes up with a new product. They tell you how you are doing with what you are doing. New ideas do come out of garages, pure creativity... You build the iPod, they will come.

On what Canadians want from their cultural institutions...

Not every institute is for everybody in the country, which is normal and fine. For institutions like the Opera, the AGO [Art Gallery of Ontario], the ROM—the sort of high-end institutions—I think audiences in Canada really want excellence. When they travel, they go to the best places and they don't want to see second-rank, under-funded institutions like the old ROMs, the old AGOs. And we don't want La Bohème done over in the same old way. They want a new way to approach at Opera House that's cool and works. Excellence, creativity, edginess, style are essential for first-rank institutions. They have to be groundbreaking, creative and expose us to the new. It's a myth that Canadians are unadventurous. This is no longer a colonial outpost. Canadians travel and they expect far higher standards than we've been delivering.

Canada is emerging again as a significant world force because of the way the rest of the world is going. These are changing relative positions and the population is changing dramatically. So we shouldn't look back too much, in looking at the Canadian psyche. The Canadian psyche is ready for much higher quality. It's much more self-confident and creative.

Our Commitment
inspire wonder, build understanding,
deliver exceptional service

Respect
• warm, engaging and attentive service
• comfortable, safe and clean

Discovery
• physical and intellectual access to our
collections and services

Communication
• clear and friendly communication

Action and Accountability
• reach out to exceed the expectations
of our visitor
• demonstrate courtesy and
be responsive

Consistency
• evaluate our progress

R O **M** Royal Ontario
Museum

Clive Beddoe

Habitat: Chairman, WestJet

Bloodlines: Beddoe, one of the founding shareholders of WestJet, immigrated to Canada in 1970 from the UK. A successful entrepreneur with his private pilot's licence, Beddoe was one of four Calgary business leaders who saw an opportunity to reinvent low-fare air travel in Canada based on the successful model set by Southwest Airlines in the US.

Field Notes: WestJet took flight in 1996 with three aircraft and 220 employees serving just five western Canadian cities. By 1999, the carrier had completed its IPO of 2.5 million common shares. By 2006, at a time when many airlines were in crisis mode, WestJet had become Canada's most successful airline and one of the two most profitable carriers in North America. WestJet now employs over 6,500 people.

On creating extreme culture...

The industry at the time was dominated by two very inefficient carriers. We called them Tweedledum and Tweedledee. It was a golden opportunity to build something that was different, along the same lines as Southwest. Southwest gave people participatory opportunities that became the core of their success. We used the same principles but modified them to fit within the Canadian context. We set out to create an even more extreme culture. From a participation standpoint, our profit sharing is much more generous. For every dollar that an employee puts into the company, we match it dollar-for-dollar up to twenty percent of their salary. That's three or four times more generous than anybody else's program. We "bribe" people to become shareholders. You're leaving twenty percent of your salary on the table if you don't take advantage of it.

The more success employees are able to create, the greater the level of participation that they get.

Human beings need a sense of participation and meaning in their lives. We got that by aligning the interests of the employees with that of the company. Everyone talks about it but few seem to achieve it. What we wanted was a fundamental shift in behaviour from the person that comes to work because he or she has to get a paycheque, to somebody who comes to work because they're passionate about what they do. They have a meaningful sense of being part of the team that's collectively building something. We are asking people to care. We are asking guys making twelve dollars an hour to care that when you check in, you're treated with respect. Don Bell came up with the idea that we should call our customers "guests." It started to change how people behave.

We empower our people to do whatever it takes to make right the experience of one of our guests. There's no limit. Once, many years ago, we were flying a couple to Kelowna to get married. Our contract baggage handlers failed to put their luggage on the flight. This poor woman arrived without her wedding dress! Our employees went out and bought her a wedding dress. They don't have to ask. They just do what they know is right. What makes people feel that this is a great place to work is that they have that licence.

Culture and brand are one and the same. The culture creates the brand. The brand is the experience that people have when they encounter us. Whether it's on the phone, at the airport, on the flight or when they have a problem, it's all the brand. Our culture is embedded in every part of the business. We have no tolerance for any great hierarchal structure. The accountants decided to call themselves "beans" so their offices are called "bean land." We have a lot of parties for our people. We celebrate successes. I was talking to an Air Canada flight attendant and I asked him about their profit sharing. He said, "I think we get a couple of hundred bucks a month." Now, two hundred dollars a month is $2400 a year but they don't celebrate it. How is it paid to him? It's paid to him in his check every month for every two weeks. But he could care less about it. What a waste! We gave out almost the same amount to flight attendants this year but we have a huge celebration. We give it to them in one check and they go, "Wow!" You see? Milton obviously thinks that it is the profit giving versus the profit sharing that makes the difference. It's not! It's the "How" not the "What." That's the distinction.

If we talk about teamwork, then we better show it. Anybody flying that works for the company helps clean up the airplane after landing: the captain, the flight attendants, the executives too. We save twelve to fifteen million dollars a year by not paying to have the aircraft cleaned between flights. I am not treated any differently; I park with everybody else on a first-come-first-serve

basis. Obviously my salary is different but I don't get any preferences. It says that we are all in this together.

If culture is what's important to you, you cannot leave it to happenstance to just occur. We have a department of culture focused on both the strategic development to continue to grow our culture and a department called "Care," focused on delivering a great cultural experience for our employees. What has amazed me is just how powerful this really is and how few people understand it. Until you live it, breathe it and are part of it, it's almost impossible to grasp. I get asked all the time, "Okay, what's the secret?" I say, "It's about culture." They respond, "Sure, but what's the real secret?" It is culture! It's about your commitment to the people. You can talk about this all your life, but until you live it, see it, smell it, taste it, it's very hard to comprehend just how powerful it is. We are all tested constantly. Our own people are watching all the time to see whether we make the right decisions or not. They want to know that we've got that emotional commitment. If it's just a cerebral commitment, then you are not going to make the right decisions when it comes to difficult issues.

On managing change...

I was looking around our executive meeting the other day and there were only two of us that were there from the start. Yet we've attracted better minds with broader horizons and better perspectives to make the best team that has ever existed here. Part of my role is to make sure that the company sustains itself beyond me and the founders. I've been conditioning the market and employees for that event progressively over the last three years. Even the model that Southwest created has changed, because the aircrafts have changed. So, change is a norm. The culture has to embrace change. It's fundamental to our success. You don't like change, but change is the norm.

On advice to Canadian entrepreneurs...

My advice to other entrepreneurs is always people, people, people. Many of the classic entrepreneurs who have a hard-driving, dictatorial, top-down, aggressive management style, can achieve a lot with that in the short-run—maybe even in the mid-run—but you cannot do the long-run. Fear of you will generate extraordinary performance in a short period of time. After that, either people revert back to performing at eighty percent of their capability or they say "To hell with you, I'm out of here." Then you've got huge turnover and you lose the very thing that is the core of your business—your people. Powerful aggressive individuals can achieve a lot with huge compensation packages too but it's costing you because you're paying them excessively or because they are not going to perform to the maximum of their capability. If, on the other hand, you focus on people, the culture, the teamwork and the pride that they get out of what they do, they'll do amazing things for you! It won't really cost you a lot to do it and you can really reward them out of the bottom line, not out of the top line.

In my past employment experiences I wasn't mistreated but I felt abused because I never felt I was rewarded for what I contributed. It's out of my own bad experiences that I focus on the things that we do today. I've had so many people who have come here and said, "I've heard about all your culture but until I got here, I had no idea how powerful it really is." That's when I recognized that we've unleashed something here with enormous potential. Look at what we've achieved with so little and imagine what would happen if you could take the whole Canadian economy and achieve the same with it. I think it could be done, I really do. The principles we've pursued are not that difficult.

We have run WestJet with eighty employees per airplane. Air Canada runs with 120. Now, apply that to this economy. Just think of what productivity could be! I absolutely know everybody in this world could put out ten percent more without even thinking about it, probably twenty percent. They can, but they don't. They are not induced to; they are not inspired to. In fact they are penalized if they do because if you put out more than your colleague beside you,

your colleagues around you really don't like it. We reward mediocrity. We don't like people who really succeed. I hasten to add that it is not what I've done with WestJet; it's what the team here has done. There is no question that we've tapped into something very powerful. The business schools will say that WestJet has got a tremendous culture, but they really don't get into how it happens. Why does it happen; what's the effect of it; what does it really do; what has it achieved, and why is it so important? That's the step that gets missed.

The mountains and the huge expansive space—that's what I came for. It's very dramatic country. When you see the sunrise on a summer cloud that's going from north to south and the sky is just a brilliant red and the mountains in the background have snow on them, it's a pretty amazing sight that's still inspiring even after being here for over thirty-five years.

How to build a reputation

(Based on the recognition we received in 2005 – a textbook year)

figure 9-b

1. **BE ACKNOWLEDGED**, as WestJet was, for having the most admired corporate culture in the '2005 Canadian Corporate Culture Study' by Canadian Business magazine and Waterstone Human Capital Ltd.

2. **DO AS WESTJET DID** and place first in customer service in the Eleventh Annual 'Canada's Most Respected Corporation's Survey.'

3. **MOST IMPORTANT OF ALL**, continue to attract rave reviews from passengers or, as we prefer to call them, guests.

Proud moments at WestJet in 2005

figure 35-A

1. **WHEN WE LAUNCHED** our transborder service from Vancouver to Honolulu and Maui.

2. **WHEN WE CELEBRATED** the arrival of our 50th Boeing Next-Generation aircraft, giving us the most advanced fleet of any major North American Airline.

3. **WHEN WE IMPROVED** our market share to 32%, an impressive growth of 3% over last year.

4. **WHEN WE INTRODUCED** Web check-in to allow 398,855 guests to print their own boarding pass.

5. **WHEN WE PROVIDED** 24 channels of Bell ExpressVu satellite programming and four channels of pay-per-view movies to help make our flights even more fun.

6. **WHEN WE REALIZED** we had so many proud moments that this list could keep going.

Mario D'Amico

Habitat: Senior Vice-President Marketing, Cirque du Soleil

Bloodlines: D'Amico has worked with ikonic brands throughout his career, starting with the legendary snack cakes May West and Jos. Louis. During his tenure with the agency Scally McCabe Sloan, he helped launch Apple Macintosh and Labatt Blue in Quebec. He was a partner at Publicis when Cirque du Soleil came calling in 1999.

Field Notes: Cirque du Soleil was founded in 1984 by Guy Laliberté. A street performer, Laliberté, with a coterie of stilt-walking, fire-breathing, acrobatic confreres, won a commission from the Quebec government to stage performances for a summer festival in the village of Baie St. Paul celebrating the arrival of explorer Jacques Cartier. Cirque made its own history during that fête. Twenty-three years later, the company, based in Montreal, has 3,800 employees worldwide including close to one thousand artists, manages six shows on world tours, two shows in arenas and seven resident spectacles (five in Las Vegas, one in Orlando and one seasonal show in New York), with a number of new projects in the works. Over seventy million people around the world have seen Cirque productions.

During a 2007 speech to the Canadian Marketing Association, D'Amico described the Cirque brand as an elaborate ecosystem whose success hinges on incubating "no compromise" quality at the molecular level. Cirque's artistic risk-taking and visceral, breathtakingly imaginative storytelling inspires intense loyalty among devotees. Celebrating its roots, the troupe created "Cirque du Monde," a program that trains underprivileged youth from some of the world's poorest communities in the arts of street theatre.

CIRQUE DU SOLEIL.

On creativity…

I love this job. I tell people I have the second best job in the world, after Guy. Creativity as defined by Cirque is a very pure form of creativity. Our creative people—whether they be the lighting directors, choreographers, directors—are pure artists. Cirque has chosen the live stage as its canvas.

The line between business and art meets at marketing because the show has to live for the next twelve to fifteen years in countries around the world. Each show's development is a two-year process. Then they hand it over to marketing to make it successful in terms of routing it properly, finding sponsorship, finding a name. We're involved in the creative process from the second year on so we're fully aware of what the intent is. Then we develop the name, the whole visual language around it. We're promoting something that has a point of view on art, on culture, on beauty, on the way people live. It's actually a competitive advantage for us. Guy might say, "I'd like us to look at alienation. What does that mean to us in the late twentieth century?"

The team will live an incredibly intense experience for two years and give birth to something that is actually unfinished. Nothing has ever been really ready on day one. The famous expression at Cirque du Soleil is: "work in progress." Even *Alegria*, which has been on the road since 1994, is still seen as a work in progress. The original twelve creators of that show actually go revisit the show and say, "You know, this part is not how I had intended it. We need to fix that." There's that constant connection to the show and the brand. Each of the shows also has an artistic

director. While that show is on tour for the next twelve or fifteen years, he has to maintain the integrity of the show and the intent of the original creators. It's a nice ecosystem that feeds itself. It's almost hermetically sealed in the sense that the creators live this process for two years and then the tour lives this for years as a unit of 150, a family that's maintained.

On the culture of storytelling…

There is an incredible culture in this company. You get a real sense that this company has an identity; it knows who it is. You'll see an incredible diversity of colour; you'll hear languages that you can't even recognize. People tell you stories in this company. And these stories get transmitted to other people. All of a sudden, I'll tell that story, actually thinking it's my story. This company is also very good at creating meeting places. On tour, the kitchen is a famous meeting place for everyone. We even take clients there. We have very defined moments where everybody gets together, whether it's a party, a luau or whatever. We have an internal communications department that is very, very good at promoting "Cirque-ness" internally. We're good storytellers, we like to tell stories.

We want to get people to feel Cirque du Soleil in an intimate way. There's quite an intimate relationship between us and our public. If we had to sell this company, our two million Club Cirque email subscribers are as valuable as our brand as far as I'm concerned. These are our best customers. It's a well-educated, wealthy, mobile audience. You've got to be careful having a relationship with a group like that. It's not about throwing offers to them. We sell tickets to commercial activities but we also use them to give us feedback on what we're doing right, what we're doing wrong. We encourage it. We have brand love scores that are in the nineties—higher than the Apples and Harley Davidson's of this world. We are this little jewel—really small but highly polished.

On authenticity…

Authenticity is one of our brand values. It's one-of-a-kind authenticity. The Broadway model is if you have a successful show like *Beauty and the Beast*, you take it on the road and you have *Beauty and the Beast* everywhere in the world. If you're watching it in Korea, there's somebody watching *Beauty and the Beast* for sure in New York or L.A. We don't have that. When you're in Rio de Janeiro, it's the only place in the world where you can watch something like *Alegria*. We make sure that our community of 2 million [members] knows that. From a merchandising perspective, you'll see T-shirts and the regular stuff. But you will also see the odd piece that is a one-off where we hired a local artist and commission art from him. That also speaks to authenticity and one-of-a-kind. We make our costumes by hand, one by one. We actually buy white latex and then we hand paint it most of the time.

You have to say to yourself, "How did Quebec become a hot bed of circus-ness?" It's pretty amazing that this culture that has no circus tradition at all has become the expert in modern, artistic circuses. Obviously, the fact that Guy's a street performer has a lot to do with it. That is more a tradition in Quebec—the street corner magician or performer, passing the hat around. There's a naïveté, that you can take this art form that doesn't really belong to you, borrow from a couple of other art forms, mix all that together and fuse it into something. Before Cirque du Soleil started it was really what was called La Fête Foraine—it means a street party, some sort of gathering. I think this is more Quebec than Canada— "fêter," to party, to celebrate. The success of street festivals in general in this province might have something to do with the bloody weather. You're inside for eight months and those four months of summer you just want to be outside and contribute to this festive environment.

On being international…

Nomadic is also part of the DNA of this brand. You'd be surprised at how few people know where we're from in the rest of the world. Clearly they get a clue when you're called Cirque du Soleil that you're French or maybe French Canadian. It actually helps us

my ikonica

*Canadian Tire.
I was born in Italy and came
to Canada when I was
about four. When I was a
kid, I wanted to be part of
"Canadiana" quickly. When
I was twelve years old,
the first Canadian Tire
store opened in our
neighbourhood. Not only
was it a hardware store—
which I loved,
being a boy—but it had
the name Canadian.
I actually thought if I
walked into Canadian Tire
a lot, it would rub off on
me and I would become
more Canadian! It's as
silly as that, but that's the
story. Me and my friends
also bought our first canoe
from Canadian Tire.*

not to be from anywhere; then we're from everywhere. We're not strangers. We're good wherever we are. That's the way the tour has to live too. They have to adapt and be part of whatever society that they're in. It's the ecosystem again. When we move into a city or into a site, we don't need anything. Really, the only thing that we need is water in, water out. We have our own generators, a school house with a teacher depending on how many kids there are on tour, our tent master is there. It's incredible. We're completely self-sufficient.

On success...

Even Guy is incredibly surprised by the success of this company and how quickly it became successful. I don't think Guy is religious at all but I do think he's spiritual and he talks in those terms—about the planets being aligned or there's some star that's clearly looking out for Cirque du Soleil. We've had some failures. When we went to Niagara Falls the first time in '86, the marketing people looked at all the tourists that come in to Niagara Falls and thought it will be like Vegas. We failed miserably. The tourists' average length of stay was about two hours. But the more philosophical thing is they changed the name. They called themselves "Circus of the Sun." Circus of the Sun just sounds so banal. I think even Guy can believe we have forty percent of the high-end ticket inventory on the Las Vegas strip. No one in their wildest dreams could have imagined that. The "Rat Pack" didn't have forty percent and they were identified as Vegas.

On Canadian brands...

In comparison to the US market, there's an overly sensitive bullshit meter in Canada. Canadians have this level-headedness that we can sense when the hype button is ratcheted a little too much. The tone of voice should be a moderate one. To me, the most successful brand is Tim Hortons. They're just telling you stories in a "Have a seat. Here's a cup of coffee. Let me tell you a story," way. That's a metaphor for how to talk to middle Canada.

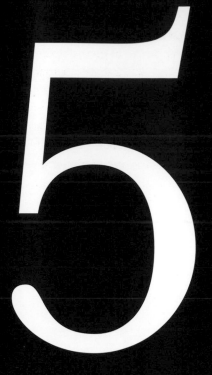

5

CLIMATE CHANGE PRIMER

OUR FIELD SKETCHES of Canada's brandscape have become clearer as we've added shadings of history and cultural comparisons, dashes of *genius loci* and the rich texture of personal stories from all parts of our atlas. The picture that's emerged is of a brandscape with its own special ecology and geography. Nevertheless, there's no escaping the seismic shifts heading our way. Environmental climate change is only one of a number of inexorable, international forces that are reshaping the world of business and brands.

"Did you Know?" is a simple PowerPoint presentation created for a faculty meeting at a Colorado high school in August 2006. This primer on the exponential acceleration of social and technological change has become a proof point for its own argument— shift happens, sometimes abruptly. It went "viral" on the web and—as of October 2007 —at least ten million people around the world are said to have seen it. Canada should get the notion of big shifts better than most places with the number of change mavens in our backyard: Malcolm Gladwell, who introduced the language of "tipping points"; Thomas Homer-Dixon, who brought us the *The Upside of Down*; Don Tapscott and Anthony D. Williams, with their cram course on *Wikinomics*.

In 2007, The Canadian Marketing Association published its own line-up of change factors entitled, *Building Brands in a Complex World*. We've added some updates to the categories they identified:

Globalization/Internationalization: International competition is here to stay but it's a blade that slices two ways. New competition poses challenges but with it comes more open markets. As Joe Chidley, editor of *Canadian Business* writes in an editorial, an integrated marketplace won't protect our ikonic firms but it can, "establish the conditions that will help Canada's entrepreneurs create more of them."

Empowered Consumers: Buyers have more choice than ever and low barriers to switching. They are well informed; expect more personalization, and can easily mobilize into powerful interest groups through websites, blogs, social media and mobile communications.

The Proliferation of Media: Breaking through the mind-numbing onslaught of messaging that we all face daily is the big barrier for marketing. The public is fighting back with tools for blocking, filtering and generally tuning out unwanted distractions.

Technology: Ten years ago, who could have anticipated the rapid rise of whole new species of innovations such as YouTube, Second Life and Facebook? Peer-to-peer networks, virtual communities and collaborations like the Wikipedia wield extraordinary clout. Canadians are fast adopters of social media. As of fall 2007, eleven of the thirty most active Facebook cities were Canadian; Toronto and London, England, swap first-place bragging rights regularly. The brand-building playbook is being constantly rewritten as marketers struggle to keep up.

Short-term economic pressures: Investor demands for quarterly earnings and short-term returns are more intense than ever. Without effective measurement tools, quantifying return on investment becomes a barrier for many brand-building efforts.

*On April 16, 2007
trend-watcher Arieh Singer
highlighted on his blog the
following post from Rannie
Turingan, a fellow
Torontonian, commenting
on the surprising growth
of the social networking
tool Facebook:*

Today I found out
how many people are
in the Toronto Network.
That number is 483,887
people… compare that to
all of California which
includes 19 networks
(LA, San Francisco,
San Diego etc)
341,433 people. NYC
(202,600 people)…
In the time it took me
to write this post the
Toronto Network has
grown to 483,944
(57 people)
…yowza.

Demographics: The sheer number of baby boomers moving toward retirement has every industry scrambling to infill skills and capacity, while businesses try to retool their offerings for greying markets. Immigration, multiculturalism, social mobility and the changing complexion of "typical" households make it more challenging than ever to profile markets and audiences.

Ethics in business: The age of transparency exposes corporate governance, reporting, treatment of employees, privacy and social policies to the unforgiving glare of public scrutiny.

Organizational Change: We know the critical role of staff in delivering the brand experience. But technology gaps, outsourcing, employee turnover and a revolving door of top brass undermine even the best-laid plans.

Community values: The rising tide of corporate social responsibility adds new pressure for brands to prove their community commitments. The greening of commerce, for example, will push many businesses to rethink their ecological "footprint" on many levels… from energy efficient buildings and production processes to new design approaches that avoid unhealthy ingredients and minimize packaging.

The Canadian Marketing Association's line-up of forces at play in our brandscape underscores the obvious (but often overlooked) interdependencies of commerce, culture and community.

As business guru Peter Drucker pointed out, we can't manage change; the best we can hope for is to stay one step ahead of it. How can Canadian brands adapt? Luckily, adaptability is one of our strong suits. In the swirling maelstrom of major disruptions—ecological, technological, social or geopolitical—meaning and authenticity provide shelter to businesses. This new world order demands that enterprises finally take full advantage of all the competitive resources that our brandscape has to offer. Let's reframe the argument for why brands matter in today's unpredictable business climate. The message for brands in Canada is a simple one: Mind the gap.

COMMERCE: THE VALUE GAP Money talks. Brand assets used to be seen as something relegated to the marketers. That notion is dying away as economics sharpen the case for putting brands on the "C suite" agenda. Optimizing valuation, risk management, investment priorities—these are all executive preoccupations where brands play critical roles. While there are many competing models for assessing brand valuation, the important point, as pundit Jonathan Knowles explains, is that these assets represent significant money: "On average, a brand represents ten percent of the market capitalization of a bank. Let's imagine a bank with a market valuation of fifty billion dollars. Ten percent equals five billion dollars but that's just the average. A strong brand might be worth more—say $7.5 billion; a weak brand might be valued at only $2.5 billion. That leaves management with a five billion dollar question: "How will we manage our brand?" CEOs and board members are beginning to take notice.

Strong brands are a form of risk management as well. Given the pace of change, five-year plans become increasingly speculative. Winning the race in volatile times demands something of a hybrid of tortoise and hare; the hare's astute hearing and quick response married to the tortoise's unflustered staying power. First movers don't always have the advantage. CEO Paul House uses the metaphor of "riding the fences" —versus sitting on them—to describe Tim Hortons' approach to monitoring shifting customer territory. Patience, tolerance for ambiguity and a healthy dose of skepticism are good qualities to have when exploring emerging markets.

Tipping points can come quickly in business but it takes time to retool well-established operations. Aeroplan is a great case study in leveraging its brand positioning to reshape its culture. Instead of abstract vision statements, their approach is to create a robust, highly personalized brand "story" to engage everyone, from investors and partners to front-line workers, in the process of change. It also creates strategic filters for smart investment. Leading business schools are now advocating the benefits of brand-based design explorations as a practical way for businesses to prototype preferred futures and ways to achieve them. Pilot programs become cost-effective ways of learning by doing.

COMMUNITY: THE RELATIONSHIP GAP Tim Hortons rarely deals directly with consumers; instead it enables its store-owner network to sell on its behalf. The real lifeblood of "Tim's," Canadian Tire and many other brands is the depth of their network relationships. We've imagined our brandscape as an ecology—a place of complex, interdependent relationships—because the tie between "consumer" and "producer" is not the only one that counts. The larger community of influencers, partners, investors and employees has always played a key role in the success of a brand. What's different in the changing business climate is the new emphasis on what brands can do for communities and what communities can do for brands.

Some call it social purpose, social strategy or corporate social responsibility. Old wine in new bottles, it's a recasting of the principle "do well by doing good." Whatever the descriptor, expectations of what organizations and their brands should be doing in communities is growing rapidly. Critics may argue about the causes—record-breaking profits, extraordinary executive salaries or frustrations born of government boondoggles —but good corporate citizenship matters more than ever to Canadians. Market researchers note a steady climb in the willingness of audiences (especially older and younger markets) to pay a premium for brands that give back in some way. There is also a self-interest rationale for organizations to wade in on social concerns. Immigration, social justice, environment, education, health—these are all issues that can affect the ability of an enterprise to thrive.

The flip side of how business can support communities is the concept of what journalist James Surowiecki dubbed, "the wisdom of crowds." Wikipedia is one example of the power of mass collaboration. Don Tapscott and Anthony D. Williams chronicle many more stories of peer production in their best seller, *Wikinomics*. The book opens with the tale of Toronto-based gold-mining firm, Goldcorp Inc., an old economy business that found new life by "open sourcing" its exploration process. The authors point out that "firms that cultivate nimble, trust-based relationships with external collaborators are positioned to form vibrant business ecosystems that create value more effectively than hierarchically organized businesses." Collaboration is clearly the modus operandi of the "Net Generation," Tapscott's term for those weaned on MySpace, Facebook, flickr and a host of other social hubs. For this cohort, community is like breathing. Tapscott and Williams make the case that, "the Internet makes life an ongoing massive collaboration, and this generation loves it... They have a strong sense of the common good and of collective social and civic responsibility."

Tapscott is not the only one who sees radical generational shifts ahead. The makeup of Canada's under-forty set, according to pollster Frank Graves of Ekos Research, is quite different than either its US or European counterparts. More pluralistic, internationally minded, tolerant of diversity, Graves dubs them the "new Phoenicians." In a *Globe and Mail* profile by Lawrence Martin entitled "Changing of the Guard," Graves is quoted as saying, "We can be the place that puts the highest emphasis on cosmopolitanism, multiculturalism, immigration—a society that can go in different directions in terms of both demographics and values." The new collaborative work ethos certainly plays well to our genius for being "team players."

Playing well with others demands a strong dose of tolerance, an attribute with clear links to economic development according to noted US urban economist Richard Florida. Florida caused a stir in many circles when he headed north to become Academic Director of the Martin Prosperity Institute at the Rotman School of Management. Best known for his groundbreaking treatise, *The Rise of the Creative Class*, he evangelizes that the secret to growth and prosperity is cultivating the three Ts: technology, talent and tolerance. We may be middle of the pack of the first two, but in Florida's estimation, we stand tall in the latter category. "Canada was not always the most open-minded place in the world, but I think right now you could number it among one of the most open-minded places in the world," Florida points out in an interview with *Canadian Business* writer, Erin Pooley. Underscoring how community values feed commerce, Florida notes how, "some of the places that have the most attractive business climates are not doing very well. Maybe your immigration policy, your border policy and your policy towards arts, culture and gay and lesbian marriage are as important as your monetary, tax and regulatory policies."

As if to prove his point, an article by Regan Ray immediately preceding Florida's profile in *Canadian Business* lays out the backstory of Microsoft's announcement of a two-hundred-employee software development centre near Vancouver. Microsoft cited the ability to recruit worldwide talent more easily in Canada as one of its reasons for the decision. Later in the piece, Ray quotes Barry Gander of the Canadian Advanced Technology Alliance: "With a tiny bit of organization, Canada can be positioned as the 'world in a nation'—the single door that opens the skills of the world to our partners."

Our brandscape breeds diverse opportunities to create offerings inspired by a new "mash-up" of multicultural and international influences that can thrive not only at home but abroad. The Umbra team, McCain Foods and Cirque du Soleil demonstrate just how successful that strategy can be.

CULTURE: THE AUTHENTICITY GAP With a collaboration-savvy, community-minded generation entering the workforce, the authenticity factor becomes an important lever for organizations to attract and retain great talent. Scott Lerman, founder of Lucid Brands, has led groundbreaking transformations for a who's who of global organizations. For Lerman, clarity, truth and emotion are the real benchmarks of ikonic brands. "There's tremendous skepticism in companies where the consultants have arrived and charged a lot of money to do something that does not touch them deeply in their hearts or changed the nature of how people do things," he explains. "People should be re-energized to approach what they do with new conviction. If you do it right, you can reach that every time, no matter how disparate the parts of the business seem. For any organization that wants to endure and build long-term value, being true and genuine is essential."

Lerman is quick to point out that getting to meaning and truth is a challenge for a lot of companies. The best door in is often through stories. "If you start to chronicle the great stories that people tell about when they have been at their best as a company—whether it was something that they created or a crisis or how they decided to grow—it gives you signposts to the character behind the behaviour. You have to push people to look beyond the surface, beyond what they would tell someone to sound more important or more interesting than they really are. Then what you find are some very genuine, important characteristics that can be significant in differentiating why someone would want to work with them. It's those stories that are at the heart of great brands."

Some of the most promising new frameworks linking brands and internal culture are coming from a new breed of Canadian practitioners who are pushing organizations to bring depth and dimension to corporate purpose and values. In her work, Mary Jane Braide connects organizational development and change initiatives to brand building through an insightful parsing of cultural values she calls "Deeps, Differentiators and Deltas." Deeps she describes as, "values that are fundamental to operating effectively and legally and that are shared across competitors or peers within an industry." They come to bear in those moments of truth that demand doing the right thing—integrity, accountability or transparency.

Differentiators are values that distinguish an organization from others as statements of intent, based on its long-term vision, such as, "co-creating with customers, or front-line decision making, or pioneering unproven ideas, or being an advocate for a cause," Braide explains. "These values tend to be more complex than the Deeps as they express qualities that are unique to one organization and so not easily summed up in a single word."

The top tier is the realm of the Deltas—new, sometimes aspirational values that need to be instilled in the organization as part of a change process. The drivers might be a re-branding, a strategic shift or a cultural initiative. But Braide is quick to add a note of caution to this category: "Values, if they can be changed at all, change very slowly, so taking on more than a couple at a time is risky. Better to select one or two really important ones and dedicate a lot of time to making them very real for people."

The benefit of Braide's taxonomy is the ability to monitor and manage organizational values more effectively. Deeps, she argues, must be constant and unwavering; Differentiators should be reinforced through explicit, highly visible programs of training and support but they must be meaningful. Given the Canadian penchant for skepticism, employee antennae are highly attuned to contrived boosterism, what Braide call "fluff-filters." "Nothing creates a worse experience than feeling that you're just an X in somebody's playbook and you're being moved up the field according to the 'brand-right' rules," she quips. Deltas, however, are values that should be on the CEO's agenda and modelled at the highest levels. On her blog, Braide underscores the fact that Deltas should be, "important, transformational values like organizational honesty, network collaboration or open systems."

Lerman sums up the importance of clarity about corporate values and purpose when he says, "If we don't have something that we can articulate clearly, and in an actionable way, what do we think we are going to do in the world? If we don't even know what drives us then we are doomed."

What will we do in the world? That is simultaneously a highly pragmatic, and profound, question. What we've learned is that great organizations and great brands are continually exploring these simple, but essential, questions: What will we do in the world? What will we mean to the world? What is our character? What is our story?

LEARNING FROM THE BEST The most exciting thing we discovered on our brandscape explorations was how rich Canada is in great stories to be shared. And we've observed how ikonic brands share a number of best practices including:

Strong, positive leadership: Their passion is not for making money, per se, but for performance that attracts customers. While good business management and profit are table stakes, what drives successful leaders and their organizations is creating value on many dimensions.

Clear brand meaning: A raison d'être that the organization must "stretch" to achieve.

Integrity in approach: Based on real values of respect for customers, employee and communities with values that come from a sense of humanity rather than the often-synthetic values of marketing.

Teamwork: The brand is not just the preview of the marketing department but is shared by HR, Finance, Operations, Sales; every part of the organization is ultimately engaged.

Learning and persistence: Ikonic brands don't happen overnight; they sometime falter and take wrong turns. But they endure by learning from successes and failures.

Measurement: Navigating the brandscape is a process of continuous calibration based on prevailing conditions. Are we on course? Brand leaders have developed numerous formal and informal feedback loops to keep them relevant and close to the prevailing winds.

POSTCARDS FROM THE EDGE

Genius Loci Tips for Canadian Brands:

MULTICULTURAL
Drink the local wine:
When in Rome… Focus on meaningful local adaptations to serve diverse markets.

COLLABORATIVE
Be partner of choice:
The fastest way to create critical mass and scale is through symbiotic (win/win) partnerships.

ENTREPRENEURIAL
Swim in blue oceans:
Explore untapped spaces on the brandscape.

COMMUNITARIAN
Build community capital:
Strong communities (local and virtual) strengthen commerce. Build community capacity where it impacts your self-interests (education, environment, etc.). Be the convener. Enable peer-to-peer relationships.

ENDURANCE
Take the long view:
Focus on critical sustainability issues. Never mistake a clear view for a short distance.

EXPERIENTIAL
Tell great stories:
Become a student of your organizational history. Analyze your business DNA. Create an oral tradition that celebrates meaning and momentum—where you've come from, heroic battles, moments of truth, authentic ingenuity, meaningful contributions and future promise.

CHAMELEON
Learn from nature:
The nature of ecosystems has much to teach us about sustainability and growth. As Mario D'Amico from Cirque du Soleil recommends: "Inject quality at the molecular level." Promote diversity in thinking. Explore "biomimicry"— looking to nature for innovative solutions.

INTERNATIONAL
Learn from the world:
Other sectors and geographies are great early-warning systems for new trends, opportunities and challenges.

ADAPTABLE
Manage the meaning, not the people:
Viable systems will self-organize given a few simple rules, a clear sense of purpose and a strong identity. Mindless consistency can be a trap. Focus on purpose and cohesion. Like open source development, many minds make bright work.

SKEPTICAL
Challenge assumptions:
Encourage people to regularly revisit the fundamentals of purpose. "Why," and "why not," should be essential parts of the organizational lexicon. Learn by doing. Create a bias for action. Experience is the best teacher. Experimentation helps the whole organization adapt faster.

HEADING DUE NORTH What we bring home from our travels is the understanding that we are, as we always have been, shaped by our landscape. Perhaps a better metaphor for brands is to think of them as places—natural environments where the connections between community, commerce and culture are as intrinsic as earth, air and water. To thrive in the new climate of global competition, new technologies and extraordinary cultural shifts we have to cultivate our own space in the world—places of authenticity where we can steward our natural resources and draw from the wisdom of *genius loci*. Indigenous Australians have navigated their vast outback for millennia with songlines. These intricate stories and music are embedded with ancient knowledge about landmarks and how to negotiate the terrain.

Adaptable, comfortable with ambiguity, hungry for experience, multicultural and curious about the world, skeptical but patient, collaborative with a strong communitarian streak—looking inside our competitive kit bag, it appears Canada's brands should be well equipped to take on whatever the winds of change blow our way. All that we're missing are some good orienteering tools for navigating and sharing possibilities ahead—our very own songlines.

A word to the wise: best stories win.

As Canadian as possible under the circumstances.

BIBLIOGRAPHY

Adams, Michael. *Fire & Ice, The United States, Canada and the Myth of Converging Values.* Toronto: Penguin Group (Canada), a division of Pearson Penguin Canada Inc., 2003. Pages 4, 6, 10, 49, 56-57, 66, 82, 87, 102, 117, 123-124, 141, 143

Benyus, Janine M. *Biomimicry: Innovation Inspired by Nature.* New York: Harper Collins Publishers Inc., 1997. Page 261

Blanchard, Robert T. "Parting Essay" 1999. Source: *Branding Strategy Insider* blog, The Blake Project: Asacker, Tom; VanAuken, Brad; Daye, Derrick. http://www.brandingstrategyinsider.com/all_brandquotes/index.html (accessed December 27, 2007)

Brown, J. J. *Ideas in Exile: A History of Canadian Invention.* Toronto: McClelland and Stewart, 1967

Collins, Jim. *Good To Great: Why Some Companies Make the Leap... and Others Don't.* New York: HarperCollins Publishers Inc., 2001. Pages 90-91

Diller, Steve; Shedroff, Nathan; Rhea, Darrel. *Making Meaning: How Successful Businesses Deliver Meaningful Customer Experiences.* Berkeley: New Riders, 2006. Pages 3, 29

Eliot, T.S. *Four Quartets.* New York: A Harvest Book, Harcourt, Brace & World, 1943, 1971. Stanza 240, Page 59

Gazzaniga, Michael. "The Split Brain Revisited," *Scientific American,* July, 1998

Gernak, Anthony; Hughes, John; Hunter, Douglas. *Building the Best: Lessons from Inside Canada's Best Managed Companies.* Toronto: Viking Canada, 2006

Hanlon, Patrick. *Primal Branding: Create Zealots for Your Brand, Your Company, And Your Future.* New York: Free Press, A Division of Simon & Schuster Inc., 2006

Holt, Douglas. *How Brands Become Icons: The Principles of Cultural Branding.* Boston: Harvard Business School Publishing, 2004. Pages 10, 28, 37, 209, 215, 220-221

Jacobs, Jane. *Dark Age Ahead.* Toronto: Random House Canada, 2004. Page 4

Kapferer, Jean-Noel. *Strategic Brand Management: Creating and Sustaining Brand Equity Long Term.* New York: The Free Press, A Division of Simon & Schuster, Inc., 1992

Kim, W. Chan; Mauborgne, Renée. "Blue Ocean Strategy," *Harvard Business Review,* October, 2004. Pages 76-84

King, Thomas. *The Truth About Stories: A Native Narrative.* Toronto: House of Anansi Press Inc., 2003. Page 2

McCracken, Grant. *Culture and Consumption II: Markets, Meaning, and Brand Management.* Bloomington and Indianapolis: Indiana University Press, 2005. Pages: 165, 167, 175, 185
———"The Value of the Brand: An Anthropological Perspective" in *Brand Equity and Advertising,* ed. Aaker and Biel. Pages 126-127

Newman, Peter C. 1995 speech to The Empire Club of Canada, published in *The Empire Club of Canada Speeches 1995-1996,* Edited by Edmison, David and Edward P. Badovinac (Toronto, Canada: The Empire Club Foundation, 1996). Pages 259-272

Neumeier, Marty. *The Brand Gap: How to Bridge the Distance Between Business Strategy and Design.* Indianapolis: New Riders Publishing, 2003

Olive, David. *No Guts, No Glory: How Canada's Greatest CEOs Built Their Empires.* Toronto: McGraw-Hill Ryerson Limited, 2000. Page 84

Pine, B. Joseph; Gilmore, James. *Authenticity: What Consumers Really Want.* Boston: Harvard Business School Press, 2007
———*Pine & Gilmore's Field Guide for the Experience Economy.* Aurora, Ohio: Strategic Horizons, 2005

Polk, James. *Wilderness Writers.* Toronto: Clarke Irwin, 1972

Porter, Michael E.; Kramer, Mark R. "Strategy & Society," *Harvard Business Review,* December, 2006. Pages 78-92

Ray, Randy; Kearney, Mark. *I Know That Name!: The People Behind Canada's Best Known Brand Names from Elizabeth Arden to Walter Zeller.* Toronto: Hounslow Press, 2002

Ries, Al; Trout, Jack. *Positioning: The Battle for your Mind.* New York: McGraw-Hill Book Company, 1981

Schull, Joseph; Gibson, J. Douglas. *The Scotiabank Story: A History of the Bank of Nova Scotia 1832-1982.* Toronto: Macmillan of Canada, 1982. Page 341

Scoffield, Heather. "Is Canada hollowing out?" *The Globe and Mail,* December 5, 2006

Tapscott, Don; Williams, Anthony D. *Wikinomics: How Mass Collaboration Changes Everything.* New York: The Penguin Group, 2006. Pages: 15, 47

Wheatley, Margaret J. *Leadership and the New Science: Discovering Order in a Chaotic World.* San Francisco: Berrett-Koehler Publishers, Inc., 1999. Pages: 50-51, 86, 132, 162

Zaltman, Gerald. *How Customers Think: Essential Insights into the Mind of the Market.* Boston: Harvard Business School Press, 2003

Page 138-140: Source TIFFG

Page: 141: Creator: Jayme Odgers

Page 142: From the collection of Carol Aida

Pages 144-147: Source: Air Canada

Pages 150-152: Source: Aeroplan

Pages 158-161: Source: Vancity, except page 160, Mike Weir. Creator: Carl Lindberg, licenced under the terms of the GNU Free Documentation License, Version 1.2 or any later version published by the Free Software Foundation.

Pages 162-165: Source: RBC, except image of the Rockies.

Pages 166-167: Source: Scotiabank

Page 168: Advertisement, "They helped Canada grow", 195-. Source: Scotiabank Group Archives

Page 169: Bank of New Brunswick, Florenceville (East Florenceville) (BNB) #70.jpg, c. 1902. Photographer: Mr. Neville C. Tompkins, Vancouver, British Columbia. Source: Scotiabank Group Archives

Page 172: Illustration: Marty Bregman

Pages 174-175: Source: Russ Kisby, The ParticipACTION archives, http://www.usask.ca/archives/participaction/english/home.html

Page 176: Illustration: Blair Drawson

Page 179: Illustration: Anita Kuntz

Pages 180-181: Source: Mount Sinai Hospital

Pages 184: Illustration: Jean Marc Coté, 1899

Pages 186-191: Source: Siemens Canada except Pierre E. Trudeau. Source: Wikimedia Commons © Public Domain

Pages 192-193: Source: Rogers

Page 196: Source: Cirque du Soleil

Page 198: Source: CIFAR

Page 201: Source: Cirque du Soleil

Page 202: Photographer: Sam Javanrouh © Royal Ontario Museum, 2007

Pages 203-204: Source: Cundari Group Limited

Pages 207: Photographer: Stephen Tasker

Pages 208-211: Source: WestJet

Pages 212-217: Source: Cirque du Soleil, except page 216, Canadian Tire

WEBSITES (accessed December, 2007)

http://www.canadianencyclopedia.ca/

http://canadianencyclopedia.ca/index.cfm?PgNm=TCE&Params=A1SEC816443

http://archives.cbc.ca/IDD-1-74-342/people/mcluhan/

http://www.canadiandesignresource.ca

http://en.wikipedia.org/wiki/Canada

http://en.wikiquote.org/wiki/Canada

http://en.wikisource.org/wiki/CIA_World_Fact_Book%2C_2004/Canada

http://www.hbc.com/hbcheritage/history/

http://www.empireclubfoundation.com/search.asp

http://www.nytimes.com/2006/12/07/arts/television/07mosq.html?ex=1323147600&en=d22f5b36a36e920d&ei=5090&partner=rssuserland&emc=rss (accessed December 28, 2007)

http://www.cbc.ca/inventions/inventions.html

http://www.mediaincanada.com/articles/mic/20070503/facebook.html

http://www.brandingstrategyinsider.com/2006/08/history_of_bran.html

http://www.brandingstrategyinsider.com/all_brandquotes/index.html

http://andreamandelcampbell.blogspot.com/

http://www.usask.ca/archives/participaction/english/home.html

http://ismaili.net/timeline/2005/20050609ts.html

http://www.participaction.com/index.htm

http://www.rim.com/newsroom/media/gallery/logos.shtml

Did You Know video: http://www.youtube.com/watch?v=pMcfrLYDm2U

http://en.wikipedia.org/wiki/Hudson_Bay_Company

http://www.jantzisocialindex.com/

http://www.townhall.com/Columnists/DineshDSouza/2007/05/21/a_canadian_philosopher_worth_reading

http://www.project-syndicate.org/contributor/214

http://www.project-syndicate.org/commentary/taylor2

http://www.jyu.fi/yhtfil/fil/armala/texts/2002a.pdf

http://www.adbusters.org/home/

http://en.wikipedia.org/wiki/I_Am_Canadian

http://www.competeprosper.ca/index.php

http://www.designcanada.org/history.html

http://archives.cbc.ca/index.asp?IDLan=1

http://www.brainyquote.com/quotes/authors/p/peter_f_drucker.html

http://itc.conversationsnetwork.org/shows/detail468.html

http://news.speeple.com/theglobeandmail.com/2007/08/07/canada-is-in-for-a-generational-shakedown.htm

http://www.canadianbusiness.com

http://mjbraide.com/index.php

Porter, Michael, 76

Positioning: The Battle for Your Mind (Ries and Trout), 57

President's Council on Physical Fitness, 174, 177

price as core value, 112, 144, 148, 149, 194

Procter and Gamble, 21, 75, 186, 192

productivity enablers, 95

profitability: at Aeroplan, 150, 153; at Air Canada, 149; and corporate culture, 60-61; at ParticipACTION, 177; at Rogers, 194; at Vancity, 158, 160; at Westjet, 211

profit sharing, 208, 210

public relations (PR), 23, 101, 102, 128, 154

Q

Quebecor Inc., 29

R

Rashid, Karim, 65, 119, 124, 128

Ray, Regan, 222

RBC Financial Group, 75, 157, 162-65

Redpath, 39-40

regionalism: at Air Canada, 144; being sensitive to, 189-90, 194; and identity, 49, 123, 215-16; at Rogers, 192, 194; at Roots, 123; at Scotiabank, 1/0; at Siemens, 185, 189-90; at Umbra, 127

Reichmann family, 28

Renfrew, G.R., 37

research: at Canadian Tire, 117; at CIFAR, 197, 198-201; on discovering brand, 154; misplaced faith in, 60, 67, 68, 206; at Mount Sinai, 183; at ParticipACTION, 177-78; at Siemens, 189; at TIFFG, 141; at United Way, 182

Research in Motion (RIM), 28, 61, 65, 195

Right to Play, 35, 67

risk management, 62, 66, 200, 220

Ritz Carlton, 66

Robertson, P.L., 40

Robinson, Peter, 72

Rogers Communications Inc. (RCI), 29, 40, 185, 192-95

Rogers, Ted, 40, 195

ROM (Royal Ontario Museum), 197, 202-6

RONA organization, 30

Roots, 31, 119, 120-23

Rowan, Paul, 119, 124

Royal Bank of Canada (RBC Financial Group), 75, 157, 162-65

Royal Canadian Mounted Police (RCMP), 35

Royal Ontario Museum (ROM), 197, 202-6

S

Sarner, Robert, 119, 120, 122-23

Sauder School of Business, 66

Schaeffer, Fred, 64, 76, 91, 92, 95-96

Scotiabank Group, 26, 75, 157, 166-71

Seagrams, 26, 40

Second Cup, 65

service costs, 57, 144, 148

service stories: at Aeroplan, 155; at Canadian Tire, 117; at Four Seasons, 74; and moments of truth, 162; at Vancity, 159; at Westjet, 74, 210

share price, 194

Sharp, Isadore, 34, 128, 143

Shoppers Drug Mart, 31

Siemens Canada Ltd., 185, 186-91

skepticism: as business trait, 61, 91, 109, 143; as a national characteristic, 62, 66, 170, 197; of organizational boosterism, 174, 183, 205, 224; tips on, 225; toward authority, 53

Sleeman Brewing and Malting Company, 26, 40

slogans, 41, 58, 68, 166, 182, 183

Smith, Ernest D., 40

Sobey, John W., 40

social activists, 173-83

social marketing, 33, 35, 160, 174, 182

social responsibility (*See also* community programs): at Aeroplan, 153; as core value, 61, 64; and corporate culture, 75-76; future of, 221-22; at McCain Foods, 96; at Mountain Equipment Co-op, 66; at RBC, 164-65; at Roots, 120; at Vancity, 160

Southam Newspapers, 29

Stanley, George, 79

stock prices, 92

stories: and the Canadian narrative, 140-41; at Cirque du Soleil, 215; genesis, 73, 98, 101, 120, 122, 124, 127; of great service, 74, 117, 155, 159, 162, 210; at Harbourfront Centre, 132, 135; importance of, 131; at Roots, 119, 122-23; at Scotiabank, 166, 168; tips on, 225; used to get at meaning, 58, 67, 68, 73, 183, 223; at Vancity, 158, 159

Stymiest, Barbara, 157, 162, 164-65

Suncor Energy, 29

Sundance Film Festival, 140

Swidler, Ann, 201

symbols (*See also* ikons; logos): as culture connectors, 74, 109; national, 79, 80-83, 102, 136

T

Tapscott, Don, 219, 221-22

teamwork, 96, 113, 122, 210, 224

Telus, 28

Thomson organization, 29

Thorsell, William, 197, 202, 205-6

TIFFG (Toronto International Film Festival Group), 131, 138-41

TIlley Endurables, 34

Tim Hortons: as ikon, 30, 109, 112-13, 170, 183, 216; success story, 18, 30, 64, 109-13, 221

Toronto International Film Festival Group (TIFFG), 131, 138-41

Toronto Maple Leafs, 35

Toy, Samuel, 37

Trans-Canada Airlines, *142*, 144, *145*, *146*

Trudeau, Pierre, 117, 195

trust, 52, 72-73, 91, 113, 116, 197, 201

U

Umbra, 31, 65, 119, 124-29

United States: and anti-American attitudes, 149, 164; Canadian firms borrowing from, 65, 208; marketing in, 113, 127; and President's Council on Physical Fitness, 174, 177; values comparison with Canada, 45, 47-53, 65, 95-96, 128, 136, 190, 201

United Way, 180, 182

V

Vachon, Arcade, 40

value/values: affordability as, 112, 144, 148, 149, 194; attempt to change, 56, 201, 223-24; of brand, 220-21; Canadian v. American, 45, 47-53, 65, 95-96, 128, 136, 190, 201, 208; core Canadian, 24, 26, 45, 47, 51-52, 68-69, 165, 198, 200, 206, 216; eleven values of top organizations, 64-66; how to create, 60, 71-76, 154, 155; importance of, 55, 56, 61; instilling within customers, 57-58, 153, 189-90, 215; and leadership, 155, 224; measurement of, 88, 224; of youth, 49-50, 66

Vancity, 64, 157, 158-61

Vanier, Jean, 88

volunteerism, 178

W

Walker, Hiram, 40-41

Weir, Mike, 160

Westjet, 57, 74, 197, 208-11

Weston, Galen, 37, 41

Weston Group, 30, 38, 41

Wheatley, Margaret, 18

Williams, Anthony D., 219, 221-22

Y

Young, Ric, 35, 60, 67-69, 173

Z

Zellers, 41

ZENN Motor Company, 27

Zucker, Jerry, 24